NELSON'S PURSE

'truly riveting...fine scholarship...a total triumph'
SIMON WINCHESTER

'Fascinating...extraordinary insights'
DAILY MAIL

'Strewn with vivid images...Well-researched and
well-written'
SUNDAY TIMES

'a gripping read'
SPECTATOR

QUEEN'S KNIGHT

'history as it should be written: a riveting page-
turner, underpinned by impeccable scholarship'
ALISON WEIR

'masterly skill...riveting'
LITERARY REVIEW

'A compelling picture of Victorian court life'
SUNDAY TIMES

'Crammed with fascinating details'
SPECTATOR

'vividly succeeds'
DAILY TELEGRAPH

The Sultan of Zanzibar

The bizarre world and spectacular hoaxes of
HORACE DE VERE COLE

Martyn Downer

BLACK
SPRING
PRESS

Published in 2011 by Black Spring Press Ltd
Curtain House
134–146 Curtain Road
London
EC2A 3AR

First published in hardback by Black Spring Press 2010

www.blackspringpress.co.uk

ISBN: 978-0-948238-46-8

A full CIP record for this book is available from the British Library

Cover design Ken Leeder; inside back cover: *Inside the Café Royal* by Adrian Allinson,
1915, by kind courtesy of the Court Gallery, Somerset.

Typeset in Baskerville by Dexter Haven Associates Ltd, London
Printed and bound in Great Britain by CPI Cox & Wyman, Reading

For Valerie

We are such stuff as dreams are made on;
and our little life is rounded with a sleep.

THE TEMPEST, ACT IV, SCENE 1

Contents

List of illustrations

Preface to the second edition

When *The Sultan of Zanzibar* was first published, a number of people approached me with their own anecdotal memories of Horace de Vere Cole. Often these stories enhanced or clarified my own account, so many are included in this revised edition with my grateful thanks.

More significantly, during the original preparation of the book, the long-lost typescript of Virginia Woolf's talk about the *Dreadnought* hoax, presented by her amid gales of laughter to the Rodmell Women's Institute in 1940, was marvellously rediscovered by a researcher at the Women's Library of London Metropolitan University. Previously known only in fragments, the publication of the full talk, so resonant with Woolf's distinctive voice, has added some vital and colourful new texture to the story of the hoax, even though, inevitably and like the reminiscences of other participants, she misremembered or confused some details of that long-ago Edwardian afternoon. Particularly striking (and possibly surprising to many readers) is Woolf's obvious, if slightly exasperated, affection for its frequently maligned ringleader. 'I liked Horace,' she says at one point, 'but I admit I always wondered what he was up to.' Unlike Virginia Woolf, you can now find out.

Martyn Downer, Anstey, 2010

Prologue

F ew people today have heard of Horace de Vere Cole, and those only of a certain age. Yet a hundred years ago he was one of the most celebrated men in England. Then he disappeared and war came, and over time people forgot until no one was entirely sure if he was alive or dead. Yet mention the *Dreadnought* hoax—when Horace and his accomplices, dressed as Abyssinian princes, fooled the Royal Navy into a tour of the greatest warship then afloat—and memory stirs. Still locked into the British subconscious is a love for the underdog, a sense of the ridiculous, the ability to laugh at ourselves and, as so exquisitely demonstrated by Horace that long-ago afternoon, an overwhelming desire to mock pomposity. It is an attitude which saved England from a Mussolini or a Hitler (both considered utterly ludicrous by Horace). It is why our premier lives in a semi-detached house, not a palace, and why we begrudge 'political correctness' and 'health and safety'. (The same prank today would surely lead to a heavily armed police response, possible bloodshed, a public enquiry and bitter political recrimination.) It comes as no surprise that, according to his friend Augustus John, the French responded to Horace's humour 'with disgust'.

Of course the real beauty of Horace's masterpiece was the utter failure of the navy to see the joke. The country roared with pleasure when the prank was exposed but those in authority, from Whitehall to Windsor Castle, felt a shiver of fear as the comfortable world they inhabited was given a jolt. Horace's old tutor at Eton deplored the act, suggesting in all seriousness that his pupil's talents would be better served in parliament. And yet official retribution for the hoax, as we will see, was restrained and no prosecutions resulted. Nineteen-ten is a century, two world wars and countless catastrophes away from us now. But if it was hardly a world of innocence, it was one in which a certain good sense, and sense of proportion, prevailed. It was understood that Horace's target was not the navy *per se* (after all, his greatest hero was his namesake Horatio Nelson) but the self-important and mediocre men who had come to staff its upper ranks. Horace thought this decline the inevitable consequence of a cumbersome and bureaucratic empire which nurtured men like Admiral May, commander-in-chief of the Home Fleet. A lifelong and incurable romantic, Horace longed for a new Elizabethan age unencumbered by bloated imperial responsibility when England would 'become again a wonderful little island (with Scotland and Wales!) in the North Sea (or East Atlantic as you choose) as she was in the famous and transcendental days of Shakespeare'. A century on, one could argue his dream has been realised, but not as he may have wished.

A profound sense of Englishness gave Horace's life shape and meaning. After all, England was not only the birthplace of Shakespeare but also of other heroes like Keats, Shelley, Tennyson and Browning. However, as he freely admitted, his patriotism was that of an immigrant, as he was in fact only half English, his mother being Irish. This gave his feelings an edge and objectivity. 'I have a love of England but not necessarily for the English,' he once declared. He judged and admired each of his native countries, and was fiercely proud of both, but not always of how their people behaved. For example, he deplored the 'mediocrity of thought' of the English with their 'moneyed snobbery' and 'classification' of accent. He tried to avoid the 'double loyalties' he saw in other 'educated people of the Irish landlord class' (he wasn't always entirely successful). Horace credited this attitude to his dispassionate English blood. On the other hand, Ireland bred his passion, poetry, mischief and sense of the ridiculous. These opposing currents ran through Horace like veins in marble.

In the early years of the last century, aided by great wealth and an even larger personality, Horace carved out his unique career as a poet-prankster. For a time between the wars he was constantly in the tabloid press. Anyone who read a newspaper knew him by name, and many by face too, for he cut a quite extraordinary figure. Auguste Oddenino, the society café owner in Regent Street, called him 'one of the three finest looking men in England' (who were the others, I wonder?). Women agreed, and fell at his feet. Thirty years after accompanying him on the *Dreadnought* hoax, Virginia Woolf still recalled Horace's 'beautiful blue eyes', his 'perfect figure' and 'beautiful soft voice'. Blessed with such looks, money and an utterly charming manner, Horace enjoyed a string of glamorous girlfriends and two striking wives. Yet he was not entirely unmistakable. Late in life, with his mane of snowy-white hair and bristling handlebar moustache à la Kitchener, Horace was sometimes confused with the equally hirsute Labour politician Ramsay MacDonald (and also, or so he claimed, with Einstein). This could give rise to some impromptu and baffling public oratory, in which he would lambast his audience with a diehard Tory speech (Horace kept one of MacDonald's visiting cards in his pocket for just such an occasion). That his brother-in-law was Neville Chamberlain merely added to the fun.

Horace could have stepped fully formed and roaring from the pages of P.G. Wodehouse. Like Bertie Wooster he had the urge to steal policemen's helmets, and he was tormented by disapproving aunts. He also wielded that effortless Wodehousian turn of phrase. The wife of an elderly Irish peer had 'a face exactly like a plaice', another friend looked 'as sprightly and ruddy as a Whitstable oyster with Tabasco on it', while an old enemy was 'an out and out cad and bounder'. His London club, the St James's on Piccadilly, might have doubled for Drones. Horace and his stories were such a feature there that his friend the Anglo-Irish author Lord Dunsany probably had him in mind when he created Mr Jorkens, the lovable club bore. Certainly Horace always maintained he inspired many of his friend's eccentric characters.

However, one reviewer has astutely observed another, darker, literary landscape for Horace's unconventional activities. Writing in the *Spectator*, Hugh Cecil commented that, with its underlying violence and menace, Horace's life was more suited to the pages of Saki than Wodehouse. I think you'll see what he means.

So many tales surround Horace that it has been difficult extracting fact from fiction. His practical jokes being, well, practical don't work well on the page, so were often not recorded. Apart from the jokes which made headlines, like the *Dreadnought* hoax, Horace's activities mainly survive as anecdote, the tales growing taller as the years pass. As he himself said, 'My hoaxes have often been told at 2nd, 3rd or 4th hand in papers, and accounts of my doings, apocryphal or otherwise, have appeared in at least ten books of our time. But that's all to the good: it's unpaid for publicity! And every account I've seen was inaccurate.' Scouring these memoirs and poring over faded newspaper cuttings has furnished his story with many hidden gems, but dozens more (and Horace claimed to have pulled off a hundred jokes) are probably lost to us forever. Moreover, almost every unexplained prank before or since has been attributed to him. How we would love to know, for instance, whether the 1912 'Piltdown man' hoax—when a prehistoric human skull discovered in Sussex amid huge excitement was found to be a fake—was down to Horace. Sadly, there is no evidence for his involvement, though he would have hugely enjoyed ridiculing the scientific establishment.

It would be wrong, however, to see Horace simply as an upper-class jester. I think his story has real depth and pathos. It certainly confounds expectation. Here was a Cambridge-educated Old Etonian who felt as happy (probably happier) drinking in Whitechapel as Whites. Who was highly cultivated, passionate and literate, and with such a strong sense of social injustice that he supported the Fabian cause, was a committed socialist and volunteered to help the poor of the East End. The many contradictions of his life, like his dual nationality, developed in Horace a divided self which found physical release in eccentric behaviour but expression in poetry, his first love. Today, he may appear remote and his jokes racist and faintly reprehensible. Yet the *Dreadnought* hoax only happened one very long lifetime ago, and minstrel shows were popular on British television until the 1970s.

In a wider sense, Horace's story is a fable on the collapse of a whole class and its manner of living. His life almost precisely spanned the decline and fall of the aristocracy in Britain, from its zenith in the 1880s to its defeat by the 1930s. Born to privilege and wealth, Horace ended his life in utter poverty and degradation. His fate was extreme but its cause was not unique. By his death, England was strewn with mansions stripped of their treasures and great estates reduced to smallholdings. The sons of the nobility, if they survived the Great War, were uprooted and scattered across the globe in an effort to make a living. When they failed, as Horace did, they ended up clustering together in places like Kenya and the South of France, where, disorientated and disillusioned, they drank and mourned their losses.

I first heard of Horace through my wife, who is related to him. Mention of a joker in the family is unnerving, but in

Horace I found a wonderful, if occasionally irascible, literary companion. It was astonishing that no one had written a book about him before. Tempted by many offers, Horace tried to produce one himself but the manuscript was destroyed, as we shall see, through his own and others' efforts. This loss has drained Horace's fame. Many of the painters he patronised and the writers he encouraged are highly regarded today, some revered. The press still occasionally wheel Horace out as the 'Prince of Jokers', usually on April fool's day. Recently he has been featured in the *New York Times* and *Daily Mail*. But for some reason his ground-breaking 'cow teat in the open trouser fly' remains still sadly neglected, while the work of his arch-enemy, the sculptor Jacob Epstein (who *did* produce a self-serving autobiography) is lauded.

In the seventy years since Horace's death, many writers (and not a few television producers) have toyed with his story. But all have been frustrated by the lack of will, money and material. His papers are fragmentary and scattered, and scooping up the debris of his life has been difficult. I was lucky, however, to meet two people who knew Horace personally: his nephew John Cole and daughter Valerie. Horace was hopeless with anybody's children but deplorably so with his own. Yet John and Valerie's memories, cast in the light of childhoods from a long-vanished age, gloriously restored Horace to life. They did so alongside an extraordinary trove of letters and papers revealed by Tristan de Vere Cole, another person to whom I owe an incalculable debt of gratitude.

Tristan was born during Horace's lifetime to Horace's wife Mavis, but he is not Horace's son. His father was, it is assumed but not proven, the painter Augustus John. It was said that the sexually rapacious Augustus treated every child he met as his own, in case it was. In Tristan's case he might have been. Augustus certainly assumed he was the father and, after Horace died, unofficially adopted Tristan. Mavis de Vere Cole was more equivocal. If she knew the truth for certain, she took the secret with her to her grave in 1970. Certainly Tristan has that distinctive later Augustan look with large features, beard and unmistakable twinkle in his eye. He co-wrote an affectionate but unsparing portrait of his mother after her death, when she was found in her chaotic bedroom 'sprawled bottom-up beneath the copy of the drawing Augustus John had done of her'. *Beautiful and Beloved* charts Mavis's tempestuous life with Horace and her many later affairs. But until now Horace himself has avoided the biographer's gaze, a strange outcome for a man who so loved and courted attention. Now, as living memory fades and the *Dreadnought* hoax is over a century old, it is finally time to tell his story.

I met Tristan for the first time four years ago. We sat drinking tea, and then Chablis, in his garden near Newbury. I had finished a book on Queen Victoria and was looking for another subject. Horace seemed too good to be true. Visiting Tristan was the obvious place to start, but I had no idea of the treasures he possessed or that, over the years, he had watched other writers (19 to date) enthusiastically embark on the quest for Horace before dropping him in agonised frustration when the trail went cold. I can see now that over that afternoon Tristan gently probed my motivation, suspecting that, like so many before me, I simply wanted to tell Horace's jokes. Yet, even then, I felt that the jokes were simply one symptom of an extraordinary and creative mind. Moreover, I was drawn to my task not only by Horace but by the world he roamed: from Edwardian London through the roaring twenties to the Great Depression. Dylan Thomas described Horace as 'absolutely fuddled with the nineties and the tens and the twenties and the rest of the between war escape'. I was to discover that it was an outward progress which uncannily matched his troubled inner life.

As the afternoon lengthened, we talked about the artists Horace had known and the writers he admired. His life crashed into the orbits of so many famous people that he is like a touchstone to pre-war English society. Tristan showed me a slightly Pooterish document written by Horace in an idle moment (he had many), grandly entitled 'Acquaintances: a mixed bag of 50', which ranges wildly from Queen Victoria through Rupert Brooke to W.B. Yeats. We wondered at his meteoric ascent to fame and then his calamitous decline; how he squandered a fortune and the love of his family. How, in a way, his life mirrored the decline of a whole manner of living which at his birth in 1881 had seemed so secure and certain. Horace's pranks, we agreed, should be set against this landscape. Without it they lose their context, meaning and, crucially, their mordant humour. As we traced his fading star, it occurred to me more than once that the trajectory of Horace's life cut an almost Wildean arc as it shot high before crashing to earth.

I was buoyed up by my conversation with Tristan, but little expected what would happen next. Before I drove away, Tristan showed me portraits of his mother and Horace by Augustus John. He then disappeared to his study and emerged with a battered tin box labelled 'M. de Vere Cole'. The box had been retrieved after Mavis's death and it contained not only her lengthy and highly charged correspondence with her husband but also a miserable handful of his last possessions. Among them was a large file of faded newspaper cuttings, fragments of autobiography, a bound copy of his mother's poems, a wallet (empty) from Asprey's inscribed 'W.H. de V. C.', a diary for 1909 and a heavily thumbed volume of the collected works of Robert Browning. Most tantalising of all was an exotic-looking silver sheathed knife bearing the label 'Horace de Vere Cole's dagger'. How could I resist? Who on earth was this man?

1

My first name is a flower sweet
Of very ancient line,
My second is a poet mete
To share his fame with mine!
My third reveals a double pun plus
A name of proudest birth,
My last is with great labour won
Up from the depths of earth!

The name Horace de Vere Cole is so exotic it is a wonder it was ever forgotten. In fact his given first name was William, after his father Willie Cole, a major in the 3rd Dragoon Guards who died of cholera in India when Horace was a boy. He in turn had been named for Horace's grandfather William Henry Cole, the youngest son of Norfolk gentry who made a fortune in the American trade dealing in quinine. The drug brought William Henry a mansion in London, an estate in Berkshire and a place in society. His son and heir Willie was duly lined up to marry the aristocratic Isabel Stracey, future Lady Kimberley. Instead Willie picked a bride from Ireland of great beauty, formidable intellect and quixotic temper. Mary de Vere was the granddaughter of Sir Aubrey de Vere and niece of Aubrey de Vere, both Irish poets of high renown. The de Veres claimed kinship with the Earls of Oxford and the right to the title Lord Great Chamberlain of England, an honour granted to the first Earl by Henry II in the twelfth century. (Horace would hanker after this prestigious role all his life. But it had long since devolved to the Cholmondeley family, and it was said that the nearest he ever came to becoming Chamberlain was having his sister marry one.)

Willie's surprising choice of bride mirrored the contradictions of his own temperament, accounts of which differ substantially. In a memoir of her childhood, his niece Mary Elphinstone described him a gentle, bookish and mild-mannered man who doted on his children. His surviving letters to Horace certainly give this impression. They radiate love and warmth in that peculiarly Victorian manner. Willie speaks of his life in India and enquires after Horace's cricket in words every schoolboy will recognise. 'You must play steadily and carefully,' he instructed his son, 'and not hit at every ball you get.' The letters display a close, loving bond. To young Horace, his father

was the exemplar of a chivalric life: by turns dashing and gentle, heroic and humble. A photograph of Willie in uniform hints at a swagger and love of display which he clearly gifted his son. His early death in far-off parts serving Queen and country was full of mystery and romance to Horace, and one he came to envy.

Willie's Irish in-laws held a very different opinion of him. Mary de Vere's sisters and mother thoroughly disliked him, but the more they had voiced their opposition to her engagement, the more stubbornly she had

Horace's father, Major Willie Cole, dashing but disliked by his Irish in-laws (Francis Chamberlain).

dug her heels in. Mary's sister Eileen was unsparing in her assessment of Willie. She wrote after his death,

> I consider his good points, namely generosity, a capacity for affection, the possession of a good deal of cleverness, were stunted and rendered of but small account by unbridled and most thoughtless selfishness. Mother offered to get Mimi out of the engagement if she at all repented, but Mimi declared herself satisfied with her choice. The fact was, her grand but undeveloped nature was as unfit to be linked with his common one as a union between a cultivated and high-born young woman and a ploughman would be unsuitable. Her extraordinary unswerving, innate honesty, and truth and nobility, found no response in his very commonplace and shallow nature, which was only perceptive enough to chafe under her passionate disapproval when, after marriage, she came to understand him.

Clearly the de Veres were not a family to mince their words.

Mary was high-spirited, red-haired and quick-tempered, with the startling blue eyes she gave her son. Walter Sickert, a good judge, told Horace she was the 'most beautiful woman he had ever seen'. Her sister Eileen recalled that Mary 'had strange romantic ideas, and was full of mystery and a love of mystery and a great tendency to hero-worship'. She passed on these characteristics to her eldest son, in whom they obviously mingled with his father's apparent selfishness to produce explosive results. Mary was ill-suited to Willie and the Coles, who preferred shooting to poetry, dogs to art. But she came with titles and class, while he delivered money and an estate in England. In Victorian marriage terms, it was a pragmatic match if not one made in heaven. Willie Cole had pursued and won Mary against the odds. Horace said later that his father had never made his mother happy and, according to Lady Augusta Gregory, Mary never failed to run her husband's memory down after his death.

It was Mary's father who gave Horace his distinctive name. Horatio de Vere was a Crimean War veteran with friends ranging from the messianic Charles Gordon of Khartoum to poet-painter Edward Lear. Lear had drawn whimsical birds for Mary as a child and one can imagine her telling her own children his nonsense poems. Horatio's life was cut short when he was murdered in bizarre circumstances by a disgruntled soldier at Chatham Barracks. Horace never knew his grandfather, but his gallant reputation filled him from an early age with romantic notions of warfare and a chivalric ideal that were quite out of step with the world around him. Horace's own military career would be brief, bloody and ultimately disappointing, as he always yearned to go out in a blaze of glory. 'The soldier's death in action is the best,' he pronounced.

Horace felt the historic legacy of the de Veres very keenly. He self-consciously assumed the name as a prefix to Cole as if to burnish its Norfolk dullness with the brilliance of his Irish ancestry. The name shaped him, defined him and added to the heroic pose he liked to strike. Unfortunately, living up to his family's poetic reputation was more difficult than simply adopting the name, and as arduous as matching its military prowess. Edward de Vere, the seventeenth Earl of Oxford, was rumoured by many (and many still) to have written Shakespeare's plays, while the work of Horace's great grand-father Sir Aubrey de Vere had been praised by no less a figure than William Wordsworth. Mary de Vere was also a gifted poetess in the Gaelic bardic tradition. Horace believed that only his mother's 'spirituality' prevented her becoming a great one. She spoke Irish, and converted to Catholicism after her husband died, as it was the only true religion of Ireland. Her writing was full of magic and wandering spirits. One imagines her reciting Irish folk tales to her young son, populating his mental universe with tales of fairies, banshees and other grotesque figures from Ireland's mystic past. A photo-graph of Horace as an infant shows him dressed as a girl, as if to stop the fairies stealing him. This oral inheritance gave him a wonderful memory and ear for language and mimicry. As a boy, he learnt the whole of *Julius Caesar* by heart, and could quote hundreds of other lines from Shakespeare. When Horace was ten, Mary wrote her children 'East Wind by the Sea' to nurture their understanding of the spirit world she inhabited.

> Little white cloud ships up in the blue,
> Sailing westward the long day through,
> Boats of the sky, where the spirits lie
> Drifting and dreaming like you and I.
> Here on the sea in a white-sailed boat
> Quite as happily we will float;
> But when we die our spirits will fly
> Up to the cloud ships in the sea sky
> And on and on to the gates of the sun
> Where alas! Our merry voyage is done.

The de Veres were very highly regarded in Anglo-Irish literary circles, with Uncle Aubrey a frequent guest at the salons hosted by the writer Lady Wilde in Dublin. Indeed, it is not too fanciful to see the relationship between Horace and his mother in the same light as Lady Wilde's all-encompassing one with her son Oscar. Both existed within artificial worlds which rejected the real and the ordinary and placed spirituality at the heart of the human experience. Like Oscar Wilde, Horace venerated his mother.

Horace as a child, in skirts to stop the fairies stealing him (Francis Chamberlain).

In his own poems Horace tried to reach towards that other world she occupied. She was the paradigm against which every other woman in his life—and there were many—would be judged and found wanting. She taught Horace that nothing was more valuable in life than art, and nothing more worth-while than a creative life. She gave him that passion for words which emerged in his love of aphorisms and his own poems. She was, he bemoaned shortly before his death, the only person who 'ever REALLY cared a damn what became of me'. His jokes were a manifestation of the same imperative for love and attention. Properly channelled, his imagination might have left a substantial literary legacy, but then perhaps we would have been denied the jokes and hoaxes which made him famous.

2

The warm West wind is crying
With the lusty voice of birth;
Old Winter is a-dying,
Spring has returned to earth;
And mother earth is sighing
With plenty, after death.

The fields will soon be glowing
With a million magic eyes;
The branches will be blowing
White buds to opal skies;
All nature will be growing
A-growing till it dies

And I am going home—aye home
Where our ancient race was bred;
Deep beneath the leagues of foam
Where lie the myriad dead
Who needed not the wormy loam
To make their final bed.

The too-good-to-be-true rumour that Horace de Vere
Cole, prince of jokers, was launched into an unsuspecting
world at Blarney Castle in County Cork, home of the
eponymous stone and well-spring of Irish wit, appears correct. His
birth was registered nearby in the garrison town of Ballincollig,
and Mary Cole may well have been staying at the castle when her
son arrived prematurely on 5 May 1881. Sir George Colthurst,
the castle's owner, was an old family friend, while his son, also
George, would go to Cambridge with Horace and stand best

man at his wedding. So it seems Horace was right to claim that he had kissed the Blarney Stone 'at a very tender age!'

Before his father died, Horace's life revolved around the Cole family estate at West Woodhay in West Berkshire and the country houses occupied by his mother's various relatives in Ireland. Apart from the de Vere stronghold at Curragh Chase in Limerick—then occupied by great uncle Aubrey de Vere, who patrolled his vast demesne composing poetry and wearing the cape his brother Horatio had worn in the Crimea—Horace had the run of Issercleran, a pretty Georgian mansion in County Galway. Issercleran, and its earlier castle, was the ancestral home of Mary de Vere's maternal family, the Burkes, founders of Galway City, who came to Ireland with the Normans and married into the 'mad' O'Haras. It was, remembered Horace's Aunt Eileen de Vere, a place of 'great solitude and silence with turf fires and warm nurseries'. Its position in the remote west of Ireland, hard to reach and difficult to find, gave the house a magical aura in Horace's mind. It was so closely connected

Issercleran, County Galway, a magical place (John Cole).

with his mother, who inherited it, that after she died he couldn't bear to go back, and it passed to his younger brother Jim. Issercleran (or St Cleran's) is now an upmarket hotel with bedrooms named after Chamberlain, Yeats and Joyce.

Even by the unforgiving standards of her day, Mary's mother Anne Burke endured more than her share of tragedy. The peace of Issercleran was frequently shaken by violent and sudden death. Anne's husband Horatio de Vere was murdered, one of her brothers killed in the Crimean War; another, the explorer Robert O'Hara Burke, died of starvation attempting to cross Australia on foot, while a third had succumbed to painful illness. With three daughters and no sons, this string of tragedies left Anne Burke in a house full of women, with no male heir. But she was a resilient, forceful woman with a great capacity for fun. Horace had planned to begin his autobiography by recounting a long-forgotten practical joke his grandmother had played as a child on her own father.

The feminine environment at Issercleran, with its emphasis on art, literature and politics, left a lasting impression on Horace. It gave him an intellectual respect for women denied to boys in more conventional Victorian households. It made him an ardent supporter of female emancipation and suffrage. But if death stalked the corridors of Issercleran, it was worse for the foxes outside. Hunting dominated Galway society: six days a week if possible during the season. The Burkes and the de Veres followed the Blazers, a daredevil hunt which took its name from the evening its members torched an inn after dinner. So many stone walls crisscrossed the Galway landscape that it was said the Blazers spent more time in the air than on the ground. The thrill and danger of hunting exerted a powerful pull on Horace's mother. She deeply resented the interruption of pregnancy to her sport. 'Hunting? *Hunting!*' she once exclaimed, 'How can I hunt when I've been having all these beastly babies!'

Horace inherited her love of the chase. Forty years later he startled a reception at the House of Commons hosted by his brother-in-law Neville Chamberlain with a rousing rendition of 'D'ya ken John Peel?' Away from the hunting field, winter passed for the Anglo-Irish in flirting, drinking, shooting, drinking, amateur dramatics, dancing and more drinking. Issercleran leavened this relentless diet with poetry, music, walking and literature. With time on idle hands, there was also a great deal of practical joking within upper-class circles, marshalled by men like Sir Hercules 'Herky' Langrishe, who lost a vast fortune pursuing a playboy lifestyle, and Lord Bandon, who surprised his guests at Castle Bernard in County Cork by secreting cockerels in their chamber pots.

In summer, there was tennis, pony racing and cricket at Coole Park, the home of Lady Augusta Gregory, a cousin of the de Veres. Her reputation as a literary hostess provided her son Robert, a childhood friend of Horace, with a unique pool of unlikely cricketers to choose from: from W.B. Yeats, George Moore and

Horace's mother Mary de Vere, standing between his Irish aunts Eileen and Maggie (Francis Chamberlain).

John Masefield to George Bernard Shaw. Then each year, as the shadow of autumn stretched over the hills of Connemara, the de Veres decamped to a villa discovered by Horace's grandmother at St Jean de Luz on the Biscayan coast of southern France. It was a place of memories, and eventually of refuge.

Ireland exerted a powerful influence on the youthful Horace. It defined his outlook, sharpened his creative senses and rooted his imagination in a magical, poetic land where the boundaries between reality and fantasy were blurred. The Irish literary revival, centred at Coole, was weaved round with mysticism and spirituality. Horace's sister Annie remembered visiting Lady Gregory as a child and gazing into a crystal ball with W.B. Yeats, where she saw strange people sweeping with brooms under an old archway. Two of Horace's closest friends in Ireland, Lord Dunsany and James Stephens (author of the bestselling *The Crock of Gold*) wrote fantasy fiction populated by elves and leprechauns. He also met the poet, critic and editor George Russell, known as A.E., who painted fantastical fairy pictures over his study walls. Russell's poem 'The Gates of Dreamland', in which 'the land of youth lies gleaming flushed with rainbow light and mirth', was a favourite of Horace's. He copied it into his commonplace book alongside verses by Coleridge and a poem dedicated to his mother by the lyrical poet William Watson beginning

> Daughter of Ireland, nay, 'twere better said
> Daughter of Ireland's beauty, Ireland's grace,
> Child of her charm, of her romance; whose face
> Is legendary with her glories fled!

For Horace the woods around Issercleran really were populated by the leprechauns and fairies he read about and had heard his mother describe. Years later, he conjured up this life-transforming, life-enhancing vision in a poem called 'Fairyland, or a Mountain Magic':

Far away on the mountain moorland where the great, green
grasses wave
You will find the home of the fairies; be your heart both wild
and brave
You will enter a magic circle, by the shower of a magic lake,
And the hopes and the fears of a lifetime for ever you will
forsake.

Your mind will become a mirage for all things that have had
no name,
For speech has no use on the mountain, where thought is a
living flame,
You will find in the fire-tongued presence of the mountain
mists at morn
The thrill of the first creation, when time and this world were
born.

You will dream all night in the stillness great, amber tinted
dreams,
Great harmonies of colour sent down on the soft star-beams
And when you awake in the morning to the hum of the insect
world
From the secret presence of nature all her garments will fall
unfurled.

And there you will stay captive, though often times you go
Back to the towns and cities with their ceaseless ebb and flow,
The fairies will have caught you to their magic world behind
Where there's dew, and fairy dancing, and the sun-awakened
wind.

This childlike innocence sustained Horace through his life,
giving him a belief that anything was possible. Add in dressing
up after dinner to perform skits for the grown-ups, overarching
confidence, and the tradition of pranking, or spoofing, in Irish
country houses, and you have all the makings of a practical
joker. The triumph of his art, and secret of his success,
was Horace's ability not simply to act a part but to absorb
it with such conviction that he really believed he was the

Sultan of Zanzibar when he donned make-up and a few tatty robes.

Ireland was entering a darker, more violent period—and a very dangerous one for the Anglo-Irish—but the country never lost this magic for Horace. He shared his childhood between two countries with opposing cultures, and although he would live most of his life in England, he never shook Ireland from his bones. 'I have a strong feeling for the Downlands of Wiltshire and Hampshire,' he said of his English home, 'but nothing like the feeling I have for Ireland.' Wherever he was, he had a craving for Irish stew, and he never failed to mark St Patrick's Day with a toast, or to ask his brother or sister to send shamrock from home.

3

The smuggest men I've ever found
Are those Success had hedged around;
Their life is like a field of grass
With conscience on it, viz an Ass
At time the Ass begins to bray
Then down our smug ones fall to pray;
At times the ass lets drop manure
They cry alone 'Well, well! 'tis pure!'
The Ass however's very smelly
And only lives to fill his belly

*I*n 1891, when he was ten, Horace nearly died of diphtheria. The illness required several dangerous operations, and left his hearing seriously impaired for the rest of his life. Although it heightened his visual sense and response to art, it impeded a longed-for army career and, unable to follow conversations in crowded rooms, made him socially uncomfortable and awkward in company. He hid his disability with bluster and an overbearing manner, driving him to ever more outrageous behaviour. His booming voice was seen as a sign of boorishness, as were his ill-timed attempts to cover his explosive farting by coughing. It also made him acutely sensitive to personal criticism or comment. The slightest insult was met with violence, the only form of communication on which he felt on equal (and usually superior) terms. I think this sense of personal injustice also motivated much of his practical joking, as if it satisfied a deep-seated but undirected desire for revenge.

Horace would admit that, as a child, he was 'thrown inside myself, largely owing to deafness and character'. Always a dreamy boy, he now constructed an alternative reality, living in a fantastical world of his own creation. With life around him muffled and distant, he built an inner space where convention was distorted by the prism of his imagination. It was populated by historical heroes like Nelson and Wellington, who jostled with a shifting cast of demons and fairies from folklore. On this interior stage, he played out fantasies in contravention of the rules outside. He was not a high-achieving boy at school largely, I believe, because he expended so much energy moving the scenery of his own mind. It made him both precocious and insecure. In a less cultivated person, such pathological introspection might have materialised in random violence (and Horace certainly had an aggressive streak, particularly when drunk), not practical joking.

As a child, the outward expression of this reshaping of Horace's inner life was the sharp deterioration in his behaviour, hastened by the early death of his father. In one of his last letters to his son, Willie Cole had exhorted him to be 'good, brave, honourable and obedient...and you must never bully anyone'. Horace was brave but, thrown back on the care of an indulgent mother and lacking paternal restraint, he struggled to meet, and then failed to keep, his father's exacting standards. As he grew up, the shy, introverted child became a bully and show-off. The ill health which blighted his childhood saved him from punishment, while the sympathy it aroused spoiled him. His prep-school headmaster, Mr Hussey, struggled to cope, so much of Horace's early education was at home under the guidance of tutors or willing relatives. This gave it an eclectic and ill-disciplined look, full of stories but weak on detail.

His cousin Mary Elphinstone wrote an account of her childhood holidays with the Coles at West Woodhay which is peppered with anecdotes of this youthful, troubled Horace. His antics appear amusing—which they were to his hero-worshipping younger cousin—but they must have been very trying to the grown-ups, particularly to his uncle, Alfred Cole, a city businessman who acted as Horace's guardian after Willie died. Several stories revolve around the various amateur theatricals the house hosted, when the children were elaborately dressed and made up to perform in plays like *Pygmalion* (W.S. Gilbert's 1871 version of the Greek myth, not Shaw's) and long-forgotten Victorian melodramas such as *Yellow Roses* and *Shades of Night*. Horace was always the best actor, but no one quite knew to what end he would put his talent. However, there is obviously a direct link between the child blacking his face and singing the Negro spiritual 'Little darkies cry cry' in the smoke-filled library of West Woodhay, as Horace did, and the man who played the Sultan of Zanzibar at Cambridge.

Even as a boy, Horace gave these harmless parlour games a subversive edge. In one performance of *Shades of Night*, for example, he nearly killed the leading lady by using real poison in the murder scene. This unfortunate woman was the first of Horace's recorded victims. The next—in a list which grew to encompass admirals, curates and members of parliament—was the children's stout German governess. She fled within a week after Horace squeezed her into the box-like luggage lift at West Woodhay and sent her plummeting to earth from the attic nursery. The episode was an early demonstration of Horace's persuasive charm and his dislike for figures of authority. It was unusual in one respect, however. As far as I know, it was the only time he ever targeted a foreigner.

The governess could be replaced, and Mary Cole faced more pressing worries than the conduct of her son. Widowed with three young children, she had retreated to a house on the Coles' estate in Berkshire. Following the death of his father, Horace, aged eleven, was now heir to West Woodhay, with its collections and acres and acres of rolling Berkshire countryside. At its heart was a magnificent Jacobean mansion, attributed to Inigo Jones, which overlooked a tranquil lake where the children could fish and row their boat. In his last years, his grandfather had 'improved' his house, as was then the fashion, with the addition of a rambling extension (since demolished). But for the present Horace's demesne ran no further than the nursery on the attic floor. Here he drew in chalk on the white plaster walls and filled the ancient rocking horse with his brother's pocket-watch, sister's best hankie and other personal treasures.

The mansion beneath the nursery was occupied by his adoring grandmother Jane Cole, whose father Alfred Brooks

The Jacobean front of West Woodhay House, the Coles' Berkshire mansion (Mike McClintock).

had founded the famed London wine merchants Justerini & Brooks. By marrying her, Horace's grandfather William Cole had consolidated his newly made fortune and acquired a faintly raffish sophistication which belied his own more modest beginnings. Jane lived in the great house with her two spinster daughters Jesse and Edith. It was a similar situation to Issercleran, one in which women also ruled. But Horace's English aunts were very different to his free-thinking Irish ones. Unconcerned by politics or modern literature, they busied themselves with the welfare of the village, decorating the church built by their father with tapestries and beautifully carved pews. Spiritual matters stopped at the church door.

A third aunt, Annie, had married Sir Howard Elphinstone, who won a Victoria Cross in the Crimea and was another hero of Horace's childhood. After Sir Howard was lost at sea in 1890, Annie was a frequent visitor to West Woodhay, her girls providing playmates for the Cole children and innocent victims for Horace. I think all three of these English aunts, dedicated religious women, gave Horace his social awareness and a moral compass which swung violently but never entirely left him. They tempered his Irish flights of fancy. Finally we should not forget the servants who tended to the family. In their different ways they too fed Horace's imagination, their foibles stored up for use in future roles he played.

In 1890, West Woodhay had 11 live-in staff, including maids, a cook and a footman. They were presided over by the butler, Charles Dobson, a lugubrious character whose only 'outlet for self-expression [was] in the soulful sounding of the gong that lived under the stairs'. Dobson cultivated carnations and was 'master of the art of arranging dinner napkins'. The contrast with arrangements at Issercleran was striking. Here, Mary Cole was devotedly attended to by the steward, Morgan Fahey, a diminutive, walnut-skinned, wiry man who had been with the de Veres for forty years at least (no one was absolutely sure). He taught the children to ride and hunt by running alongside their ponies, holding them down in the saddle. Fiercely loyal, he had a wicked sense of humour, remembered Eileen de Vere, 'combined with a hot, violent temper, a bitter criticism and hatred hoarded up for people he disliked or disapproved of, and an entirely unforgiving desire for revenge for any injury done to himself or those he cared for'. It's a description that might have fitted Horace, who adored Morgan and returned to Ireland to be by his side when he died in 1918.

Grandma Cole loomed large in Horace's childhood. She was highly cultivated, well travelled and great fun: unafraid, for instance, of appearing at one of her grandchildren's 'dressing-up' dinners wearing a black mantilla to play the castanets. She had been devastated at the death of her son Willie. 'I want nothing to be restored to me but my own boy with all his faults and nicenesses,' she had written. Now Jane Cole's hopes for

The Victorian rear of West Woodhay House, added by Horace's grandfather William Henry Cole with money from quinine (John Cole).

West Woodhay rested on Horace, in whose favour her other son Alfred had been passed over. It was a rigorous exercise of primogeniture, but it also hinted at disapproval of Alfred, who, like his dead brother, seems to have earned few admirers. He was very combative and prickly. As a child, Alfred had raised his fists at the slightest provocation, and he still liked to mock, belittle and bully his opponents. Whereas Willie had entered the army to mark time before inheriting West Woodhay, Alfred followed their father into the family business, rising through City ranks until he eventually became Governor of the Bank of England (he was dismissed by Lloyd George within two years for characteristically, but ill-advisedly, speaking his mind).

Uncle Alfred presiding over Horace's English aunts at West Woodhay, attended to by Dobson (author).

Though based in London, at the Cole residence in Portland Place, Alfred was often at West Woodhay, using the house for large-scale shooting parties. When he wasn't killing things or making money, Alfred would spend hours rummaging through the family tree looking for a title to claim. He clearly resented Horace's youthful position as heir to the estate. Nor did he fail to disguise his irritation with his spirited Irish sister-in-law Mary de Vere, who fitted uneasily into West Berkshire society. The feeling was mutual.

Unfortunately, in a family dominated by highly accomplished and forceful women, Uncle Alfred was now Horace's principal male role model. He was not a good one. Alfred was pompous, boorish and uncultured. His sole aim was to make money, yet he kept his widowed sister-in-law so short of funds that she was forced to sell her jewels to pay for her family's keep at West Woodhay. Horace shared his uncle's, and presumably his own father's, belligerent outlook. But he deplored his greed and his unsympathetic treatment of his mother. Uncle Alfred came to represent, then to define, everything Horace agitated against in life. This was the 'Alfred Clayton Cole,' he later told his brother Jim, 'who persecuted mother and hated our father.' All he could do as a child to retaliate was to fill Uncle Alfred's bath with frogs. But he never forgot or forgave him, setting his face against everything his uncle stood for. Ironically, the only thing he trusted was Uncle Alfred's financial advice, and this had disastrous consequences.

Alfred was soon joined in Horace's mind by another villain. To his horror, barely two years after his father died, his mother married a twenty-three-year-old officer in the Coldstream Guards called Herbert Studd. Mary's hasty decision to marry a man closer in age to her children than herself upset the Coles and caused comment in society. On the face of it, Mary's choice of second husband closely resembled her first, and that marriage had been far from successful. Herbert had followed the same path as Willie Cole—Eton, Cambridge, army—but he could never replace a father who, since departing on his final, fatal mission to India had been much mythologised by his grieving son. He shattered that special understanding Horace had with his mother, and when two half-sisters arrived, he lost her full attention too. Lady Gregory, recently widowed herself, sat next to Uncle Alfred at Mary's wedding. She observed Mary's over-exuberance and Herbert's pleasant though steely manner. To her surprise, she saw Herbert firmly contradicting an instruction Mary gave her children before the ceremony. It was a sign that they were all under a new regime, with the freewheeling, slightly chaotic household of old a distant memory. The only compensation for Horace (and it was a significant one) was his stepfather's reputation as a first-class cricketer. Herbert's younger brother Charles had even scored a century against the Australians and had played for England in the inaugural 'Ashes' series. But sporting glory could never outweigh the loss of a mother. Horace decided his stepfather was not in his mother's class 'in mind or spirit'.

4

Horace was bundled off to Eton just weeks after his mother's wedding. It felt like another rejection, and was more cause for later resentment.

Why the devil, with such a handicap, was I sent to Eton where no deaf boy could hear anything in form? Callous cruelty to an innocent boy with £600 a year, I call it. I should have been taught a trade or profession. However, I expect I was too stupid. I remember, *before I became deaf*, winning a mathematical prize at Hussey's, my first term. What chance afterwards was I ever given by my guardians of learning mathematics or anything else, deaf as I was? *None whatever!*

At the time, Eton was still in thrall to its energetic, reforming headmaster Dr Edmund Warre, who was steadily dragging that medieval institution into the modern age. Horace's housemaster was the genial Arthur Ainger, a keen athlete and amateur lyricist who encouraged his pupil's poetry and involuntary singing. Otherwise, correspondence with the college librarian has established that Horace's career at Eton was marked by a singular, one might say purposeful, lack of achievement. He failed to make 'Remove' with the clever boys; instead, he was in a lower form alongside Lawrence Oates, who would one day walk out of Captain Scott's tent in the Antarctic. He won no prizes, played in no school teams and occupied no high office (inevitably Uncle Alfred had been Head of School). Being Irish he was not expected to work too hard, so didn't.

However, despite all its fagging, ragging and undercurrent of brutality, Eton did cement Horace's love of learning, particularly of history. This passion was aided by inspiring teachers like poet A.C. Benson, Edward Austen Leigh—known as 'the Flea' because of the blood he drew with his thrashings—and 'Mad Muggins' MacNaghton, who taught Greek before he committed suicide by walking into the Thames. He was also a popular boy, making a string of lifelong friendships, among them with Teddy Mulholland, son of Lord Dunleath, Reggie Bastard and Oliver Locker-Lampson, who kept a revolver at school. The lack of parental control at home, an instinctively rebellious nature and a self-conscious effort to overcome the handicap of his deafness resulted in a devil-may-care attitude which schoolboys find appealing. We can be sure he led the high jinks which haunt every housemaster.

In many ways which matter, Horace never left Eton, nor it him. The school's simmering anarchy, otherworldliness and

constant agitation between oppressed and oppressor suited his combative spirit. After his disrupted childhood, he was drawn to the fierce loyalty of the boys and their shared code of conduct. Good manners, sportsmanship, honesty, gallantry and kindliness bonded them together. When a boy breached the code, he took the punishment cheerfully and without protest. Horace's

Horace the Etonian, still conventional (Francis Chamberlain).

friend Walter Keppel, Viscount Bury (known as 'Gooseberry') was caned ten times one term, and it is unlikely Horace fared any better. Yet they did expect fair play: unjustified punishment was intolerable and, worse, somehow foreign. When Horace and a naval officer ritually caned each other after the *Dreadnought* hoax both men were honouring this unspoken rule.

An opportunity to demonstrate the virtues implanted at Eton came sooner than expected. The outbreak of the Boer War in 1899 signalled an outpouring of national fervour. The pacifist Lady Gregory complained that even Mary Studd was swept up by the jingoistic mood and was almost hysterical with nervous excitement. Her husband sailed with his regiment, and her schoolboy son eagerly pressed to follow him. Deafness might have barred him from the army, so he looked enviously towards the Imperial Yeomanry, a series of volunteer companies raised by private subscription which had sprung up around the country to meet the call to arms. Even Uncle Alfred was impressed by Horace's determination not to miss the action. He told a friend,

> I did not want to throw cold water on his enthusiasm as this really is the first thing he has ever shown himself really keen about. Mary did not want to stop his going and...I felt on the whole it was an opportunity of him seeing some service which he would not get in the ordinary way. Also I was very pleased with his spirit.

So, with the blessing of Dr Warre, Horace left Eton in February 1900 on 'indefinite leave' and travelled to St James's to enlist in the elitist Duke of Cambridge's Own, essentially a volunteer cavalry company for hooray henrys. By May, Trooper Cole, the youngest cavalryman in the whole British army (or so he claimed), was in Cape Town. 'I never expected Table Mountain to be so flat,' he reported on arrival, 'it really is absolutely flat on the top with the town right underneath it.' The place itself was disappointing, and 'very like any English provincial town', while saluting officers, many he recognised from school, rankled deeply. He dined at the Mount Nelson hotel with friends from school like John Christie, shared coffee with the Duke of Norfolk, and pitched tent with an Elphinstone cousin. He told his mother, 'I should say it is much the same sort of life as any Tommy Atkins gets in camp on Salisbury Plain except maybe it is hotter and there is not such a variety of provisions.' In truth, it felt more like a jolly excursion to the Eton versus Harrow game at Lord's than a war, and with less chance of bloodshed. It was a great adventure. Horace even found time to play a joke on his commanding officer involving a dead donkey.

While in camp, he was commissioned in the Yorkshire Hussars, his deafness apparently proving no bar, first as lieutenant, then, as losses mounted, as acting captain. He may have benefited from family connections, but he had also plainly demonstrated an

Going to war with the Duke of Cambridge's Own (Francis Chamberlain).

ability to command. Where Horace led, others tended to follow: beguiled by his charm and browbeaten by his persuasiveness. After several frustrating weeks enduring the heat, dust and rumours of camp, his regiment finally headed to the front line in the eastern Orange Free State. It was as exciting as going to a meet at Issercleran. The Yorkshires were tasked with escorting a convoy through enemy territory in support of an attack on Bethlehem, a Boer stronghold. At about midday on 2 July, the enemy engaged the convoy near the town of Lindley. Horace and his troop peeled off to hunt down the attackers in the surrounding hills. As they cautiously returned, they almost rode over some concealed Boer snipers. Horace was hit immediately, though he clung to his horse's neck long enough to gallop away before tumbling to the ground.

Typically, his wound was unusual, even freakish. The bullet, the deadly 'dum-dum' variety, had entered his back, where it shattered into fragments before exiting through his shoulder blade. Only a slight ricochet from his slung rifle saved him from instant death. 'The sensation of being shot was terrible,' he reported to his mother, 'but after a few seconds one felt quite sleepy.' He lay peacefully, without feeling anything, 'on my back and seeing the sky full of stars, although it was a cloudless winter's day in the Veldt with a blazing midday sun'. Who can know what passed through Horace's mind as he lay alone and bleeding? Resignation to his fate? That he had achieved a glorious end? The physical scarring never left him, and probably accounted for his early death, but those few transcendental minutes acquired an even greater significance over time. They marked the end of innocence and an agonising breach with the past, with its hopes and dreams. Horace was still Horace. But the boy knocked from his horse would arise a man determined to confront the world, no longer fearful of death or the consequences of living. 'What a pity to have missed such a happy end!' he would write in 1932. 'What chance the whole damn business of life is.'

Horace was taken to a field hospital, then to the Red Cross hospital at Kroonstad. ('It was curious coming here on the Lord's match day,' Horace wryly remarked in his first letter home. 'I hope Eton won this term.') The numbness was shortlived, and by the time he was attended to Horace had fallen into a delirious fever, with his life hanging in the balance. Internal bleeding had dislodged his heart, causing his right lung to collapse, while an X-ray revealed no less than eight pieces of shrapnel embedded deep within him. The doctors punctured his side and extracted over two pints of blood to return the heart to its proper position and ease his breathing. The procedure saved him, but for the rest of his life Horace knew that a heavy fall might kill him. It failed to, and many other things contributed towards Horace's early death: drink, despair, loneliness, poverty. But that bullet played its part, giving Horace—and how he would have enjoyed this—a post-mortem claim to be the last casualty of the Boer War. Living on the edge of oblivion made him careless of the future and hungry to experience life in every shape and form. Far from limiting his behaviour, it liberated him, as if every day was a victory over death.

News of Horace's wound was treated phlegmatically at home. 'Poor Horace,' said Uncle Alfred, 'he was so anxious to get to the front and so depressed to think he had started too late.' Horace remained at Kroonstad until September 1900, when he was transferred by train to Cape Town and then by hospital ship to England. After barely three months' active service and only eight in the army, his adventure was over. He had a medal to join those of his ancestors and he had a pension of £2 a week for life for his wound. This he immediately cashed in, giving the proceeds of £1800, as he always had his army pay, to the fund for war widows and orphans. Horace's wounds healed over a long convalescence at West Woodhay. The only outward sign of his short but eventful military career was his moustache (obligatory for officers at the time). This treasured wartime souvenir was nurtured by Horace until it became his most distinctive feature, rivalling the Kaiser's in luxurious growth and vitality.

Coronation day 1902 found Horace playing a riotous game of billiards with his Elphinstone cousins at West Woodhay. As oaths were sworn in Westminster Cathedral, a flying ball broke the glass on Grandma Cole's print of Frith's *Derby Day*. The Edwardian era had begun in appropriately noisy fashion. But for Horace it meant the bitter realisation that, at just twenty, the life he had planned was over. The only career he had ever desired—that of a warrior—was closed to him. His epiphany in the dust of the veldt had removed his fear of death; and life without the dread of death loses momentum and meaning. A mischievous, even malicious, streak had been evident in him before the war, but Horace emerged from it with the motivation for revenge against a world which had left him fatherless, deaf and crippled by injury. Soon he would have the means and method to exact it. He only lacked a stage. That year he found that too. He went up to Cambridge.

5

Old William Cole, the progenitor of the family fortune and Horace's grandfather, had carved his own way through life. Within a generation, his industry, perseverance and the public's appetite for the wonder-drug quinine had lifted his family from a Norfolk backwater to a lavish Berkshire estate. William's social expectation had also risen with prosperity. His own education was modest and patchy but his two sons Willie and Alfred were sent to Eton then Trinity College, Cambridge, one of the most elite colleges of an already exclusive university. Despite the distractions of war, a lack of application to study, and the doubts of Grandma Cole as to 'how he might get on' there, it was unthinkable that Horace would not follow in their footsteps. After cramming with a private tutor, he scraped past the entrance examination and went up in October 1902, settling into first-year lodgings in King's Parade.

The university then was nothing like the well-ordered, career-focused institution of today. It was small, insular and predominantly male, with an air of disorder which occasionally erupted into anarchy. A visit of the King and Queen to Cambridge during Horace's second year was met with rioting and a vast conflagration of broken furniture on Parker's Piece. Town and gown viewed each other with little less than loathing. The closest the privileged undergraduates came to mingling with their fellow Cambridge residents was in their use of the town prostitutes.

Uncle Alfred had maintained strong connections with Cambridge since his own days there through friendships with the university librarian Francis Jenkinson, known as 'Jinks', and, intriguingly, with the Rabelaisian Oscar Browning. Browning was a fellow of King's College and, like the other Oscar, a flamboyant seducer of undergraduates and shop boys. Before his dismissal for improper conduct, 'The O.B.' had taught Alfred at Eton, and he now lorded it over Cambridge. His squat, dissolute figure must have been a familiar one to Horace as it bustled in and out of King's College below his window. Today, Browning is seen as the guiding light for a whole generation of free-thinking students, many contemporary with Horace, who came to be associated with Bloomsbury. Browning exerted his influence through the Cambridge Conversazione Society, or 'Apostles', a self-selected coterie of half a dozen or so young intellectuals called 'Angels' who met weekly in an affected aura of secrecy to debate a chosen topic. As unofficial Archangel, Browning lent proceedings a narcissistic and self-indulgent air where (homo)sexual innuendo could flourish, snobbery was encouraged and superiority assumed. If the O.B. set the tone of the meetings, the brilliant young philosopher G.E. Moore, a fellow at Trinity, provided the intellectual framework. Looking back, Moore shaped the outlook of a whole, golden generation of Cambridge undergraduates who in their different ways would haul Britain into the modern age.

The year Horace went up, the Apostles included, from his own college Trinity: Lytton Strachey, Leonard Woolf and Saxon Sydney-Turner; and, from King's College: fellow-freshman John Maynard Keynes. Another Trinity man, Clive Bell, was omitted as he was thought too worldly and hearty. These were not the sort of men Horace particularly warmed to or could admire. He was wary of their sexuality, disdainful of their academic posturing and indignant at their intellectual arrogance. Yet in the small society of the university (there were only three thousand undergraduates at the time) and the narrow confines of college life their paths often crossed, as they would for the next twenty years. Horace was on the fringes of their intellectual set but he shared some of their academic curiosity, joining the less distinguished Sunday Essay Society, which, it was said, converted 'puppyism into dogmatism'. As a counterweight he was also a member of the less-than-earnest and heavy-drinking Magpie and Stump, a debating society named after a notorious local brothel which took a more sardonic look at the world. It was at Trinity, too, that Horace most likely first encountered the Ghost Club, a London-based society which had its roots at the college. Its earnest investigations into paranormal activity no doubt appealed to his spiritual side, though he could also see humour in the subject. Apparently a lifelong member, he later delighted in turning up for meetings in bizarre fancy dress and based several jokes around ghosts and haunting.

Undoubtedly the intellect which Horace most admired at Cambridge belonged to his tutor and mentor George Macaulay Trevelyan, whose iconoclastic lectures drew large crowds and ruffled traditionalist feathers (forcing his resignation from Trinity in 1903). Trevelyan nurtured Horace's deep love of history, layering his passion for myth and legend with meaning and context. He shared with his student his passion for Italy, telling his romantically minded pupil that he could have been one of Garibaldi's officers. Trevelyan's untimely departure from Cambridge disrupted Horace's education and weakened his enthusiasm for study. But his tutor had radicalised him politically, completing his journey away from the comfortable Tory world of the English upper classes. Despite the progressive thinking of his mother and Irish aunts, Horace had so far been shaped politically by Uncle Alfred, a fierce Tory and stalwart of the Conservative Association of the City of London. At Eton, Horace had even been reprimanded for entering his matron's room and turning a portrait of Tory *bête noir* William Gladstone against the wall. But the experience of warfare, when he had lived cheek by jowl with tommies from the working classes, seeing many of them killed, liberalised him.

Now when a voguish wave of Fabian Socialism swept Cambridge, Horace was among the first to convert, its utopian message suiting his imagination. Like many university men at the time, Horace felt discomfort at his personal good fortune and was strongly idealistic about the future. There was something heroic and noble about the working classes. By contrast, the bourgeois obsession with career, domesticity and accumulating money struck him as undignified, vulgar and immoral. Life was a gift, and it was a duty of the recipient to use it wisely, generously and creatively. A cynic, of course, might say that Horace, like many well-heeled socialists, could well afford to take this view. Yet he brought real passion—and humour—to the radicals' cause. For instance, finding himself in a house party in the South of France with a terrifying upper-class matron, he printed then pasted all over town posters announcing a suffragette demonstration, forcing her to flee.

His curiosity with socialism led Horace to the Working Men's College, set up in London by theologian F.D. Maurice in 1854 to further the education of the working man (and still going strong). Original sponsors of the college had included John Ruskin, Dante Gabriel Rossetti and John Stuart Mill. But by its golden jubilee, as Horace bitterly complained, the college was staffed by 'terrible prigs [who] desire earnest tête-à-têtes with men, about "intellectual" subjects. They have little humour and no idea of talking amusingly and with interest about every day and ordinary things.' Horace much preferred the congenial and collegiate atmosphere of Toynbee Hall in the East End of London, where undergraduate volunteers eased their conscience by providing social work to the local community. Contact with progressive socialism, albeit of a rather genteel variety, shifted Horace's moral horizon and opened a breach with his family. 'Reform comes not from the rulers but from the rank and file,' he announced to a mystified Grandma Cole. His new-found zeal for reform found a target in the college dons. 'They are monastic and dictatory, attaching ridiculous importance to trifles and overlooking grave things.' Grave things meant art, life, love. Trifles were rules, laws, convention. It was a statement of intent. Over time, the much-maligned college authorities would be joined by policemen, politicians, naval (never army) officers, ecclesiastics and modern artists.

Horace's opinion of his fellow students was equally coloured by his strongly held views and personal experience. Like the post-war intakes of 1919 and 1945, the university was split at the time between those undergraduates who had and those who hadn't seen active service with the army. The age difference was small—a year or two at most—but the gulf in outlook was significant, not least in sexual matters. Horace's war had been short, but several weeks in camp with thousands of red-blooded working-class troops and with the brothels of Cape Town nearby quickly knocked off any repressed attitudes. In contrast, many of his fellow undergraduates had come straight up from public school, and except for family members had no knowledge of girls, but rather too much of boys. The onanism of the clever-clever Apostles, with their cultish behaviour, sniggering and juvenile sense of humour, was easily ridiculed by men who had repeatedly faced death. An incident on the Cam with Clive Bell illustrated this difference. According to Lytton Strachey, Horace 'saw some hair apparently floating on the river, pulled it up and found a female attached to it. Cole denied that he'd pulled the lady by the hair, and said he'd done it by taking hold of her under the arms; on which Bell, who was there, said, "Surely that isn't incompatible".'

The point is that Horace had saved the girl while Bell stood by with a clever quip.

Horace's friends shared a similar background to him and were less angst-ridden than the college clique surrounding Strachey, and also a great deal less earnest. Many had been at Eton and most were good sportsmen, an ability for which Horace always retained the very highest respect. Their names can be glimpsed in his letters home: George Lyttelton, father of jazz trumpeter Humphrey Lyttelton; Robert Longman, scion of the eponymous publishing house; the exotic and scholarly Stephen Gaselee, who played tennis in a hair net; Irish peer Lord Moore; Dick Sheppard, later a much-loved Dean of Canterbury; Irish childhood friend George Colthurst; Oliver Locker-Lampson, son of a popular Victorian poet; and John Christie, founder of the Glyndebourne festival of opera and one of only two undergraduates to own a car, a beloved Georges-Richard. In an era when men addressed each other by surname, close friends used nicknames. Horace's was 'Molar', in tribute, no doubt, to his self-confessed 'ugly mouth', though it seems it was also Uncle Alfred's nickname at Cambridge. Nevertheless, it is as 'Molar Cole' that Horace often appears in his friends' memoirs.

But it was a former pupil of Westminster School who would become Horace's closest intimate at Cambridge. Adrian Stephen was the son of the author and critic Sir Leslie Stephen, whose gaunt, lanky figure he had taken after. Adrian's elder brother Thoby, called 'the Goth', was also at Trinity when Horace went up and, although not an Apostle himself, was an acolyte of the philosophy of G.E. Moore and close to Strachey, Leonard Woolf and Keynes. Both Thoby and Adrian were keen sportsmen, enjoying hunting, beagling and cricket at Cambridge, down-to-earth characteristics which appealed to Horace. Adrian was also an accomplished actor, excelling on the stage at school and college. Meanwhile, the Stephens' beautiful sisters Vanessa (later Bell) and Virginia (later Woolf) caused even Apostolic hearts to flutter when they wafted into Cambridge for May Week. Like Horace, Adrian had been encouraged to think for himself since childhood, and to challenge convention. 'It had seemed to me since I was very young,' he admitted, 'just as I imagine it had seemed to Cole, that anyone who took up an attitude of authority over anyone else was necessarily also someone who offered everyone else a leg to pull.' Here was the perfect foil for Horace: someone sympathetic and encouraging yet unafraid to take him on. There was something subversive about Adrian which motivated Horace. He played a leading role in both the Zanzibar and *Dreadnought* hoaxes, and I doubt very much that Horace would have attempted either without Adrian by his side.

Horace didn't work very hard at Cambridge. In fact, after George Trevelyan left, he hardly worked at all. 'Looking back on my years at Trinity,' he recalled in the 1930s, 'how long each day seemed: and yet we had long nights of sleep too!' Initially there had been no obvious signs of the man who would one day terrorise the Café Royal. He was serious-minded and well-intentioned. For instance, at a May Week ball in 1903, Horace was to be found not on the dance floor but playing bridge in an anteroom with the classical scholar Walter Headlam. He took tea with the Darwins—the most highly respected family in Cambridge—founded a croquet club and practised his real tennis so much that he was considered for a Blue. Nobly, 'I stood down for a better man who in his turn refused to play and Oxford won.' But imperceptibly things were changing, as surely as the old century was turning into the new. The ragging familiar to every undergraduate was escalating, with Horace now more often than not ringleader. Drink played its part. John Christie was woken at 3 a.m. one morning to the alarming sight of Horace thrusting a dagger into the pillow on either side of his head, a sign of the violence that always lurked beneath his behaviour (George Lyttelton recalled with a shudder how Horace always kept a shillelagh—a traditional Irish cudgel—in his rooms as a warning to unwelcome visitors).

An accomplished and daring athlete, by night Horace went roof-climbing with the Cambridge Alpine Club, earning the considerable distinction of being the first student to conquer the vertiginous Great Gateway of Trinity. During the day he organised fake funerals for rusticated students, such as that of poet-philosopher T.E. Hulme, sent down in 1904 for idleness and disruptive behaviour. Together with Adrian Stephen, he also started playing practical jokes 'on a small scale', though the details of most of these are lost. In his notes for a lost autobiography, Horace mentions only antics involving examinations and the college kitchens, but we can be certain there were many more. And already, as his Eton contemporary Robert Vansittart later observed, Horace was achieving 'a standard higher than the increasing imbecility of students' rags'. Anthony Buxton, for instance, loved to relate how Molar Cole slipped incognito into the annual Newmarket to Cambridge walking race and won by a huge margin, to cheering crowds. Religion provided a rich seam for humour, its rituals, costumes and posturing proving irresistible to a burgeoning imagination. He bullied the staunchly atheist Adrian Stephen into Christianity at the point of a sword and, very theatrically, converted to Catholicism himself while stretched out on a coffin in his rooms. It was also said that he visited a leading public school dressed as the Anglican Bishop of Madras to confirm the boys in the chapel. He was, it is fair to say, building a reputation.

He was also developing an earthy taste for music hall, circuses and boxing matches. The colours, noise and pungent smells of sex, drink and sweat in the halls were irresistible. He loved sensation and all that was modern and artificial. They met a need to counter the mundane tragedy of life with the fantastic and bizarre. The halls were an escape valve from the stultifying world of aunts and drawing-rooms. They were strange and outlandish and sexually charged, the cacophony of sound reaching through his muffled hearing. There was the New Theatre in Cambridge, but it was a pale and sanitised version of the London halls. So although he still dutifully joined Uncle Alfred for recitals at the Wigmore Hall, he now much preferred to slip away afterwards to the cavernous Alhambra, Bedford or Empire music halls to thrill at the acts, gawp at the chorus girls and be assailed by the prostitutes in the lobby. It was a world of role playing, lurid colours, crude knockabout humour, cross-dressing and impersonation. Where 'swells' like Horace could mingle with 'mashers' from the working classes, sharing in their crude entertainment and plebeian tastes. He soon counted their greatest star, Marie Lloyd, among his acquaintances. Society's rules and the hierarchy of class meant nothing in the flickering gaslight. The strange make-believe world of the halls, with all its fakery, glitter and gloss, offered a refuge from the real. Black-faced minstrels, cockney dressed-up sultans and the poking of fun at authority were standard fare in the Edwardian halls. Horace's talent was to take such acts away from the West End and play them out on a public stage and to an audience unfamiliar with the variety tradition. It was daring, shocking and great fun.

6

I knew a man who said that love, and hate, and fear
Were but unmeaning words that had no life;
No heart had he, no sympathies, and near
Where should have been his soul, I found a knife,
And on its blade, deep-bitten in by rust,
I read four words engraved: 'Life, life is lust'.

*I*n their second year at Cambridge, Adrian and Horace moved into college rooms near each other in palatial Neville's Court. Down the corridor lodged Prince Yugala of Siam, a satisfyingly exotic figure for two overactive imaginations. According to Adrian's sister Virginia, 'Horace turned up in his rooms one day and said, Hullo Stephen, what are you doing with all those books? Reading for my exam, said my brother, Oh nonsense said Horace. Let's do something amusing. Well, my brother was only too happy to throw away his books. And so they amused themselves.' Adrian later claimed his own inspired suggestion was to travel to Alsace-Lorraine, don German uniforms and cross the border into France with a detachment of hastily assembled troops. With tension then running dangerously high between the countries over control of Morocco, such an escapade could have caused, in Adrian's own words, an 'international incident' (Quentin Bell opined that his uncle would, more than likely, have been shot).

That such a preposterous stunt could even have been considered, Adrian admitted, threw 'an odd light on the world we lived in before the War' (odder still today with the hindsight of two world wars, a cold war and the attack on New York's Twin Towers). Horace pooh-poohed the idea: not on the basis of risk but because he considered it impractical, lacking in spontaneity and too costly. According to Adrian, Horace proposed using a planned private visit to England by the young, English-educated Sultan of Zanzibar—the flamboyantly named Sayyid Ali ibn Hamud Al-Busaid—as cover for targeting someone closer to home, and his was the plan adopted. Horace would impersonate the Sultan on a state visit to Cambridge. The thrill would be cheaper, the audience larger and the celebrity more rewarding if they could pull off such a stunt under the very noses of their student friends and the college authorities.

Bizarrely, the plan which Adrian had originally mooted would be executed—but not by him. The following year, in October 1906, a German petty criminal dressed up as a captain in the imperial army commandeered some genuine troops and marched into the Berlin suburb of Köpenik. There he held the mayor hostage and fleeced the town for 4000 marks. The public applauded the feat, and even the Kaiser was said to have been amused at the audacity of the heist. In London, the *Daily Mail* copied the feat by marching men dressed in German uniforms down Oxford Street to promote the serialisation of one of the 'invasion scare' novels so popular at the time.

The coincidence of Adrian's thought and the deed of the so-called 'captain of Köpenik' is striking. Adrian was writing thirty years later—is it possible he muddled or glossed his recollection? Interestingly, the captain of Köpenik and Cambridge hoaxes succeeded for the same reason. Both targeted that universally ridiculed figure of pettyfogging parochialism the town mayor. Choosing an unsympathetic victim is essential to a successful prank, and in Mr Campkin, a pharmacist and mayor of Cambridge, Horace chose well. He calculated, as Adrian admitted, that the university authorities 'would be more likely to be lenient if we were satisfied with hoaxing the mayor'. Cleverly, Horace was trading on the mutual dislike between town and gown to secure his triumph. In other words, he was exploiting snobbism of one kind to humiliate pretension of another.

The plot was simple. Adrian and Horace would assemble a group of like-minded friends and visit Cambridge in the guise of the Sultan and his suite. Horace told the press afterwards that the prank had been 'entirely and absolutely original'. Yet, despite his denials, it bears a very close resemblance to a similar hoax carried out in Cambridge in 1873 when Horace's father Willie had been up at the university. On that occasion, a telegram had been sent to the mayor of Cambridge purporting to be from the equerry to the Shah of Persia warning of his imminent arrival in the town. Crowds gathered, bunting was unfurled, troops lined up and dignitaries assembled before it became painfully apparent that the Shah was never going to show up. This is not the sort of story a devoted father would forget telling an impressionable son who loved acting and making mischief.

The tale of the Shah of Persia hoax surely played on Horace. But the Sultan of Zanzibar was also an agreeably exotic vehicle for his fantasies. The very name Zanzibar exuded romance and mystery. It was a word familiar to countless Victorian children through swashbuckling tales of piracy and derring-do. Its richness and remoteness satisfied the imagination while its colourful spiritual leader fulfilled expectations of the strangeness of foreigners. It was perfect material for the music hall, where *The Sultan of Zanzibar*, said to be 'the worst comic opera on earth', had been playing from the 1880s and *Zanzibar*, 'a comic opera in two acts' had been performed by a troupe of minstrels since 1903.

Apart from Adrian and Horace, two other 'Zanzibarees' were conscripted from Trinity. Fellow Irishman Robert Bowen-Colthurst was a willing accomplice, as was Leland Buxton, who was fascinated by the exoticism of the Middle East and Orient. Leland, like his cousin Anthony, who would figure in the *Dreadnought* hoax, came from the Quaker tradition. Though not a Quaker himself, this family tradition had given him a strong desire for social justice, fairness and equality which chimed well with the aims of the Fabian movement. Leland's brother Noel Buxton, later a minister in the first Labour government, had founded the Balkan Committee to investigate recent Turkish atrocities against Macedonia. This was a cause which had exercised the Byronic liberating fantasies in both Leland and Horace, who reported home that he was 'very much interested in this Macedonian question'.

Most importantly, both Robbie Bowen-Colthurst and Leland Buxton had been at Harrow with the Sultan, so they could provide valuable insight into his manner, looks and personality. Furthermore, the then prince had earned a much-reviled reputation at school for standing on his dignity, adding to the motivation for mocking him now by imitation. On one occasion he had even threatened to cut off the head of an older boy who asked him to run an errand (one of the hoaxers perhaps?).

The fifth member of the party would play the Sultan's official 'interpreter' (although, in reality, none would have been required for the public-school-educated potentate). Another Old Harrovian was selected for this key role, although this time from Oxford not Cambridge University, as he was less likely to be recognised out of costume. Lyulph Walter Howard, paradoxically known as 'Dummer', was probably already familiar to Horace. Among the jokes for his lost book, Horace lists several under the general heading 'Oxford', including 'Revolvers', 'the Randolph Hotel' and 'the Salvation Army'. Details are sketchy, but the hotel incident might refer to a story he recalled for the *Daily Express* in 1911. This described how Horace walked up to the manager of an hotel and pointed a revolver to his head. The manager—responsible, one supposes, for some slight to Horace such as evicting him from his establishment—trembled as a horrified crowd gathered to watch. Then Horace calmly pulled the trigger. 'The pistol was empty!' declared the paper with a flourish. 'It was another joke!' Yet the episode sits uneasily in Horace's canon of works, an unpleasant reminder of the bullying aggression that always lurked beneath the humour. Presumably he enjoyed the feeling of power over his victim. Today, Horace would face prosecution for assault (if he wasn't shot by armed police first). Yet in an era when revolvers were freely available and carried by many men, he merely raised an uncomfortable laugh. It is another reminder that he operated in a very different world to ours.

From their base at Trinity the hoaxers plotted carefully; too cautiously, perhaps, as someone warned them that unless they moved quickly their plan would be foiled. Hurriedly the prank was brought forward to Thursday 2 March 1905, when it was known the Sultan would be in London. The day before, Adrian and Horace travelled up to London from Cambridge to attend a housewarming party in Bloomsbury hosted by Adrian's sisters Vanessa and Virginia. The others followed on the milk train, meeting Horace at Willy Clarkson's theatrical costumiers in Covent Garden early the next morning.

Clarkson's plump figure, with its curling red moustache and rouged face, was a familiar one in theatrical circles. He had fitted costumes for productions as far afield as New York and Paris and provided wigs to all the leading ladies of the Edwardian Age, from Marie Lloyd to Sarah Bernhardt. Clarkson had even supplied the wardrobe for performances at court, with Edward VII officially appointing him 'Royal Perruquier and Costumier'. Yet he was also a mildly sinister individual with a mysterious past and troubled future, who kept unsavoury company and in the end was probably murdered.

The real Sultan
of Zanzibar,
Old Harrovian
Sayyid Ali ibn
Hamud Al-
Busaid.

Robbie Bowen-
Colthurst,
who played
'Srikwar, a
servant' in the
Cambridge
hoax, shown
later as Vice-Chamberlain to the Viceroy of
Ireland (courtesy of Harrow School).

Lyulph 'Dummer' Howard, the Oxford man
who was 'Henry Lucas, the interpreter' in
the Cambridge hoax (courtesy of Harrow
School).

Leland Buxton, who played 'Ham, a noble'
in the Cambridge hoax (Judith Lister).

The Zanzibar hoaxers before they set off for Cambridge, official portrait signed by
Horace, Adrian Stephen and Leland Buxton. From left, Adrian Stephen, Robbie
Bowen-Colthurst, Horace, Leland Buxton, Dummer Howard (Francis Chamberlain).

From now on the mephistophelian Clarkson would be inextricably linked to Horace's notoriety, their talents touching in many of the coming years' stunts and jokes. Each glowed in the other's reputation before dying in similar states of wretchedness within months of each other. 'Willie,' Horace would recall, 'gave me the freedom of his world-famous shop, i.e. he dressed me up or lent me costumes for nothing!' Uncle Alfred would not have approved. On the first occasion they met, however, Clarkson, as he recalled in *The People* newspaper a quarter of a century later, knew Horace simply as 'plain Mr Brown'. 'No one could have suspected that under that gentlemanly front of reserve,' he wrote, 'that tall spruce exterior, with its trim moustache, and that bland, cultured countenance there lurked an ever-active impish mischief.'

Clarkson was a master at creating disguise and of understanding the psychological need for it. 'How many people there are,' he observed in an article for *Strand Magazine*,

> who yearn passionately to be, not themselves—although that is sometimes difficult, too—but somebody else! Of course, this yearning can be satisfied by going on the stage. On the stage you can pretend to be a millionaire (with only a shilling in the world), or an Abyssinian prince, or a solicitor, and look exactly like each of these characters and people will believe you—for a couple of hours or so. And then the curtain falls; you go out by the stage door, and you are yourself again. But the stage is not life. In real life your yearning is apt to go unsatisfied, because you have never heard of anybody disguising themselves but a detective, and you have no ambitions, or, maybe, no gifts, in that direction.

Horace felt such a yearning intensely. He naturally assumed the role of Sultan for the hoax, and was dressed and made-up convincingly by Clarkson, as were Buxton and Bowen-Colthurst as his retinue. The bedders at Trinity later revealed that the costumes had already been sent to Cambridge for approval. But Adrian's disguise, an ill-fitting robe topped off by an incongruous headscarf, was less convincing. Compared to the others, his make-up also looked patchy, as if it had been applied hurriedly. This suggests to me that Adrian might have arrived late, and hungover, at Clarkson's following the party the evening before, when—according to his sister Virginia—lots of champagne had been drunk and lobsters consumed.

There was another hitch. The hoaxers not only learned that the real Sultan was going, very publicly, to the Palace later in the day—making his appearance in Cambridge awkward—but that his photograph had appeared prominently in the press, making things impossible. Unfortunately, a telegram announcing the Sultan's intention to visit the town for a tour of the university had already been sent to Cambridge, and been politely acknowledged by the mayor. The telegram, which was

left Master of disguise and make-up artist to the stars, Willy Clarkson, photograph by Bassano (© National Portrait Gallery, London).

right The hoaxers in alternative pose (Valerie Crosia).

sent from the nearest post office to Clarkson's about midday, was signed Henry Lucas, 'simply because someone said that high colonial officials always bore that name'.

Reply paid: Strand, Southampton Street
To the Mayor of Cambridge

The Sultan of Zanzibar will arrive today at Cambridge at 4.27 for short visit. Could you arrange to show him buildings of interest and send carriage?

HENRY LUCAS, Hotel Cecil, London

Now with the Sultan splashed all over the newspapers, Horace had to think quickly or abort the mission. Hastily he re-cast himself as the Sultan's uncle, 'Prince Mukasa Ali', a name possibly inspired by Ham Mukasa, a Ugandan whose lively account of his visit to England for Edward VII's coronation was a recent bestseller. Adrian would play the Grand Vizier, 'Prince Abu el Arab', Leland a noble called 'Ham' and Robbie a servant, 'Srikwar'. By this time, they had missed their train, so another telegram was dispatched delaying their arrival into Cambridge until 5.43 (wisely, Horace also declined the mayor's polite invitation to dinner). Another cause for the hold-up was Horace's desire to have the hoaxers photographed for posterity and, as it transpired, publicity purposes. However, in the two pictures that survive—taken at a photographer's near Liverpool Street Station—they all seem tense and uncomfortable. Dummer Howard looks particularly forlorn in his drab mackintosh beside his colourful and towering accomplices (all four were well over six feet tall). Nevertheless this clever use of technology became the hallmark of Horace's success as a prankster. Who could say whether his two greatest hoaxes would have survived so long without the wonderfully evocative images of the perpetrators? The formalities completed, Horace finally led his troupe into the station where, needless to say, they caused quite a stir before embarking for Cambridge. As they settled into their seats, 'it occurred to us that Eastern princes did not usually travel with their servants'. So the hapless Howard was dispatched to second class.

As instructed by the hoaxers' telegram, the mayor sent a carriage to meet the town's distinguished guests. Mayor Campkin himself waited behind at the Guildhall, his anxiety hardly relieved when he heard that the Sultan had been replaced by his uncle. 'When we got there,' Horace told the newspapers afterwards, 'we had only to grunt and the Mayor and Town Clerk bent their heads and welcomed us.' As most Edwardians viewed Africans as simple-minded, they were playing the role perfectly. Fortunately the clerk affected not to hear one of the royal visitors exclaim 'Shit!' as he got out the carriage and stood on his robes. After a difficult opening exchange during which the hoaxers salaamed repeatedly, the mayor presented Horace with a guidebook to Cambridge and offered them all champagne. More mindful, I suspect, of their make-up than their Muslim religion, this was refused by his guests. However, Horace solemnly reciprocated the gift by handing Campkin a portion of 'the dorsal fin from the Sacred Shark of Zanzibar'. He then cheerfully followed the mayor to a charity bazaar in the Guildhall, bowing reverently as he passed a bust of Queen Victoria on the stairs.

Accounts differ as to how generous the Prince was at the bazaar. In 1936 Adrian wrote that Horace made 'enormous purchases at all the stalls', but his recollection may have been coloured by his friend's reputation as a spendthrift. In contrast, as the *Daily Mail* reported after interviewing Horace, 'the Prince made no purchases' at the bazaar. It did give him a scare, however, when an elderly woman pursued him professing to speak his own language. Dummer silenced her by sternly informing the woman that she couldn't possibly talk to the Prince without first entering his harem. But it was a close shave, and a good moment to leave. With the cheers of the small crowd gathered outside the Guildhall ringing in their ears, the royal party began their tour of the university. By now thoroughly enjoying himself, Horace's only worry was that someone might see the distinctive initials 'H de VC' engraved on the gold ferrule of his umbrella.

King's College was naturally the first place to visit. Like everyone they encountered, Irishman Shane Leslie, then an undergraduate at the college, was 'completely deceived' by the pranksters though he knew several of them well. He watched the head porter rush to open the gates. 'The tall swarthy sons of the Prophet in their splendid turbans,' he wrote in his memoirs, 'their portly tread and the polite gesticulation with which they lifted their arms in mild amazement at all the sights which they were shown, made a lasting picture.' They declined to enter the glorious chapel, however, on religious grounds. Their prize was Trinity, which, after pausing at Clare and passing Trinity Hall, they reached by the Queen's Gate. To Horace's glee, the Bulldogs, or college porters, with whom he had conducted a long-running feud, doffed their hats to him as they entered. The royal sightseers widened their eyes and lifted their hands in wonder at the sight of the Great Court. They were now in their own college: at the greatest risk of exposure but with the keenest pleasure in deception. The clerk even muttered to the mayor how 'these people seem to know their way about'. Several friends saw the exotic visitors as they toured the college, but none recognised them in the gloom of the late afternoon. Cecil Kent, who went on to establish the Embassy nightclub, ran into them in New Court as he was returning from the river. 'All the Cambridge four were personal friends of mine,' he confessed, 'but I was hoodwinked as much as everybody.'

By now, his aim achieved, Horace was growing cold, bored and slightly 'hysterical', a condition he often suffered from during a hoax or period of high excitement. After a cursory look at the 'backs' and the 'Bridge of Sighs', he demanded to be returned to the station. The hoaxers had been in Cambridge less than an hour but they now faced the difficulty of an elegant exit. Dummer had told their hosts that they wanted to catch the 7.05 train back to London. But Horace had no intention of catching it, as all four Cambridge undergraduates had to return to college by ten to avoid detection. So after some more extravagant salaaming on the station platform, the Zanzibarees turned and fled, abandoning Dummer to make his own way back to Oxford. One account has the hoaxers boarding the front of the London train before walking its length and exiting by the rear. Whatever the method of escape, 'the stately calm of the Eastern Potentate gave way to the impatience, shall we say, of an undergraduate'. Children were thrust unceremoniously out of the way as Horace and his accomplices rushed for the exit.

Outside the station, all composure gone, two cabs were hailed and ordered to drive into the countryside. A mile away, on a deserted road, the deeply suspicious drivers were ordered to stop. A violent altercation over the fares was only narrowly avoided when Horace stepped magnificently into the road and, still in character, declared, 'Me pay you.' He then led his bedraggled crew to a safe house on the Trumpington Road. This can now be revealed as belonging to Leland Buxton's sister Victoria, who was in on the act. Here, laughing and joking, the hoaxers dined and toasted their success before changing into caps and gowns and racing back to college. Two of the Trinity men made it home in time, the others were forced to scale the tall iron palings surrounding the college, rolling their gowns into balls to impale on the spikes to avoid injury. Elsewhere, the college slept on, oblivious of their feat.

7

There once was a Sultan and suite
Who made progress to Liverpool Street
By all were observed
Took a carriage reserved
Since their caste was the highest elite!

The Mayor sent a carriage and pair
And the people around them did stare
But their bearing so proud
Quite delighted the crowd,
And they drove off in state to the Mayor!

(written in train returning next day from interview with *Daily Mail*!!)

*T*he day after the Cambridge joke, a triumphant Horace declared his intention to give the story to the *Daily Mail*. The others hoaxers had agreed to keep it secret but, as Adrian put it, Horace was keen for 'publicity'. He was a little older than his accomplices and, if no wiser, more worldly and less worried by the consequences of their actions than they were. His decision also shows cunning and an instinctive grasp for public relations even before such a term had been dreamt up. By telling the story first, he controlled it. Horace never doubted the power of the press, nor its ability to foster his fame. His choice of paper was inspired. The *Daily Mail*, under its thrusting young Anglo-Irish proprietor, Alfred Harmsworth, later Lord Northcliffe, had revolutionised the newsstand. It was bold, brash and punchy, printing sensational stories with an editorial emphasis on sex and money. Harmsworth even coined a term for this new, in-your-face journalism: the tabloid. It brought music hall to Fleet Street. Used to an unpalatable diet of close-typed broadsheet, the public responded with gusto. By 1905, the *Daily Mail* had a circulation of a million and an influence on government second only to *The Times* (which Harmsworth promptly bought).

Despite his misgivings, Adrian accompanied Horace, 'to see that...what got published was the truth'. The *Daily Mail* was sceptical at first, tomfoolery of this sort was always being offered up for publication. 'How do we know you are not hoaxing us as you say you hoaxed the mayor?' Horace was asked. His forceful reply persuaded the editor to send a reporter back with them to Cambridge to check the story. It broke the next morning under the headline 'Mayor Hoaxed. Cambridge Undergraduates Daring Trick. Supposed Royal Visit. Imposters Received With Civic Honours.' The paper spared no embarrassing details as it told its readers of the 'Gilbertian comedy' which had unfolded in the town. No sympathy was shown to Mr Campkin, who when ingenuously interviewed by the *Mail*'s reporter had 'repeatedly expressed regret at being unable to receive the visitors more fittingly'.

The *Cambridge Daily News* ran the story later the same day, but dutifully sought to exonerate the mayor, who after the prank was exposed had changed his tune significantly. In striking contrast to the *Mail*, the *News* captioned the story 'A Stupid Hoax! The Mayor Victimised by Undergraduates. Shah of Persia Joke Revived.' In the report, the mayor tried to shuffle blame onto his clerk by weakly suggesting that he had thought something was amiss all along. Suspecting a repeat of the Shah of Persia hoax he claimed he only sent a carriage to the station to collect his guests, not appearing there in person as protocol dictated. Defiantly, he declared that the hoaxers 'have not scored much of us because we have not spent a penny. I

Two postcards of the
Cambridge hoax, the one
above signed and sent to
Horace's sister Annie by
'Mukasa Ali, Princeps
Zanzibaris' (Francis
Chamberlain, above, and
Tristan de Vere Cole, left).

don't think they knocked any spots off me or the Town Clerk.' In gleeful reply, Horace brandished the presentation guidebook and, spinning the story back in his favour, gave his own far more entertaining interview to the same paper, under the heading 'The Prince tells his story'.

Horace's name was never released but, as the *News* coyly put it, it was already 'well known to this paper'—in consequence presumably of his previous exploits. In any event, it soon leaked out and before long, as Cecil Kent recalled, the whole university was beating a path to Horace's 'famous "Zanzibar" rooms'. Here, surrounded by 'enormous stores of fruit—pineapples, melons etc.' which, according to George Lyttelton, Horace kept extravagantly in his room, the university's chief jester held court, flamboyantly sporting heavily scented diosma in his buttonhole and dispensing photographs of the hoaxers, signed 'Mukasa Ali, Princeps Zanzibaris'. The copy sent to West Woodhay was additionally signed by Adrian and Leland. *Tatler* picked up the story and published the photograph, while an enterprising printer in the town produced postcards of the hoax. A London publisher even offered Horace a book deal for, as he marvelled, '"3 years at Cambridge" or some such title!'

As Horace no doubt hoped and expected, the university authorities did nothing. Adrian believed they would all have been sent down had the mayor insisted. But Campkin was advised 'for the sake of his own reputation to think it over'. Powerless to act, the mayor preached against the hoaxers in the pulpit of the local Methodist church and set detectives on them in the hope of entrapment. It was all to no avail, and after what Shane Leslie described as a 'nine days' laugh' the story blew over, leaving the students to their finals, the mayor with egg on his face, and Horace with a fateful taste for celebrity. (Gloriously, Campkin's name lives on in Cambridge, as his chemist shop—now a supplier of photographic equipment—

still thrives below the window of Horace's former student lodgings in King's Parade).

News of the hoax filtered back only slowly to Horace's and Adrian's families, as neither were habitual readers of the *Daily Mail*. In her journal, Virginia Stephen noted how her brother Thoby told her over breakfast at their house in Gordon Square of the 'grand practical joke' played by Adrian three days before. Then Adrian himself turned up to tell them all about it. 'We all said, What a very silly thing to do; now you'll be sent down; you won't pass your exam; and how will you ever become a lawyer if you haven't got a degree? But that blew over. The Vice Chancellor of the University said it didn't matter hoaxing a Mayor. He said in private Mayors are rather ridiculous; they give themselves great airs, and we don't much mind if you do play practical jokes on them.' Horace wrote excitedly to West Woodhay about the hoax. 'What fun it was at the time!' he reported excitedly to Grandma Cole, who also received a photograph of the hoaxers. Even Uncle Alfred eventually entered into the spirit of the joke. After seeking assurance from Cambridge that there would be no repercussions, he conceded that 'It seems to have been fun for the undergraduate performers and apparently the dons decided to treat it as a good joke, as in fact it was.'

The 'Zanzibar joke' set the course of Horace's life but, needless to say, played havoc with his studies. Adrian scraped through his law finals and left Cambridge with a third (and, according to his biographer, possibly also with syphilis). Horace didn't sit his exam, but graduated instead with, in his own words, a 'First Class, Practical Jokes Degree (Honours)'. He had wanted to go into the army. Uncle Alfred envisaged a legal career. Disability and shortage of qualification prevented these, and lack of will any other profession. Horace had, however, discovered one thing he was good at whilst at

Cambridge. 'And so,' recalled Virginia, 'instead of going to the bar or becoming a man of business, he made it his business simply to make people laugh.' Many would—if they were not his victim. Nevertheless, there was still an earnest side to him, despite the head-turning fame of the Zanzibar joke. After Cambridge, as Adrian headed on holiday with his brother and sisters, Horace travelled to East Anglia to help on a boys' camp run by Thomas Harvey, the charismatic sub-warden of Toynbee Hall, the educational settlement for the poor in the East End. Harvey was a Quaker whose pacifism and strong social conscience chimed with Horace's new-found politics. He soon learned that living alongside the working classes was very different to debating them in the panelled calm of Trinity. In particular, he was struck by the warmth and affection the boys showed towards each other compared to their aloof public-school counterparts. Tanned and healthy after a week playing cricket and sleeping in a Norfolk barn, he returned with Harvey to Whitechapel as a resident volunteer.

Toynbee Hall was fast developing a reputation as an intellectual powerhouse for a broad church of progressive thinkers. Within its cloistered ivy-clad walls—in imitation of an Oxbridge college yet incongruously set within one of the poorest districts in England—residents like William Beveridge and Clement Atlee laid the path for the modern Labour Party. But Toynbee Hall was not simply about agonising over social justice. When Leland Buxton was resident there he dressed up as Ali Baba for the college's pantomime. It was also cheek-by-jowl with a host of raucous music halls. Gilbert's, the Eastern, the Apollo, the Cambridge, Wilton's, the Queen's, the Eagle and the Empire were all on, or within a short walk of, the Whitechapel Road. The halls were a warm, noisy and colourful retreat from the degradation and hopelessness which lay all around them.

If much of the political theorising at Toynbee Hall went over Horace's head, what he found in the East End left an indelible mark on his outlook. He later expressed his shock and anger at the poverty in Britain after a visit to the equally destitute poor of Glasgow:

I went in search of Britain's hells,
Where mankind has no shame,
And found them in a mighty town
Amidst dark smoke and flame,
Beneath great obelisks of soot
Pulsated their ill fame;
And all the time a clamour went
Up to the smoke-spun skies,
It beat into my heart and rent
The veil that held my eyes:
One day, I thought, some awful vent
Will silence all these cries;

These cries from mean-bred multitudes,
Slave-born to earn their bread
In bondage to some vast machine,
Until their souls are dead,
Until their bodies rot, and they
Are hurried useless back to clay;

'Tis Economic laws I'm told,
(Hark! To the moorland breeze)
Their lives in balance are to gold,
(How glow the Autumn trees!)
The maw of the machine, tho' cold,
Yet breeds death and disease.
Hark! How the moorland's whirlwinds rise
On yon empurpled fells,
One day from the avenging skies,
They'll swoop upon these hells
And free the places once again
To air and sunshine, dew and rain.

Horace worked hard at Toynbee Hall visiting homes of the poor and helping its Charity Organisation Committee select deserving cases to support. He was particularly affected by one little girl he had seen at the London Hospital who was not expected to live. He immediately ordered flowers from the best florist in London to cheer her up. He wrote to Grandma Cole,

> Some families I have seen recently were very near being starved...one learns a good deal and realises that perhaps those people who say that there is more charity in London than in any other city in the world, are right. *But the Government should do more especially for the children.*

His compassion for children did not always match his own behaviour towards them. Children were terrified of Horace, and he was generally bemused by them (particularly his own). John Cole still recalls with a shudder how his uncle would leap out from behind a sofa with a yell, hair flying. Horace's goddaughter Jane Madden (who was given an item of Zanzibaree clothing as a souvenir) received an even greater shock. At tea with Horace one day, she proudly showed him some coloured paper boxes she had made. Without a word, her godfather popped them into his mouth and ate them. Childlike himself, Horace gave children none of the patronising respect of other grown-ups. But he did rally to their defence, and hated the cruelty he witnessed in the East End. He could never understand why the English doted on animals but treated children so badly. He would thunder,

> I don't admire the necessity for a 'Society for the prevention of Cruelty to Children' which has to deal with 100,000 cases a year and these only the ones that come to light. No other country needs such a Society. Italians have often said to me 'why do you English make such a fuss about cruelty to animals, they have no souls' (that is Catholic doctrine). 'We have no need in Italy for a Society for the prevention of cruelty to children'. And indeed they haven't.

The sympathy shown by Horace to others was in stark contrast to his wilful disregard of his own safety. In his autobiography,

Geoffrey Young, a famous mountaineer and author of *The Roof-Climber's Guide to Trinity*, related a terrifying story of climbing Scafell with Horace while they were staying with George Trevelyan in Cumbria. Fresh air and rigorous exercise were essential ingredients for progressive socialists but, like most things he did, Horace went a little too far. After enquiring 'Are you sound?' Horace dived headlong off the cliff, putting his full weight on the belay holding both men to the mountainside. 'It was the jester's way of challenging my veracity,' recalled a still shocked Young, 'and it was playing the fool in dire earnest!' Such reckless, devil-may-care behaviour was a symptom of the mounting boredom and frustration Horace felt since leaving Cambridge. It was also evidence of a deep-seated melancholy which found expression in sudden, violent acts. Today he might be termed manic depressive.

The death of Grandma Cole in 1906 exposed Horace to a danger of a quite different kind than mountaineering. Her passing brought Horace, prematurely, into his inheritance. At twenty-five he was, in his own words, master of:

1 Country House, larger than Sandringham	1 School-mistresses' house
	1 village club-house
2,500 acres	1 Steward's house & Home Farm & Buildings
5 Gardens (English, Italian, Dutch, Rose, Rock)	1 Laundry
1 Lake	5 Farms & Farm buildings
1 Roman Camp	1 Omnibus
4 Chalk pits	1 Shooting cart
9 Woods	2 shut & 2 open carriages
14 Estate Houses	1 pony carriage
1 Rectory	1 jaunting car
1 Church	2 motor cars
1 School	many horses

On another list—too lengthy to reproduce here—Horace listed all the treasures of West Woodhay's 43 rooms from its 116 oil paintings to its twenty thousand bottles of wine, eight thousand books, three pianos and a Chippendale bookcase. All were his. The trouble was he couldn't afford it, particularly as income tax had shot up since the Boer War. As he all too soon discovered, the estate was too expensive and too great a responsibility for him to manage without the stream of revenue enjoyed by his grandfather from his many business interests. These had been managed since William Cole's death by Uncle Alfred, who showed no enthusiasm for Horace to join him, even had he wished to. He was more drawn to the garish lights of London's *demi-monde* than the dull world of board meetings, shooting parties and estate management. For a time, he tried his best to act the country squire, inveigling his friends down from London to stay for noisy weekends and burgling West Woodhay himself for a bet. Poor Dobson had never seen anything like it. But his heart was never really in it, nor did he have the money to support it.

Uncle Alfred was sceptical from the outset. 'What Horace will make of West Woodhay remains to be seen,' he told Jinks in Cambridge. But he also offered a solution. To everyone's great surprise, at the age of fifty-seven and seemingly a confirmed bachelor, Alfred met and married a Canadian widow called Lilian Chamberlain. As he also now sat on the board of the Bank of England, a seat of a quite different kind was urgently needed. At first, Uncle Alfred only rented West Woodhay. Then, when it became obvious Horace could not afford to live there, he bought the estate lock, stock and barrel from his nephew. With the proceeds Horace rented a town house in Cadogan Place and splashed out on a smart new motor car for himself. Advised by Uncle Alfred, and presumably encouraged by his Canadian aunt, Horace then invested the balance of about £50,000 (or roughly £3 million at today's prices) with the Georgia Investment Co. Ltd, a development business set up by a fast-talking young entrepreneur called John Drinkle. Drinkle proposed building a series of ambitious residential and commercial buildings in the

left Horace (standing, right) and friends larking about at West Woodhay after he inherited the house in 1906 (Francis Chamberlain).

below Adrian Stephen (left) at West Woodhay, August 1906 (Francis Chamberlain).

bottom Games at West Woodhay, 1906 (Francis Chamberlain).

booming prairie town of Saskatoon in the western provinces of Canada. Drinkle frequently visited London to drum up funds, so it is likely he met Horace to pitch the investment in person. By 1912, when Horace invested his money, Drinkle had already completed one block in Saskatoon—dubbed the 'grandest building West of Winnipeg'—while another two buildings were under construction. All were built in brick and steel and fitted with the latest mod cons, including elevators, central heating and roof gardens (but little in the way of fire protection).

The rental income from the buildings was intended to keep Horace in the style of living to which he had all too readily become accustomed. Meantime the properties were expected to double in value over the coming years, offering the possibility that he might even buy back West Woodhay one day (though Uncle Alfred refused to add a clause to this effect in his terms of sale). It seemed a win–win situation. Mountstuart Elphinstone, a distant cousin who had already invested in Saskatoon and had a hand in the transaction, bet Horace £100 that his Canadian property would rise 50 per cent value within five years. Elphinstone, the younger son of a landless earl, had been farming in the western provinces of Canada since the 1890s. The whole scheme, as Horace cheerfully admitted, was to make him a 'big profit' with zero effort. He need never worry about money ever again. Horace could return to his 'Best Occupation'—idleness.

I like to rest in the open air
With arms upon some gate
Regarding with a vacant stare
The earth and sky. The Fate
Of nations may turn men's
  hearts to lead
Nor would I even try to turn
  my head!

Where Horace's money went: Drinkle Block Number 1, Saskatoon, Canada.

Alfred's was a generous but not selfless act which released Horace from the burden of West Woodhay and removed (or so he thought) any need for him ever to work. But it also left him rudderless with too much money and in the company of people all too willing to exploit him. For now, however, the perils were far from apparent. Instead, Horace revelled in his good fortune, status and rising fame. Self-styled Horace *de Vere* Cole, he set out on a grand tour of Europe to seek adventure and write verses in tribute to his illustrious name. He had always loved poetry—how could he not with such a mother—but was Horace a good poet?

It depends whether you like his unfashionable and easily-sneered-at Edwardian style. At the least I think we can agree that he was a very accomplished versifier and that some of his lines achieve a memorable resonance. He certainly lived through interesting times for poetry, witnessing a profound shift from the elegiac to the modern. Born in the era of Tennyson, Arnold and his great hero Robert Browning, Horace came to poetic maturity under Newbolt and Kipling and lived into the age of *The Wasteland*. In the middle came the First World War—and its poets—which opened a breach in literary sentiment and swept away the nostalgia, cosy sentimentalism and formal rules of the Edwardians. Artistically, Horace remained firmly lodged in the idyllic, neo-romantic world of his youth, upholding traditional techniques of metre and rhyme even when they were deemed hopelessly archaic and conservative. As late as the 1930s he considered the almost unknown Sir William Watson, an ancient, reactionary poet of the old Victorian school, to be 'our greatest living lyric poet'. In this light, it is no surprise that his own poems were published by the radical *New Age* literary magazine before the war—but not afterwards.

Like many of his Edwardian contemporaries, Horace's poems are fixated with love and death. What sets him apart from the hundreds of other long-forgotten English recreational poets of his generation was his Irishness. This defined his poetic outlook as much as it shaped his personality. It was his creative well-spring and an artistic burden. Nursed by his mother in the Irish folklore tradition, Horace's poems, like those of his friends Lord Dunsany and James Stephens, are saturated with Celtic myth and fantasy. All of them, however, laboured beneath the shadow of 'the greatest living Irishman', as Horace slightly sarcastically called W.B. Yeats, who personified the revival in Irish arts in the late nineteenth century but evolved his style to the modernism of the twentieth.

Away from Ireland, poetry (like school) played an important social role in binding upper- and middle-class Edwardians together in a manner now quite foreign to us. It was an age when young men wrote poetry earnestly, unashamedly and without embarrassment. Within Horace's closest circle of friends, many considered themselves poets or writers, and behaved accordingly with a wilful disregard for convention. No less than six of the nine veterans of the Zanzibar and *Dreadnought* hoaxes would have poems or books published during their lifetimes or posthumously, most famously, of course, Virginia Woolf. The exceptions were Robbie Bowen-Colthurst and Dummer Howard—who both died young—and Duncan Grant, who expressed his creativity with a paintbrush not pen. So Horace was part of a culture and a community of friends well used to writing and working with words. Indeed, one pictures them hammering out verses and ideas in pubs, on trains and smoke-filled sitting rooms. Poems sustained such men in an emotional crisis and were an effective means of communicating their feelings in a less openly confessional society than ours.

8

*H*orace tasted Paris first. At the time, it was the summit of high bohemia; a Mecca for the creatively dispossessed where would-be painters, poets and writers jostled to get noticed but more often simply got drunk. Horace took a beautifully decorated apartment at the Grand Hôtel near the place Vendôme, where he soaked up Maupassant 'the greatest short story writer that has ever lived'. 'One must *think* in French,' he told himself as he lay back decadently on a crimson couch. However, it was hard to hold this affected pose for very long when Montmartre and the Moulin Rouge beckoned. Even for a man steeped in London music hall, this famed theatre was beguilingly seductive, corrupting and erotically charged. The Russian poet Andrei Bely, in Paris at the same time as Horace, left a vivid impression of a similar journey in a letter to a friend:

Sometimes I would venture from my sepulchre to the jazz of night Paris, where having gathered the colours, I would think them over in front of the fire. I could be seen walking through a funeral corridor of my house and descending down a black spiral of steep stairs; rushing underground to Montmartre, all impatience to see the fiery rubies of the Moulin Rouge cross. I wandered thereabouts, then bought a ticket to watch a frenzied delirium of feathers, vulgar painted lips, and eyelashes of black and blue. Naked feet, and thighs, and arms, and breasts were being flung on me from bloody-red foam of translucent clothes. The tuxedoed goatees and crooked noses in white vests and toppers would line the hall, with their hands posed on canes. Then I found myself in a pub, where the liqueurs were served on a coffin (not a table) by the nickering devil: 'Drink it, you wretched!' Having drunk, I returned under the black sky split by the flaming vanes, which the radiant needles of my eyelashes cross-hatched. In front of my nose a stream of bowler hats and black veils was still pulsing, foamy with bluish green and warm orange of feathers worn by the night beauties: to me they were all one, as I had to narrow my eyes for insupportable radiance of electric lamps, whose hectic fires would be dancing beneath my nervous eyelids for many a night to come.

Horace threw himself headlong into this maelstrom. The art dealer Hugh Lane, a fastidious nephew of Lady Gregory who was in Paris sourcing paintings for a new gallery in Dublin, viewed his distant cousin's antics with horror. Lane was aghast to hear how Horace had won a bet by staying up continuously for three nights enjoying the pleasures of Paris.

Among the many rich young Americans crowding Montmartre's colourful streets was Oxford-educated Royall Tyler. Tyler was a scholar in Spanish history and Byzantine art. Over many evenings at his luxurious rooms on rue Vaugirard, Tyler revealed the glories of Spain to Horace and shaped his collecting eye by curating his purchase of a medieval stone bust. Often they were joined by an Andalusian guitarist called Fabian de Castro, whom Tyler had discovered. Dark-eyed and fierce-tempered, Fabian was a romantic figure who had wandered Europe as a troubadour, leaving as many broken hearts as noses behind him. Convinced he was descended from the pharaohs, Fabian sang ancient gypsy songs, mixed with the likes of Picasso and Modigliani, and painted pictures in a weird El Greco manner. Horace thought the work freakish, but collected a few examples—'he'll be worth money when he's dead! I mean his canvasses will be.' (They aren't.) Sometimes, 'El Gyptano' (as Fabian signed his paintings) would be accompanied in his guitar playing by La Macarona, a celebrated Flamenco dancer of the 1890s who had been intimate with Henri de Toulouse-Lautrec. Her vigorous, sensual dancing combined with Fabian's strange, anguished music to produce a sensation of longing and regret.

Horace later travelled to Spain with Tyler and Fabian. The heat, raw physicality and voluptuous colours of the south were a revelation; one to which he was drawn again and again. It pulled him away from the washed skies of Ireland. He prized a photograph of himself and Fabian in the Ronda Mountains, composing a verse in tribute:

> Ye violet mountains rising in the west
> Sharp-outlined by the glow, immense and sheer
> Behind your giant mass the sun fares on its guest;
> From that red furnace now projects a spear
> Of golden flame, as herald of return!
> Long ages since no suns your peaks did burn,
> Long ages hence once more beneath the tide
> You will be cool and secret, sunset-free,
> And green sea-monsters down your cliffs will glide,
> Your caverns yield strange matings of the sea!

There were friends from England in Paris too. Dummer Howard was studying architecture at the École des Beaux-Arts, while the incongruously named Tudor Castle, an acquaintance of Horace's from Trinity days, was also in town. Like Horace, Tudor was a dreamer and enthusiast, writing poetry and volunteering for Toynbee Hall. 'He has a noble character,' Horace defensively told his sister Annie, 'so noble as to be unique and therefore not easy for outsiders to see.' Virginia Stephen described Tudor as 'tinged with romanticism' but he also shared Horace's impetuosity and spirit of devilment. Leaving Cambridge in 1904 he had missed the Zanzibar joke, but reunited with Horace they were soon up to their old tricks. Augustus John, who met Horace in Paris, painted a vivid picture of Horace, 'dressed like a "milord"' striding down the wide Parisian boulevards 'on the lookout for a chance to indulge at any moment in some mad prank'.

Unfortunately Horace's French jokes are largely forgotten, though in a letter he admits to being in a French gaol in consequence of one escapade. Under 'Paris' in his notes he simply mentions bicycles, motor cars and swordstick fights in the Bois de Boulogne, the last probably the duel recalled elsewhere as settled by 'scared seconds'. Rumours swirled around about his intentions. Wyndham Lewis, also in Paris, heard that Horace was planning 'a Grand New Hoax some think that he will abduct the President, some think it will be a prowess of a more difficult, subtle and local nature'. (What could be more difficult?) One spectacular heist, however, was always denied. In an interview for the *Daily Express* in 1926 he distanced himself from the 1911 theft of the *Mona Lisa* (and other crimes), quipping,

> I never took the Mona Lisa
> Nor the jewels from the castle
> Nor overturned the tower of Pisa
> Nor put the Gold Cup in a parcel

One jape that does survive concerned a wager that Horace could not lie in the middle of a busy road for an hour. Winning the bet was as elegant as it was simple. Horace hired a lorry and drove it down the Champs Elysees. When it 'broke down' in the middle of the place de l'Opera, Horace clambered beneath it to tinker with the engine while the traffic veered around him. Like many of his best jokes, Horace repeated this one. Oliver Locker-Lampson paid up after Horace pulled off the same trick in London. 'He simply drove his car' Oliver ruefully recalled, 'into Piccadilly, produced a loud "bang" and stopped. He then crawled underneath and pretended to tinker with the works. Nobody looked at him twice. They thought that his car had broken down. I had to pay.' Motor cars, like weapons, figured often in Horace's jokes. They both fascinated and appalled him. He was always buying the latest model and crashing it spectacularly. On one occasion he careered into a cartload of people, injuring several, one critically. Cars almost killed him too, whether he was on foot, at the wheel or on a bicycle. It was a difficult relationship, and eventually, like a scorned lover, he turned against them, preferring bicycles. With all the passion of a convert, he accused motor cars of mowing down thousands of people every year 'in a messy way', going as far as blaming the demand for oil for the First World War. He was ill suited to the machine age, which lacked beauty and imagination. Machines were logical, practical and coldly systematic: the complete opposite of him. Wistfully he yearned for 'humanity…to start all over again from the jelly-fish forms'.

Finally replete with the pleasures of Paris, Horace delved deeper into Europe. For several years he was constantly on the move, sampling life in every form on his picaresque travels.

In North Africa he travelled incognito 'as a deaf and dumb Arab', a journey inspired perhaps by Leland Buxton, who after Cambridge had been on a daring expedition to the Yemen with the dashing Old Etonian Aubrey Herbert, the model for the John Buchan character Greenmantle. Back in London, Herbert recounted the adventure over lunch with Horace,

Travelling 'as a deaf and dumb Arab', circa 1908 (Valerie Crosia).

who was transfixed by its danger and excitement. Leland also fought the Turks for two years with a band of Macedonian guerrillas. In contrast, Horace's only efforts at freedom-fighting ended when he was shot in the knee by a Corsican fisherman after becoming mixed up in a local uprising.

Ever since listening to George Trevelyan extol the country, the main object of Horace's wanderings was always Italy. The Italian mode of living, the history, the timeless culture, the landscape and the theatrical manners of its people matched his vision of perfection. It was his spiritual home. Arriving in Venice in April 1907, he bumped straight into Lady Gregory, her son Robert and W.B. Yeats. They had all travelled to Italy to escape the furore provoked by the staging of J.M. Synge's controversial drama *The Playboy of the Western World* under Lady Gregory's patronage at the Abbey Theatre in Dublin. The surprise at seeing Horace was mutual, though Robert enjoyed racing his friend around St Mark's Square. While Yeats drifted off to look at galleries, Horace crawled all over the Ca' Rezzonico, where his great hero Robert Browning had died. Horace could never bear to be apart from Browning for too long. The poet's highly dramatised and gothic romances, often on an epic scale, appealed strongly to his sense of theatre, while his 'lyrics are wonderful'. Horace knew the lengthy poem 'Oh, to be in England' by heart, and carried his 1901 Oxford Miniature Edition of Browning's poems around with him till his death. Between its pages are still pressed the flowers collected on his travels.

Horace lingered in Venice some months. He spent too much money on tacky Murano glass, and on this visit, or perhaps one later, played a nice little joke by surreptitiously depositing neat piles of manure behind the famous bronze horses mounted on the facade of St Mark's. He also trained as a gondolier, to ferry pretty female tourists around the city's canals. Gilbert and Sullivan's *The Gondoliers* had been a hit of his childhood. Now he 'was admitted to their brother-hood', joining a muscular band of young Venetians who were much admired and lusted after by the city's visitors, both male and female. 'As an exercise it is incomparable', but it could be dangerous too. One day he narrowly avoided death (again) when a bullet whizzed past his head on the Lido. It hardly mattered whether it was an unlucky accident or an assassination attempt by a jealous rival. Eventually, it appears he was driven out of Venice by the over-amorous attentions of one of his passengers, who stalked him and sent 'strange' letters.

He escaped to Sicily—where he climbed to the summit of Etna and returned in an impressive five hours—then to Naples, Capri and Genoa. From Genoa he walked the two hundred and fifty miles to Rome, in under eight days. It was a remarkable feat. Word of his exploit soon spread, with every village and town he passed through greeting the 'great English walking champion' with cheers and music. Horace loved to take on the earth and elements in this way. Walking great distances was liberating, Homeric and utopian. To a man muffled from the world by deafness, the rhythm of the road beneath the feet was sensual and invigorating. Walking was a rejection of the modern and celebration of the ancient. Since the 1905 publication of the perambulatory verses of 'Supertramp' poet William H. Davies (much admired by Horace) it was also fashionable for the Edwardian literati. Again and again Horace repeated the feat, leaving large footprints across Europe as he crisscrossed mountains, plains and forests.

Horace carried his laurels into Rome, where he was warmly welcomed by Roman high society. As was usual now, he took an apartment at the best hotel in town, the Grand, where the visit by two separate foreign delegations 'in regulation Cambridge Eastern costume' made him feel, he told a university friend, 'quite homesick'. At the hotel he developed the alarming habit of firing his revolver through the ceiling while reading Shelley aloud in bed. He was then arrested as a spy while sketching some ornamental ruins near a military installation. His response to his detainment was typical: 'I felled one official and routed two others and had great difficulty in clearing myself. However there was no danger for I know a secretary of the Embassy here (an Old Etonian).' Horace's tendency for violent demonstration was evident again when Lord Dunsany called on him. After some good-humoured banter, Dunsany ill-advisedly put marmalade on Horace's hairbrush. The retaliation was swift and violent. Horace drew his swordstick and, pointing it at Dunsany's throat, demanded, 'If you don't apologise you won't leave this room alive.' 'Was it a real threat?' thought Dunsany anxiously. He decided not, backing out of the door with Horace still glaring at him, brandishing the sword. That Dunsany hesitated at all shows the menace he felt. Yet by facing down the threat he earned Horace's respect and, Dunsany later commented, 'immunity' from his friend's jokes. It was a lesson others failed to learn—at their cost.

9

She came and asked me for a flower,
I gave her one the wind had blown,
She wore next her heart an hour
When all its gentle life had flown;
Its wings lie folded as a cowl
Like sheets upon some formless thing,
And from its petals comes a foul
Smell of decay, and burying.

U ntil now, Horace had never experienced a full-blown love affair. In Rome he lurched painfully into one. Out hunting with a pack of Roman hounds, Horace fell and broke a couple of ribs (happily, not on the side he said would kill him). He was quickly scooped up by two Italian aristocrats, the Marchese Calabrini and Count Paso Pasolini, and taken back to his hotel by car. There he lay, receiving visitors like some wounded champion of the joust. 'Several ladies used to come to tea with him,' remembered Lord Dunsany, 'to enquire how his romantic figure was mending.' Among them was the beautiful Contessa Pasolini, wife of his rescuer and formerly Mildred Montague, the twenty-one-year-old daughter of a railroad baron from Chattanooga, Tennessee.

Shane Leslie, who was a friend of the Pasolinis, described Mildred as different 'in every way' from her lofty but impoverished Italian husband. She was young, vivacious, wilful and rich. Her very name Montague resonated with the romance of Shakespeare. Fatally, she was also dying of boredom within the rigid confines of Roman society, so flirting with Horace was a welcome distraction. She teased him, calling him her 'Pocket Hercules'. However, it was only when Horace returned to Italy two years later in 1909 that a passionate affair began, with far-reaching consequences.

Horace charted the romance in his diary for the year. It is the only one of his to survive, indicating a desire to preserve the memory of an affair which bears all the hallmarks of a Henry James novel. This tiny, green leather-bound document opens at New Year in Cumbria, where Horace was staying with George Trevelyan in a party which included the young Aldous Huxley. By all accounts they had a very entertaining time, scaling mountains built of wine cases and singing raucous songs (being deaf, spaces were left in the songs for Horace to fill with his own impromptu and scatological verses). In March, Horace left for Italy with Jasper Ridley, son of a former home secretary and another distant cousin. After a month-long whirlwind tour, which covered Milan, Pisa, Florence and Venice again, Jasper returned to England, leaving Horace behind in Italy in a state of 'horrible melancholia'.

By May he was installed as a guest at the Pasolinis' country

Mildred Pasolini, *née* Montague, on her marriage to Count Paso Pasolini (Richard Kimball).

residence at Coccolia near Ravenna. It was here, between games of tennis and snatched conversations in the shade of the trees or under a 'golden moon', that Horace fell in love with Mildred. In his own words, he was seized by a 'terrible passion' for her, made worse by the impossibility of the situation. If the count suspected anything, he said nothing. On Horace's last day, the lovers had 'a wonderful and very familiar talk', each of them unable to disguise their feelings any longer. Mildred told him she had been forced into a loveless marriage by her parents, who barely knew Pasolini but craved his title. She revealed the cruelty of her husband and 'the hideousness of the vice he made her practise on him *before marriage*, telling her it was alright'. How she had loved Horace from their first meeting and did so with 'her whole being'.

Horace arrived back to London alone and in a highly emotional state, waking in the night calling out Mildred's name and 'stretching out my arms for her'. The violence of his infatuation was extreme, overwhelming all other thought and action. He wrote to Mildred every day, confided in his mother and consulted lawyers on Italian divorce law. Mary Studd was encouraging, indulging her son's mad passion, advising him to tell Mildred he loved her. But legal opinion was unanimous. There was no provision for divorce in Italy, while an annulment was impossible without the co-operation of the count. Friends rallied around. Tudor Castle, studying German in Munich, travelled to Switzerland to meet Mildred, who had gone there for a cure under the chaperone of a French woman called Madame d'Ermont. Adrian Stephen, who had recently been called to the Bar, took a closer personal interest than many. Not simply for abstruse legal reasons but because he too was miserably submerged in a clandestine love affair; though his was with a man, the painter Duncan Grant. In choosing a married woman and another man as the focus of their affections, Horace and Adrian were pursuing dangerous paths in Edwardian England. It was another form of rebellion, more subtle perhaps than hoaxing but with greater risks.

Matters came to a head in the autumn. In September Horace returned to Rome with Tudor at his side to resolve the issue, one way or another. On the twenty-fifth they went sightseeing and then to the theatre with Francesco Ruffo, a friend of Tudor's and close to the Pasolinis. Horace confided in the young aristocrat, telling him of his pact with Mildred and his determination to free her from the count. In doing so, Horace inadvertently set in motion a devastating chain of events. The next day Francesco, distraught at what he had heard, shot himself for the love of Mildred. To avoid a scandal, a hysterical Mildred fled to Paris, hotly pursued by Horace and Tudor. When they arrived they heard she had gone missing. 'Mildred meditated suicide,' Horace told his sister Annie afterwards, 'and we had to search for her through Paris, that gave me a shock I am still suffering from. When we met I said I wouldn't let her out of my sight again.' Helpfully, Tudor offered to shoot Pasolini.

This was the moment of sublime drama Horace had been heading towards his whole life. He had been brought up on tales of knights in armour and dragons to slay. Like Lancelot he had ridden to the rescue.

Tudor Castle, whose mind was 'tinged with romanticism' (courtesy of Harrow School).

Huddled together in the Luxembourg Gardens, Mildred and Horace planned their elopement together. Shane Leslie pictured Mildred descending 'secretly from a window with only her jewels'. As usual with Horace, the truth was more prosaic, but no less dramatic. That night he took the boat train to London, leaving Mildred behind at the Hotel Regina. They had agreed that she should go home to America, appeal to her parents and, if they refused her separation from Pasolini, she would illicitly meet up with Horace in New York.

As soon as Horace reached London he consulted his mother and stepfather. Mary, who knew her son better than anyone, still listened sympathetically but, to Horace's disgust, gave way to her husband's view. And Herbert Studd's opinion was fiercely different. He knew where Mildred's duty lay, and it was not with Horace. He was also airily dismissive of Horace's fears for Mildred, saying that people who threatened suicide rarely committed it. The horror of a scandal and family disgrace hung over Bertie's every word. That sealed it. Horace did not like, respect or admire his stepfather. He was still more upset that his mother had apparently deserted him in his hour of need. Her suggestion that the faithful Tudor was 'acting from motives of excitement' bitterly angered him, as he knew it was as much a reflection on himself as on his friend. So back at his house in Cadogan Place he changed his mind, and the plan: 'The terror of the situation came over me and I decided to immediately return and carry her off.' Horace was terrified Mildred would commit suicide in his absence, regardless of his stepfather's bland reassurance.

After dining with Tudor and Guy Ridley—Jasper Ridley's cousin and also a lawyer—and yet another sleepless night, Horace took the first train to Paris. There, this time abetted by Dummer Howard, he bought a sapphire ring, hired a car and spirited Mildred away. After driving through the night (and briefly breaking down) they reached Boulogne in time to catch the morning boat to England. Barely thirty-six hours after leaving Cadogan Place, Horace was back, but this time with Mildred. She was on the verge of collapse, and he 'semi-delirious'. Still he would not rest. Fearful the lovers were being pursued by Count Pasolini, Horace collected some things, consulted a doctor, and after just a few hours in London, whisked the exhausted Mildred away to Ireland. Ireland was a place of refuge and safety. It was a long way from his glowering stepfather, despairing mother and the vengeful Italian count. He had everything mapped out. He hurried Mildred to Derrybawn House, an elegant and appropriately italianate villa he had rented some forty miles from Dublin in County Wicklow. (Like Issercleran, Derrybawn is now an upmarket hotel.) This was where they would live together in defiance of the world and convention.

Now Horace faltered. In his own words, 'I cut the Gordian knot and carried her off…to have left her with *him* would have been impossible, any man who would have been capable of doing so would have been a cad.' But having acted so precipitously, his next move was uncertain. He had scandalised society and cut himself off from his family without any clear aim, and the cold light of day was dawning. Horace expected Herbert Studd to be furious, and he was, but he could still cause trouble for the young lovers. Tudor Castle gamely rallied to his friend's defence. 'If he was not unfortunately so delicate physically,' Horace defiantly told his sister Annie, 'he'd have gone round and attempted to thrash Herbert—he nearly sent him a challenge to a duel.' But both men knew Tudor was no match for the towering guardsman.

Bertie could be ignored for now, but Horace was bewildered and hurt by his mother's attitude.

Before I carried her off you said to me 'Tell her I love her'; you also said 'write to me'. When we came unexpectedly to London it was surprising to find everything handed over to Herbert. He is no blood relation of mine, it was to you I looked for help… you told me once that perhaps you couldn't judge that you had failed in your life—of course you have not—but I will say that Mildred and I have succeeded triumphantly, and that we are and always will be gloriously happy, as much as one can be where death and illness always threaten.

Meanwhile Mildred began fretting. 'What can I say to my mother?' and 'What can I say to my father?' she repeated over and over again. Fortunately calmer heads prevailed. While the elopers were holed up in Wicklow, vowing to kill themselves rather than surrender, Tudor Castle summoned Madame d'Ermont. Horace swore that during the elopement his relationship with Mildred was 'as brother and sister'. Nevertheless, Madame d'Ermont could act as a chaperone, lending a degree of respectability to the runaway couple while simultaneously opening up a dialogue with the enraged count. Her sensible advice was to meet Pasolini as soon as possible to defuse the crisis and avoid still worse repercussions. It was agreed, by telegraph, that Horace and the count would meet in three days on a platform at Gare de Lyon.

So for the third time in ten days Horace, together with a growing party of refugees including Mildred, Tudor and now Madame d'Ermont, found himself in Paris. Over dinner with Dummer the bedraggled party drafted an ultimatum for Pasolini. Then Mildred and Madame d'Ermont went back to London, leaving Horace, Tudor and Dummer to while away the hours before the showdown with the count by playing cricket in the hotel corridors. At six in the morning they all went to the station.

Pasolini's train was late. When it did arrive the two men found themselves face to face for the first time since those leisurely afternoons at the Villa Pasolini. Far from the nightmarish vision of a cuckold bent on bloody revenge, the count cut a pitiful figure. He was like 'wax' in Horace's hands as he listened meekly to the details of his wife's betrayal and his humiliation. Pathetically, his only concern was how to break the news to his mother and father back in Italy. Horace's anxiety turned to derision, then hate for his rival. 'He is no man,' he snorted in a triumphant letter to his own mother, 'he is, as Madame d'Ermont said of him, "the shadow of the shade".' Only the thought of Mildred stopped him running Pasolini through with his swordstick there and then, he claimed. The defeated count returned to Rome, never to see his wife again. The victor headed in the opposite direction, eager to re-join Mildred in London. 'No power on earth can now rob us of great happiness,' he proclaimed, 'If love such as ours is sin, then we both agree that we are in love with sin, but I somehow think that God reads hearts not legal codes.' They dined at Toynbee Hall, where Thomas Harvey was calmly reassuring. Afterwards Mildred symbolically threw her wedding ring into the Thames. Only one thing remained to be done. Horace had to see Mildred's father.

On 16 October 1909, still barely three weeks since Ruffo had killed himself, triggering the crisis, Mildred and Horace sailed on *Lusitania* for America. By now they were enjoying their great adventure. They still had doughty Madame d'Ermont in tow, but no one and nothing could reach them at sea. Horace had Mildred to himself for a whole week, possibly the happiest of his life. Wherever he was and whatever he did, Horace had never really fitted in. He was the toff drawn to the *demi-monde*, the country squire who stayed in town, the soldier who wrote poetry. Now drifting between two continents and two cultures—the old and the new, the romantic and realistic—with a woman he loved, he felt finally at peace. It was a revelation. 'When one suffers deeply and gets beneath the surface of life,' he mused, 'when one comes into contact with deep feelings and passions one gets to realise the real values of different people as opposed to their accepted values.' This feeling lasted beyond their arrival at New York, where Mildred, for propriety, checked in to the Wolcott Hotel (still there but now faded), Horace the Imperial. Barely had they drawn breath before they were summoned to Washington by Dwight Montague for their anxiously awaited interview.

Horace might have assumed that Mildred's father had come to terms with her elopement by now. He had not. 'I have never in my life seen anyone in so tremendous a rage,' he wrote to Annie, 'and thought at first he would have liked to kill me.' Yet assailed by the tears of a much-loved daughter and the Irish charm of her lover, the old man gradually relented. He listened in silence as they described how they loved each other, how Horace had saved Mildred from a brutal husband and how they wanted to marry and live together forever. He heard about the suicide of Ruffo, the escape from Rome and of the cruelty and cowardice of Pasolini. Then Dwight Montague ignored the strict instructions he had quite obviously been given by Mrs Montague back in Tennessee. He forgot the hefty dowry he had given the Pasolinis. He agreed to the lovers' plans. But on condition that Mildred's marriage could be annulled. 'My daughter's happiness—that is all I want,' he said with great dignity, 'now let us leave these two silly billies together.' And with that, an ecstatic Horace and Mildred were left to say their farewells, before she left with her father and he sailed home to complete arrangements for their life together.

Horace was in buoyant mood. The annulment of Mildred's marriage was impossible without the backing of the Pasolini and Montague families. He had now secured both. Back in London he lunched with Adrian Stephen, Tudor Castle, Jasper and Guy Ridley. He was in such high spirits that he even tried out a little joke. He tricked Jasper's father, former Home Secretary Lord Ridley, into a surprise visit to Vine Street police station, the police being one of Horace's favourite targets. Then he stayed up all night writing to Mildred. In the morning, everything settled in London, he took the boat train to Ireland, riding the crossing on the upper deck in heroic pose, the spray on his face. After seeing the agent about Derrybawn, he visited the house again with George Colthurst, who was wildly excited by his friend's plans. Everything was falling into place.

But two letters from America were waiting for him back at Cadogan Place which would shake him violently out of his idyll. The letters are lost, but we can assume they told him tersely that he was not to see or try to contact Mildred Montague ever again and that the affair was at an end.

There then followed the most extraordinary feature of this bizarre episode. Adrian Stephen travelled to Chattanooga on Horace's behalf to plead face to face with the Montagues. Until now, Adrian's inexplicable visit to America had puzzled his biographers, but it was a typically impulsive act by one of Horace's closest friends. It was also unsuccessful. On 1 December, while dining with Guy and Tudor, Horace received a cable from Adrian admitting defeat. The game was up. The last comment in Horace's diary on the matter summed up his devastation. 'Sick to death at heart,' he scrawled. He never saw Mildred or visited America again, and the affair remained a deep scar across his early life. Harsh reality had again clashed with fantasy. Mildred was dragged back to respectability by her parents. She secured her annulment to marry a wealthy, and safe, American. Meanwhile, her parents consoled themselves by wedding their other daughter to Count Pasolini's cousin.

Horace was still mourning Mildred at Christmas when he called on Adrian Stephen for one of the regular 'Thursday

Evening' gatherings hosted by his sister Virginia at their house in Fitzroy Square. Tudor Castle was already there, having 'bored' Virginia over supper, and during the evening the party grew to include Duncan Grant, Maynard Keynes and Lytton Strachey. 'Cole, of course, was disastrous,' Virginia reported to her sister Vanessa, 'he began telling stories about shooting policemen…Then he stayed till 2 talking about Mildred and the Pasolinis.' Shooting policemen was not the usual fare for these early Bloomsbury group events, when a shifting set of close-knit friends joined by a cat's cradle of sexual relationships would meet up to shape a whole new way of living. But, then again, Horace had never been a fully fledged member of a self-regarding sect which had its roots in the Cambridge Apostles, from which he had equally kept his distance. He hovered on the fringes of Bloomsbury, connected to the group principally through his friendship with Adrian. He was never part of it, nor in sympathy with its aims. He believed in action not words. I suspect he viewed the whole sainted Bloomsbury enterprise as slightly absurd, rather tiresome, mildly juvenile and occasionally insulting. On the whole the people involved were supercilious, self-obsessed and undemocratic. The feeling of dislike was mutual. An unpleasant episode when Annie Cole accompanied her brother to a soiree at Fitzroy Square illustrates this tension between the Coles' world and Bloomsbury.

That evening Strachey, Vanessa Stephen, her husband Clive Bell, Duncan Grant, the painter Henry Lamb and Saxon Sydney-Turner had assembled as usual in Virginia and Adrian's drawing-room with its red-brocaded curtains and lime-green carpet. The conversation meandered until Annie arrived, presumably after dining, at around half eleven. She sat in a wicker chair, with Virginia and Clive Bell on the floor beside her. Then, as Adrian recounted in his journal,

Virginia began in her usual tone of frank admiration to compliment her on her appearance. 'Of course, you Miss Cole are always dressed so exquisitely. You look so original, so like a seashell. There is something so refined about you coming in among our muddy boots and pipe smoke, dressed in your exquisite creations'. Clive chimed in with more heavy compliments and then began asking why she disliked him so much saying how any other young lady would have been much pleased with all the nice things he had been saying but that she treated him sharply. At this Virginia interrupted with 'I think Miss Cole has a very strong character' and so on and so on. Altogether Miss Cole was as unhappy and uncomfortable as she could be; it was impossible not to help laughing at the extravagance of Virginia and Clive and all conversation was stopped by their noisy gestures, so the poor woman was the centre of all our gaze, and did not know what to do with herself.

For Horace's sake, Annie bravely stuck it out until one. ('In those days,' Virginia said later, hinting at hero-worship, 'she was very proud of her brother. I don't think though she was proud of him when she became the wife of a Prime Minister.') However, as soon as Annie had gone, continued Adrian, 'a great discussion was started, I know not by whom, about vice.' Within this context, maybe shooting policemen was quite a diverting and original topic of conversation.

Horace's sister Annie Cole, later Mrs Neville Chamberlain (Francis Chamberlain).

93

10

When I went on board a Dreadnought ship
I looked like a costermonger;
They said I was an Abyssinian prince
'Cos I shouted 'Bunga Bunga!'

Music Hall ditty, 1910, sung to the tune of 'The girl I left behind me'

*J*ust eight weeks after Adrian's shattering telegram from America, Horace gathered together the men who had sustained him through his ill-fated love affair—Guy Ridley, Tudor Castle and Adrian himself—to embark on the hoax that would make his name. It was a bold decision and a remarkable turnaround in his state of mind. He did so to prove to his friends, himself and to Mildred in far off Tennessee that he was undiminished, unconquered and still unafraid. He risked all because he felt he had nothing left to lose. He would call it his 'navy joke' but the papers broke it to the world as 'the *Dreadnought* hoax'.

In his book on the affair, Adrian Stephen said it was a naval officer who gave Horace the idea of impersonating the Emperor of Abyssinia and talking his way onto the British battleship HMS *Dreadnought*, flagship of the commander-in-chief of the Home Fleet, Admiral Sir William May. Thirty years later in her talk about the *Dreadnought* hoax to the Women's Institute, Virginia Woolf suggested that this unnamed officer was serving in HMS *Hawk*, a battlecruiser attached to the Home Fleet alongside *Dreadnought*.

In those days the young officers had a gay time. They were always up to some lark and one of their chief occupations it seemed was to play jokes upon each other. There were a great many rivalries and intrigues in the navy. The officers liked scoring off each other. And the officers of the Hawk [sic] and the Dreadnought had a feud. The Dreadnought had got the better of the Hawk, and Cole's friend who was on the Hawk had come to Cole, and had said to him: You're a great hand at hoaxing people; couldn't you do something to pull the leg of the Dreadnought? They want taking down a bit. Couldn't you manage to pull off one of your jokes against them? That was a red rag to a bull.

This explanation for the hoax is highly plausible, although it quickly developed, as we will see, more personal motivations. In addition, I think Virginia may have mis-recalled the name of the slighted officers' ship (strangely, like Duncan Grant subsequently, she also dated the hoax to a Thursday in springtime and not, as in reality, to a dank, dark Monday in February. Perhaps their memories were forever cast in the soft warmth of youth?)

I say this because the most likely candidate for such a mischievous suggestion is Bernard Buxton, a seafaring cousin of Leland Buxton's who was later listed by Horace as a 'semi-principal' in the cast of characters for his lost autobiography. At the time Bernard was flag lieutenant in HMS *Indomitable*, a cruiser in the Home Fleet recently returned from conveying the Prince of Wales to Canada for a royal visit. On board the ship for that voyage, as executive officer, had been thirty-four-year-old William Fisher, who had since moved to *Dreadnought* as Admiral May's flag commander.

So Fisher was a plausible link between the two ships, and Buxton to the hoaxers in London. And there is another persuasive reason for supposing that Fisher was the principal target and motivation for the *Dreadnought* hoax. As the priggish son of their maternal aunt Mary, Fisher was a much-ridiculed cousin of Adrian and Virginia Stephen. As children there had been bitter rivalry between them, with the clever, sardonic Stephens tormenting the earnest and patronising Fishers. The Fishers embodied middle-class respectability and conformity: everything Adrian and Virginia—encouraged by their father—fought against, so they loved nothing more than playing April Fool's jokes on William. 'We fool ee we fool ee we fool it cousin Willy,' Virginia remembered calling out. After entering the Royal Navy at thirteen, William had risen effortlessly through the ranks, in reproach to his stubbornly uncompetitive and low-achieving cousins. A letter written by William to Adrian's mother in 1891 may even have sown the seeds for both the Zanzibar and *Dreadnought* jokes. In the letter, William recounts a visit to his ship, then cruising off East Africa, by the Sultan of Zanzibar (the real one). 'We fired guns and torpedoes,' he rather pompously related, 'and performed such like naval operations for his edification.' Now that William was a senior officer in *Dreadnought*, these details might have been recalled by Adrian, though he did not admit as much when he wrote about the hoax in 1936. William Fisher, by then a highly respected admiral, was still alive and Britain was again on the verge of war, so ridiculing a senior officer in print was inadvisable. A biography of Fisher appeared after his death, but it was so obsequious that it is impossible to discern why the man generated so much dislike among his relatives and subordinates.

A frank impression of Fisher is given by another officer Adrian knew by chance on *Dreadnought*. When he eventually visited the ship in disguise Adrian discovered to his surprise that the Captain was an acquaintance from a weekly walking club he attended. But Herbert Richmond was quite unlike either Admiral May or Commander Fisher, both of whom, it seems, he heartily loathed. He saw his fellow officers in *Dreadnought* as dogmatic, outdated in strategy, and uninspiring. In contrast Richmond was well read, highly cultivated (he was a Cambridge don after the war), a little theatrical and plainly rather arrogant. His diary gives a candid insight into the bitter rivalries on board *Dreadnought* at the time of the hoax. 'Lack of imagination is a most deplorable deficiency in a man,' he declared of May.

> He reads nothing. He never looks at a paper. Lady May sends him cuttings which may interest him 'Curious Case of Breach of Promise by a Man' or 'Cat Attacked by a Thrush' but of serious or sustained reading he is incapable. Yet he is a man charged with this supreme trust. On him rests the security of our coasts...He will spend hours over some very minor, usually easy, tactical question, because it involves no deep thinking and enables him to spend hours on the bridge making signals to people and finding fault with their manner of handling ships, but the really big things which require concentration of thought and real brain work never touches him.

Richmond's distrust of William Fisher is equally palpable:

> I have a suspicion that Willy can't get it out of his head that I am too young...and I dislike not being trusted more than I can say...I know nothing more unpleasant than the feeling of a lack of sympathy between my Chief [Admiral May] and myself. We look at things in very different ways and our interests and amusements are different...abstract thought he is incapable of.

In his book *The 'Dreadnought' Hoax*, Adrian labelled May 'Admiral X', Richmond 'Captain Y' and Willy Fisher 'cousin Z'. The pseudonyms fooled nobody in the know.

But if Adrian encouraged the *Dreadnought* hoax, Horace made the joke gloriously his own. The visit to England in November 1909 of a Chinese Naval Mission—when exotically dressed orientals, including a prince, had toured the fleet—showed it was possible. Clearly, the Royal Navy was very amenable when it came to impressing its allies. Apart from family rivalry and a naval grudge, there were other compelling reasons for choosing this particular ship. *Dreadnought* was the most powerful, complex and aggressive machine in the world. The ship was a potent and expensive symbol of state power and authoritarianism. *Dreadnought*'s launch in 1905 had significantly raised the stakes in Britain's dangerous arms race with Germany. It spawned a whole new, eponymous class of ships. A patriotic public demanded eight of them; in his 1909 budget the Liberal chancellor David Lloyd-George had promised four (at £1.5 million apiece) alongside a far-reaching welfare scheme for Britain's teeming poor. All this would be paid for by a new super-tax on the rich and a land tax on estates. The 'people's budget' produced howls of protest from the aristocracy and landed gentry. One imagines Uncle Alfred choking over his breakfast at the news.

Lloyd George's budget was thrown out by the House of Lords in November 1909, the first time the upper house had defied the will of the Commons since the Glorious Revolution. In response, the fiery Welsh Chancellor proposed flooding the Lords with new peers to dilute its inherent Tory majority, so clearing the way for social reform. As he wittily remarked, a fully equipped duke cost twice as much as a dreadnought. But without a budget Herbert Asquith's Liberal government could not survive. A general election was called early in 1910 (the first of two that year). It was fought over the budget with, at its heart, the totemic issue of the dreadnoughts.

In those more leisurely days, the election ran from 15 January to 10 February. The *Dreadnought* hoax took place on 7 February, so it should be set against this highly charged background. It was not the first time Horace had become embroiled in a general election campaign. Before the 1906 Liberal landslide he had organised hustings with Dummer and Tudor, all of them posing as politicians. At the first interruption of Horace's long-winded and nonsensical speech, his colleagues had turned and pelted the audience with rotten eggs. It was a neat reversal of expectation; one many real politicians would relish.

By exposing *Dreadnought* to ridicule at such a politically sensitive time, was Horace deliberately highlighting the wilful extravagance of building battleships and courting war with Germany when there were so many other more deserving calls on the public's (and his) purse? He certainly held views on titles and privilege, the other subject then preoccupying the nation. For a man with so many titled friends, his opinion, as usual, was unexpected and steeped in romantic nostalgia. He declared later,

> It would be better to abolish all titles, they mean nothing. *Most* of the House of Lords is descended from corrupt lawyers and placemen, from butchers [and] swindling tradesmen as Chesterton pointed out years ago. There are few historic titles in the *male line—not* 6. The only advantage of a title is to spur the imagination, I think...it's all damned silly...I spit on such 'royal-favour' and think the Socialists when they come in would be well-advised to declare all titles *illegal*.

Horace was commenting in the aftermath of the Maundy Gregory scandal—when Lloyd George used a middleman to sell titles to bolster his own political fortunes—but his meaning was clear. Modern life had devalued the chivalric origins of the peerage, leaving it the preserve of self-seeking placemen and vulgar *parvenus*. I think it would be wrong, however, to give the hoax one overarching grandiose theme. Like the people assembled to execute it, it was a blend of personal and political interests fused by a common desire for adventure.

Adrian and Horace decided to follow the successful formula of the Zanzibar joke. But whereas that had been a largely spontaneous event lacking detailed planning (and risking disaster during the chaotic escape from Cambridge Station) the *Dreadnought* hoax would be carefully prepared. With the likelihood of failure so much greater, and the risks higher, every precaution had to be taken to secure success. No one apparently considered that the consequences of successfully fooling the Royal Navy were likely to be worse than failing to. For the new hoax they would impersonate Abyssinian nobility led by 'Ras 'el Makalen', a fictitious cousin of the Emperor of Abyssinia. The cover story was that they were in England viewing Eton as a potential school for the princely children (this could have been verified by the authorities but never was). In 1936 Adrian claimed that they had posed as the Emperor of Abyssinia and his suite, a falsehood which has stuck in the popular imagination. In fact, not only was the real Emperor lying gravely ill in Addis Ababa at the time of the prank, but Horace had learned the lesson of the Cambridge hoax, when his attempt to impersonate the Sultan of Zanzibar had come unstuck forcing a last-minute change of plan. No one was likely to ask too many questions about an obscure prince.

Why did they choose to be Abyssinians (Ethiopians)? Interviewed in 1962, Tony Buxton, one of the hoaxers, said that none of them knew a 'single thing' about the country or its language. Most likely Abyssinia was chosen as it was a valuable ally of Britain against German ambitions in North Africa. Horace may have calculated that representatives of that country were likely to be warmly welcomed on board a British warship, as the Chinese had been. Acting on intelligence, he set the date of the hoax to early February 1910, when *Dreadnought* would be anchored off Weymouth in Dorset. This gave him two or three weeks of detailed preparation. The day of the hoax shifted as the time approached—and volunteers dropped in and out—causing confusion in later accounts. In the end Horace plumped for 7 February (not 10 February, as is sometimes stated, presumably on account of Virginia's faulty recollection). Conveniently, this was a Monday, giving a weekend of preparation beforehand—and the possibility of a full week of press coverage afterwards.

The vital element of the hoax—the disguise—was again entrusted to Willy Clarkson. With ample time to organise costumes, Horace went to greater efforts than with the Zanzibar joke to ensure authenticity. Over meetings with Clarkson at the costumier's lavish new shop premises in Wardour Street (still there, and now a Chinese restaurant) Horace planned the elaborate costumes. Virginia remembered visiting Clarkson, who 'liked hoaxes too', and how 'we rummaged through all his great trunks for the clothes; and I remember standing among jewels and turbans and splendid eastern dressing gowns and putting on one after another'.

The end result was a bizarre and gaudy collection of outfits more suited to a pantomine dame than a prince, and quite unlike the restrained and elegant dress of a real Abyssinian. Yet the ensemble fulfilled Western expectations (largely drawn from music hall) of how Africans bedecked themselves, so the costumes worked and were never challenged. Recruiting the princes was more difficult. Horace knew from Cambridge that there was safety in numbers, as much to divert the attention of the victim as to give the regal imposters sufficient dignity. But several friends who volunteered to join him got cold feet and backed out as the day approached. 'Those damned fools have let us down,' Horace bitterly complained after bursting unannounced one evening into Fitzroy Square, 'it's all up.' According to Adrian's sister Vanessa Bell, even Horace grew 'frightened' at the enormity of the undertaking. As the day approached only her brother Adrian 'was really keen about it'. Was Adrian egging Horace on again, as he had in Cambridge? It is obvious from his lovemaking to Duncan Grant that

above Visit to London of an Abyssinian royal delegation for the coronation of Edward VII in 1902, photograph by Lafayette Studios (© V&A Images, Victoria and Albert Museum).

below HMS *Dreadnought*: 'smaller than I expected,' recalled Adrian Stephen, 'and uglier' (author).

above left Anthony Buxton, who played 'Ras 'el Makalen' (John Buxton).

above right Duncan Grant, photograph by Alvin Langdon Coburn (courtesy of George Eastman House, International Museum of Photography and Film).

right Guy Ridley, press image (Matt Ridley).

below left Virginia Stephen, who agitated to join her brother in the *Dreadnought* hoax, photograph by George Beresford (© National Portrait Gallery, London).

below right Willy Clarkson at work (*Strand Magazine*).

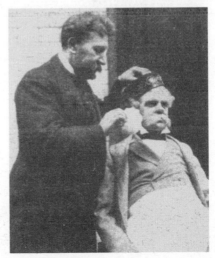

Adrian was a risk-taker but, unlike Horace, a surreptitious and secretive one. He was also toying with becoming an actor, so perhaps he was excited at the prospect of testing himself under the closest scrutiny.

Apart from the ringleaders, none of the original Zanzibarees was available for the new hoax. Dummer Howard was still in Paris; after all his adventures, Leland Buxton was sheep farming in South Africa while Robbie Bowen-Colthurst was now on the staff of the Lord Lieutenant of Ireland in Dublin. With a few days to go, only Guy Ridley and Tudor Castle had committed to join Adrian and Horace in their adventure. Guy, the son of a High Court judge, had been at school and college with Dummer Howard and shared Horace's love of fantasy. He wrote a strange Tolkeinesque novel called *The World of Teregor* in which all the characters were trees, and listed his occupation in *Who's Who* as 'Assistant Master in Lunacy', a genuine legal position. Nevertheless, it looked like the hoax would have to be cancelled. Then Anthony Buxton, another member of the Buxton dynasty and a friend of Adrian and Horace's from Trinity, was persuaded to take part, encouraged perhaps by the influence of his cousin Bernard on the scheme and by his own desire to upstage the earlier efforts of Leland at Cambridge. He was followed into the hoax by Duncan Grant. He was motivated by loyalty to Adrian and, as a resident of Bloomsbury, by a visceral dislike of the sort of establishment pomposity encapsulated by his father, a senior army officer. Duncan also relished playing jokes, having once fooled an elderly aunt by dressing up as a German schoolmistress.

With four accomplices, Horace judged he could make the hoax work, so he set the date and asked Clarkson to begin final preparations. However, he had not reckoned on the appetite for adventure of Adrian's sister Virginia who, according to Willy Clarkson, 'pleaded continuously' to join the hoax while watching Clarkson and his assistants practise the make-up on her brother and his friends at Fitzroy Square in the days beforehand. 'When cajolery failed,' the costumier recalled, 'she employed Portia-like argument: teeming, stormy, insistent and permeating.' The men dismissed the idea out of hand. The risk of taking her on the expedition was far too great, and anyhow there was no role for a woman in the planned charade. But Virginia loudly persisted, and years later Clarkson recalled in *The People* newspaper how she eventually got her way 'in a quaint and unexpected way' while the men discussed their plans in the drawing-room of Fitzroy Square. Horace

> had just said 'You know what we're in for. If we're found out we'll be thrown overboard for certain. They'd pitch us overboard without a thought.' One of the fake princes replied in a foreign voice for by now it seemed that it was impossible for him to act out of character—: 'Well that's all right. We're all good swimmers.' Then the lady's voice broke in: 'I can swim as well as any of you. Better. You all know that. I'm willing to take the risk. Why can't I come into the plot?' There was silence for a moment and then the company broke into a spontaneous and prolonged laugh. Her persistence had won.

Horace subsequently blamed Clarkson for 'inaccuracies' in his account of the hoax (he was also furious, even in 1932, that the newspaper mentioned Virginia Woolf by name). But the story has the ring of truth. It is unlikely that either Horace or Adrian would ever have considered asking Virginia to join them in the hoax, so she presumably had to force herself in. Moreover, Vanessa Bell was horrified at her sister's involvement, voicing her family's wider opposition. Virginia had recently suffered a serious mental breakdown and, with her emotional state so fragile, Vanessa feared the excitement could tip her into another. Despite having enjoyed Horace's hospitality at West Woodhay, Vanessa thought him 'an intolerable bore...very rich and very vulgar [who] throws his money about'. She suspected Horace of trying to ingratiate himself with Virginia. Horace was already hanging around Fitzroy Square, and Vanessa now dreaded he would 'pervade' the place. (Is there a suggestion that Horace had been making clumsy advances towards his best friend's sister? Virginia herself said, 'I liked Horace; but I admit I always wondered what he was up to.' 'Like most Irish people he had a way with him,' she recalled with fondness, whilst also admitting, without apparent disapproval, that he 'was a bit of a scapegrace'. But she was wary, tellingly, of his 'very wheedling way', and if Horace did harbour hopes towards her they were horribly misplaced.)

Apart from a desire for risk-taking and excitement—symptomatic perhaps of her emotional instability—Virginia was motivated, like Adrian, to join in the humiliation of their much-loathed cousin Willy Fisher. But which part would she play? There were objections to taking a 'princess' on the men's escapade, so Virginia volunteered to be dressed and disguised as a man. As Clarkson remembered,

> Her first make-up was a failure, the project was almost abandoned; but I felt piqued at being thwarted from an effect which I knew could be obtained and made a fresh start. This time the result was astounding in its realism. The beautiful girl had vanished, and in her place was a slim, dignified, dusky nobleman with a sombre countenance and a flowing regal beard.

Duncan stayed with Adrian and Virginia in Fitzroy Square the night before the hoax (despite living only a few doors away), so he was already there when Horace, Tony Buxton and Guy Ridley arrived at the house before dawn on 7 February to be dressed and made up. Tony had a slight cold, which caused trouble later when his sneezing dislodged his false beard. Towards seven o'clock Willy Clarkson and his assistants arrived. Clarkson later claimed he had no idea what was afoot: 'For aught we know, a beard may be desired for amateur theatricals' (at dawn, on a Monday morning, in February?). The similarities with the earlier Cambridge joke were so great it is impossible he did not suspect another hoax was being planned. In fact, as Virginia revealed, Horace had already 'sworn him to secrecy'. Clarkson certainly milked his involvement afterwards, selling his story to the *Daily Telegraph* for £100 when Horace's triumph was confirmed. One significant difference between the *Dreadnought* joke and the earlier Sultan of Zanzibar escapade was Horace and Adrian's decision not to go in costume as foreign potentates. This time Horace would play 'Mr Herbert Cholmondeley' of the Foreign Office (presumably a name derived from his unsympathetic stepfather Herbert Studd and the family which had supplanted the de Veres as Lord Great Chamberlains). Adrian would pose as the official interpreter to the royal party, the role assumed by Dummer in Cambridge.

Clarkson's men set to work, supervised by the great man himself. He took pride in his skills of deception and was an avid self-promoter. 'Clarkson's Lillie Powder: The Greatest Beautifier in the World' (named for Lillie Langtry) was a very popular product at the time, as was Clarkson's 'Kleeno' for removing make-up. But his activities were not restricted to the stage, or necessarily always to legitimate clients. In the 1880s he assisted Scotland Yard in their attempts to catch 'Jack the Ripper' by disguising male police officers as prostitutes. It has also been suggested that he was mixed up in the infamous Dr Crippen murder case, when Crippen's mistress escaped England dressed as a boy. Rumours of Clarkson's own double-life abounded. After his death, Virginia, who maintained an interest in his career long after the *Dreadnought* hoax, would describe Clarkson's 'sexual kink'. Now he was in her elegant drawing-room directing his assistants as they applied beards, fixed moustaches and blackened faces. One imagines them trying out different robes and struggling with their turbans.

Clarkson outlined his art in an article he wrote in 1905. From this, we can picture him arriving at Fitzroy Square with his large 'expanding make-up box' containing 'grease-paints, powders, lip-salve, nose-paste, rouge, hare's foot, crêpe hair, scissors, brush and comb, mirror, sponge etc'. The various grease-paints would have been neatly lined up, ready for use. After applying some foundation cream, the Abyssinians would have been coloured with 'No. 12 Black' or, more likely, a special preparation called 'Nigger-black' which Clarkson preferred to 'Burnt cork used as a powder', which was the traditional method of making up minstrels. The princes' moustaches and beards, or 'face-fittings' as Clarkson called them, were created using 'crêpe-hair and spirit-gum'. It sounds an uncomfortable process. First, the face was carefully spread with the gum, and then strands of hair attached and pressed on with a towel. Clarkson advised against trimming the whiskers with scissors, as this could make them look artificial.

As the interpreter, Adrian recalled receiving 'a little sun-burn powder' from Clarkson (possibly his grease-paint No 3½ 'Slightly Sunburnt'). This gave a nice impression of a European unused to the Abyssinian sun. Clarkson then applied a beard to disguise him. A battered bowler hat and long, shabby overcoat completed Adrian's garb, making him look, he remembered, like a 'seedy commercial traveller'. Horace's outfit was more straightforward. He simply donned a top-hat and tailcoat to play Cholmondeley of the Foreign Office (appropriate attire for the ringmaster). He also carried a silver-topped cane which, as Tony Buxton recalled nearly fifty years later, he constantly brandished about.

When the disguises were finished to Clarkson's satisfaction, a photographer arrived from Lafayette's studio on Bond Street to record the event for posterity (improbably, but not impossibly, Virginia recalled the hoaxers re-assembling in costume and make-up to be photographed the day after the hoax). Irishman James Lauder had only established his London studio in 1897 but he was already well known in Dublin, where he had been operating under the more glamorous name of Lafayette since 1880 (the image of Willie Cole in uniform is also by him). Lafayette was the Patrick Lichfield of his age, photographing actors, celebrities and society ladies. Visiting royalty inevitably beat a path to his door, all eager to follow in the footsteps of the British royal family. In 1902, Ras Makonnen and a suite of Abyssinian dignitaries had called at Lafayette ahead of the Coronation of Edward VII. The image which resulted, portraying the berobed Abyssinians flanked by tailcoated British officials, so closely matches the photographs now taken of Horace's troupe of hoaxers that it seems impossible that he was not aware of it when he arranged the photo shoot.

They were on a tight schedule. Weymouth was a great deal further away than Cambridge, and with fewer trains they had to make the 12.40 or else call the hoax off. However, unlike the Sultan of Zanzibar joke, when the timings had gone awry, Horace judged it perfectly. There was still time for at least two carefully posed photographs of the hoaxers. One version, which was circulated among the participants afterwards as souvenirs, shows all six standing, with Tony Buxton as 'Ras 'el Makalen' in the centre. (Tony's personal copy of this photograph, apparently lost for decades, reappeared by strange chance on the day I visited his son John in Norfolk.) This famous image, which was used by the *Daily Mirror* as a poster when it broke the story, has since come to represent the joke in the popular imagination.

However, a less familiar version, formerly in the possession of Virginia's nephew Quentin Bell, survives at the National

Anthony Buxton's copy of the official photograph of the *Dreadnought* hoaxers by Lafayette Studios (John Buxton).

A more relaxed version of Lafayette's photograph of the *Dreadnought* hoaxers, later annotated with their assumed names. From left, Virginia Stephen (seated), Duncan Grant, Horace, Adrian Stephen, Anthony Buxton (seated), Guy Ridley (© National Portrait Gallery, London).

Portrait Gallery in London. This has Horace standing non-chalantly in the middle of the group, hands in pockets, framed by Buxton and Virginia, both sitting. It is annotated in an unknown hand and titled 'The Princes of Abyssinia and suite February 1910 with the compliments of the Foreign Office'. The photograph clearly identifies the roles each played in the charade. So, besides Buxton as 'Ras 'el Makalen', we learn that Guy Ridley acted the part of 'Ras 'el Mikael Golen', Virginia of 'Ras 'el Singanya' and Duncan Grant of 'Ras 'el Mendax'. Apparently the princes picked the names themselves. 'Makalen' was a near anagram of the real emperor's name Menelik; 'Mikael Golen' combined a traditional Abyssinian noble name with that of the ancient Syrian city Golan, while 'Mendax' was a mischievous use of the Latin word for untruthful. Virginia's choice of 'Singanya' is more obscure, and suggestive of her joyful love of words, real or not. No fading black-and-white photograph, however, can ever give us a true idea of the vividness of the costumes. These have to be coloured by our imagination, as the reports are contradictory. For instance, one newspaper noted how Virginia wore a 'sky-blue robe, beautifully embroidered', although she herself remembered being dressed in 'royal red satin with a turban on my head'.

With the photographer's work finished, the hoaxers were hurried by car to Paddington. 'People were going to work with their bags and baskets,' said Virginia looking back. 'The milk carts were rattling along the road. I did feel very queer… Everybody stared.' But at the station, 'everybody took us seriously.' Horace had arranged a reception committee from the railway company, and after a brief ceremony, the princes were ushered into a first-class reserved carriage. Minutes later, the train eased out of the station. It was too late to turn back now. For Virginia this meant her nervousness disappeared and she no longer cared what happened: 'It was clear everybody believed we were Abyssinians; and one began to believe it too.' For the next three-and-a-half-hours Horace and his accomplices would be out of contact with the world, uncertain how their journey would end. They had been meticulous in their preparation, but the trap itself had yet to be set.

Now Tudor Castle swung into action. Since chasing Mildred Pasolini around Europe, he had found work with Thomas Harvey at Toynbee Hall. He is the invisible man of the hoax, but his role was critical. An hour after the Abyssinians departed for Weymouth, Tudor walked calmly into a post office in St James's Street with a carefully drafted telegram. It was addressed to Admiral May, commander-in-chief of the Home Fleet, and signed Charles Hardinge, Permanent Undersecretary of State at the Foreign Office. Timed at two minutes past three, it read:

To: C in C Home Fleet Portland

Prince Makalen of Abyssinia and suite arrive 4.20 today Weymouth he wishes to see Dreadnought. Kindly arrange meet them on arrival regret short notice forgot wire interpreter accompanies them

Hardinge Foreign Office

Adrian and Horace had fretted beforehand whether the telegram needed some form of official coding. In fact, as was subsequently pointed out, the telegram should have been sent 'OHMS' ('On His Majesty's Service'). It wasn't, but the message was still taken completely at face value when it was transcribed at Portland half an hour later at 3.31p.m. This document still exists in the National Archives in Kew near London. I found it tucked inside the slim file of papers relating to the *Dreadnought* hoax in the Admiralty papers for February 1910 (the hoax itself has been carefully excised from the ship's log). The telegram's wording was so bureaucratically matter-of-fact that no one thought to challenge it. A further vital fifteen minutes elapsed before the message was handed to Admiral May aboard *Dreadnought*. This delay was a stroke of luck for the hoaxers. With only half an hour before the scheduled arrival in Weymouth of his foreign guests, May had no time to wire the Admiralty back for confirmation (he didn't think of telephoning). In any event, the Admiral was—taking Captain Richmond's assessment into account—an unimaginative man, not given to querying orders.

Horace and Adrian soon found the dining car in the train (which was emptied for their exclusive use by obliging stewards). The Abyssinians were forbidden from eating for fear of disturbing their beards and make-up. Clarkson's parting words to Virginia had been, 'Madam, you're the very image of an Abyssinian prince. But remember this: if you eat

The telegram received by Admiral May in Weymouth, with misspellings following transmission (National Archives).

or drink you're done. For any liquid or food warmth will make the dye run.' So for the princes hunger was the overriding impression of the day. Horace did purchase some buns for them at Reading, which they nibbled behind the drawn blinds of their carriage, but their starvation matched his growing anxiety. So many things could go wrong. Apart from concern that the telegram would be questioned, it had slowly dawned on Adrian that Willy Fisher might possibly recognise him, 'and then we should get into trouble'. To while away the journey, and distract such thoughts, Horace and Adrian tried to learn a little Swahili, using a grammar from the 'Society for the Propagation of the Gospel' bought especially for the purpose on the Charing Cross Road. But their efforts were lacklustre. They half expected the whole thing to be called off or prove a damp squib. They would then, as Adrian put it, 'slink back to London' with no harm done. How wrong he was.

11

The shudder of fear and excitement as the train slowed for Weymouth was palpable. 'Like a plunge into the cold bath,' recalled Adrian vividly, and far worse than arriving at Cambridge five years before. The stakes were so much higher and the territory unknown. Virginia felt in a 'trance' of excited apprehension. Would there be police at the station? Or, indeed, anybody at all? 'But no,' recalled Adrian, 'there on the platform stood a naval officer in full uniform, and the hoax had begun.' 'The greatest relief I have ever known,' said his sister years later. Admiral May had sent his flag lieutenant Peter Willoughby to meet the princes, with an eager smile and a detachment of marines neatly lined up on a red carpet. A cordon kept back a small, expectant crowd. Hats were raised, people bowed and a small cheer raised for the royal visitors who, according to Virginia, tried hard to remain 'severe and dignified', as princes should. Outside the station, cabs waited to transfer the princes the short distance to the quayside.

Weymouth today gives little impression of the drama of that now-distant day. The Victorian station has been swept away. It is a typical run-down but proudly defiant English seaside resort. But the magnificent clock on the esplanade, erected for Queen Victoria's Jubilee, is still there, as unmistakable now as it must have been in 1910. When Lieutenant Willoughby—who was 'lovely', Duncan reported lasciviously to Maynard Keynes—took *Dreadnought*'s guests past it, the clock read half past four. Within the hour they would see it again, their triumph complete.

At the quayside the princes were led on to the Admiral's steam launch that would take them out to *Dreadnought*. The immediate danger of exposure was past. Horace's fears receded with the shore as the launch swept out into the bay. He chatted amiably with Willoughby, certain now that the hoax could work. He was back in that fantasy world of his own making, where he made the rules. Adrian, too, relaxed. 'The expedition had become for me at any rate almost an affair of every day,' he recalled. Both men were benefiting from their experience in Cambridge. As Adrian put it, 'Everyone was expecting us to act the Emperor and his suite, and it would have been extremely difficult not to.' In modern parlance, they were method acting. It was a more nerve-wracking experience for the others, who sat mutely in the back of the launch. Virginia, in particular, was afraid to speak 'in case my voice, which I made as gruff as I could, should fail me. I found I could easily laugh like a man, but it was difficult to disguise the speaking voice.'

Soon the battleship loomed up in the February gloom ('smaller than I expected,' Adrian remembered, 'and uglier'). Bizarrely, the strains of 'Yankee Doodle Dandy' drifted across the water, played by a band of Royal Marines drawn up on deck. Then gloriously—considering Horace and Adrian's earlier exploit—the band launched into a lively rendition of the national anthem of Zanzibar. Not knowing the Abyssinian version, the bandmaster considered it a good substitute. The ship was festooned with flags and chains of lights in honour of the royal visit. Beneath them stood Admiral May and his staff, waiting patiently to receive their guests, all in full dress uniform with gold braid and medals. Horace led the princes on board, with Adrian trailing discreetly behind. 'We came near disaster on boarding the ship,' recalled Tony Buxton, 'I nearly tripped on coming over the side onto the deck and only just recovered my balance.' A similar incident had occurred on reaching

The officers and crew of HMS *Dreadnought* await the arrival of the King for an official visit in 1909. The hoaxers met a similar scene (author).

The officers of HMS *Dreadnought*. Willy Fisher is standing in the centre behind Captain Richmond and beside Lieutenant Willoughby (author).

The wardroom on *Dreadnought*, where Horace had a tea which the Abyssinians had declined, for fear of upsetting their disguises (author).

the Guildhall in Cambridge five years before. Virginia was delighted when her cousin then smartly saluted her. 'I thought I should burst out laughing, but happily I managed to preserve my Oriental stolidity of countenance,' she said.

The hoaxers had only finally settled on their names on the journey down from London, so Horace might be forgiven for garbling them now in his introductions. Tony remembered in particular how Horace repeatedly and loudly misspelt his own assumed name, 'Cholmondeley', to the assembled officers. Of course Tony may have forgotten Horace's deafness, which made him muddle names and speak with an unnaturally booming voice which could be disconcerting to his listeners. Adrian, meanwhile, was horrified to be presented as Herr Kaufmann. He had agreed a similar-sounding but English name, which Horace had accidentally (or not) misheard. Introducing a German to proceedings on a British battleship in 1910 was a risky move but one typical of Horace. 'Invasion stories' were all the rage, with frequent reports in the papers of Germans hiding in suburban streets. Indeed, just as Adrian had feared, his cousin stepped forward to query the presence of a German on board. Fortunately, the navy's 'proverbial tact', as Adrian described it, and Horace's noisy bluster avoided a confrontation, and the moment of crisis passed. Horace rattled on about how he had recently been at the Embassy in Rome; how the princes were in England to see Eton and how they had all left Paris in a hurry due to flooding. If pressed, these were all subjects which Horace knew something about. Above all, he expressed heartfelt regret at the short notice of the Abyssinians' visit.

Admiral May then led the princes on an inspection of the guard of honour. Feigning interest, Adrian quizzed the Admiral, in a hastily improvised German accent, on the various differences of uniform. It being a favourite subject of his, May did so—at length. He then unnerved Adrian by asking him to translate his answers for the princes. Turning to an expectant Tony Buxton, and trying not to laugh, Adrian began 'Entaqui, mahai, kustafani'. But then his nerve, and his improvised pidgin Swahili, completely failed him. Knowing he had to rapidly produce a stream of gibberish, Adrian fell back on Latin and Greek, reasoning, correctly, that his expensive classical education was better than May's naval one. By mangling his words and avoiding any obvious phrases, Adrian manufactured a workable lingo from the classical texts he had been force-fed at school, starting with passages from the *Aeneid*. Several officers commented on the strangeness of the language. But they were reassured when one officer, probably Fisher, declared that their guests had 'the real nigger smell'. (Hearing this, Willy Clarkson joked, 'Perhaps it was some of Clarkson's dark stain that stimulated the naval imagination!') Fisher had been on the Africa station for three years as a young midshipman, and even thirty-five years later in a memoir he claimed to recall 'the odd sickly smell of native life and sandalwood which permeated the narrow streets' of the towns he visited along the east coast.

After a statement of such authority nobody was prepared to challenge the princes. Instead, they were invited to tea in the wardroom. Horace, by now thoroughly enjoying himself, readily accepted. But Adrian, sensing calamity, wisely declined on behalf of the princes. He excused them on religious grounds, saying that their food had to be prepared in a special way. He then made the error of informing his hosts that at sunset the princes would have to prostrate themselves on the deck towards Mecca. As it appears from photographs that all four fake Abyssinians were wearing crucifixes—as they should, as Coptic Christians—Adrian was tempting fate. Fortunately May's religious education was as weak as his classical, and his prejudice stronger than both. Alarmed at the prospect of holding a strange Muslim ritual in his flagship, the Admiral officially delayed sunset. All across the fleet, bugle boys were left out in the cold as they waited perplexed for the flagship to signal the end of the naval day.

So Horace disappeared below decks, leaving Adrian and the Abyssinians to fend for themselves. It was a sign of growing confidence and his trust in Adrian. Nevertheless, sitting with the officers in the wardroom, he surely must have wondered when the door would burst open and he be unmasked. He need not have worried. Adrian and the princes were coping very well. Captain Richmond was showing them all over the ship, suspecting nothing and waiting patiently as Adrian translated his comments. The guns were especially admired, though the offer of a royal salute was waved aside. Adrian magnanimously replied that as the French Fleet had failed to salute the Abyssinians at Toulon, there was no need for the British to do so now. He later claimed he was worried about dirtying the guns and causing unnecessary work for the sailors. 'Besides, it was almost as grand to refuse a salute as to accept one.' Then Adrian faced a real crisis. The wind rose and it gently began to rain (as it had in Cambridge). He watched in horror as Duncan's moustache started to lift off in the breeze. Beside him, Virginia clearly saw the pale skin beneath the flapping hair. With the Captain distracted, Adrian undertook running repairs, but with only one umbrella between them— Horace is shown carrying one in the Lafayette photograph— there was now an urgent need to seek cover. Thinking quickly, Adrian told Richmond how cold it was compared to Abyssinia. The Captain took the hint, ushering the increasingly bedraggled party below to show them the wireless room and, unexpectedly, the officers' bathrooms, causing momentary panic among the hoaxers that they were about to be discovered and ducked.

Fortunately for them all, however, time was running out faster than their luck. Horace was anxious to catch the six o'clock train back to London, aware that an uncomfortable and awkward delay in Weymouth would result if they missed it. So, to the rousing strains of 'God Save the King' and three cheers from the crew, Willoughby escorted the princes back to the steam launch. To their delight, Horace and Adrian discovered later that Prince Battenberg, a cousin of the King, was officially reprimanded for steering another vessel across the bows of the Abyssinians' launch during their journey ashore. During the return trip, Willoughby amiably questioned a clearly baffled Tony Buxton on his many wives. Only afterwards did Tony learn that Horace had regaled the Lieutenant with wild stories of the Abyssinians' unorthodox domestic arrangements over tea in the wardroom. With the end of their adventure in sight, the princes grew relaxed and playful. They expressed 'the astonishment of simple natives' as Willoughby turned on and off the launch's electric lights. Horace, too, was becoming dangerously over-confident. He pressed money on the crew, then tried to award the fake Abyssinian decoration hanging around Tony Buxton's neck to Willoughby. 'This was an awful looking bauble,' shuddered Tony, 'borrowed I think by Ridley from his mother's hat.' What a Foreign Office mandarin was doing even attempting such a thing seems not to have occurred to the guileless Lieutenant. But wisely he followed protocol, politely declining the order on the grounds that he lacked permission to accept it.

For Adrian this summed up the ambiguity he felt at the success of the *Dreadnought* hoax, 'at mocking,' as he put it, 'even in the friendliest spirit, such charming people.' Unlike the mayor of Cambridge, with his petty-minded bitterness at being tricked, the officers of *Dreadnought* were men of their own class, with manners to match. Willoughby was the son of an earl, while the charming Captain Richmond shared many of Adrian's interests. With the exception of Willy Fisher, he had no axe to grind against such men. This nagging sense of betrayal spoiled his fun. Tony Buxton shared the unease.

He thought the hoaxers should have written a letter of apology to Admiral May. Although in later years he enjoyed telling the story of the hoax, his son John Buxton recalled his father's embarrassment, even shame, at being involved in the humiliation of the Royal Navy, particularly in the light of the war which so swiftly followed. As late as the 1950s John was cut dead by a naval officer after revealing a family connection to the incident. Admiral May, Commander Fisher and Captain Richmond all went on to higher things. None of their highly respectful biographies mention the hoax.

Like the flight of the Zanzibarees, the departure of the Abyssinians was undignified, despite the better planning. With minutes to spare, Horace bundled them into the train for London, leaving a bewildered Willoughby on the platform and cabbies clutching large tips. They all sank exhausted into their seats, hurriedly pulling the blinds down as a sneeze removed half of Tony Buxton's moustache. 'The only thing we could think of,' recalled Duncan Grant, 'was a meal.' 'I hadn't realised till that moment how tired I was,' Virginia said. 'My lips were parched. I could taste the paint on them. My dress was heavy. My wig made my head hot. Oh, if we could only take our things off and have a meal!' Only the incorrigible Cole had the will and energy left to continue the charade. He insisted that the train stewards wear white gloves to serve the princes, causing the train to be delayed for a time while some were purchased. ('That shows you what a very serious business a hoax was to Horace Cole,' Virginia ruefully remarked.) As the train rattled through the darkness, they swopped stories of their extraordinary day. One thing they all agreed. The officers had been so charming and the hoax such a complete success that they would not give the story to the press to embarrass the navy further. Naively they assumed that it was the end of the matter. But they had not counted on Horace's indiscretion, or his appetite for publicity.

12

*H*orace, fired up from the day's events, had gone straight to his club when he reached London, to celebrate. The others arrived home exhausted, grateful to have the chance to remove their smeared make-up and frayed whiskers (with Vaseline, cold cream or Clarkson's famed 'Kleeno'). Before parting they had sworn themselves to secrecy, but Horace could not resist relating the tale to his astonished friends at the St James's. Unfortunately, someone in his audience was sufficiently alarmed, outraged or sceptical about what they heard to inform the Foreign Office. Hearing this, Horace immediately decided to confess. Like a naughty schoolboy, Horace went to Whitehall the following day to own up (also, according to Tony Buxton, to see the effect of his joke). He was not believed. The officials thought he was mad. No one in Whitehall had heard of the Abyssinians' visit to England, or indeed of any official request to tour a British battleship.

Nevertheless, as a matter of routine his confession was referred to the Admiralty, which passed it down to Admiral May in Weymouth for comment. May's feelings at learning he had been duped can only be guessed at. He had just sent a message to his superiors informing them of the success of the visit. He was not happy. The Admiral gathered together his officers to grill them on their recollections of the Abyssinians. Lieutenant Willoughby helpfully volunteered that he had always suspected the interpreter was wearing a false beard. This was not what the Admiral wanted to hear. In a highly defensive reply to the Admiralty's enquiry, May confirmed the visit to his ship. 'The Abyssinians were in native dress and appeared to be genuine,' he reported tetchily. A seaman on *Dreadnought*, voicing the more forthright view below decks, called the hoaxers 'hounds' and 'villains'.

Four days had now passed since the hoax, and the Admiral might reasonably have expected the incident to pass without further embarrassment. But on Saturday 12 February the story broke on the front page of the *Express*, making May and the navy a laughing stock. Under the headline 'Sham Abyssinian Princes visit the Dreadnought' the hoax was revealed to the world. Rumours of the 'lunatic affair', as Maynard Keynes termed it, had been circulating among the hoaxers' friends all week. It was only when they saw it in print that they finally believed it. Horace was immediately blamed for leaking the story—for letting, as Duncan Grant so succinctly put it, 'the cat out of the bag'. Adrian never doubted that it was Horace who had given the game away, claiming Horace never contradicted him when he said so. All the newspaper would reveal about its source was that 'the majority of the young men sought seclusion, but one of them, bolder than the rest, has remained in London to tell the tale'.

The report was certainly very well informed—giving a detailed outline of the day's events—but not comprehensively so. Its description of the Abyssinians' make-up and costumes was sensationalised, and so outlandish that it can only have been written to satisfy an Edwardian racial stereotype. It spoke of 'black woolly mats' for wigs, false 'nigger lips' and 'enormously long, pointed, elastic-sided patent-leather boots', none of which are visible in photographs of the hoaxers. Other facts were also misleading or wrong. There was a suggestion that the 'commander-in-chief' of the prank spent £500 (many thousands today) furnishing the princes with real gems and decorations. But none are visible in the photographs of the hoaxers. In his book Adrian mentions only the 'fancy-dress' order which Horace tried to press on Willoughby and which Tony Buxton recalled had been purloined from the hat of Guy Ridley's mother. In one glaring slip, the report stated that the hoaxers had been dressed at Clarkson's shop and not, as several could testify, at Fitzroy Square. Whoever spoke to the press first—and Vanessa Bell thought it was someone from Clarkson's—it was not Horace. He was a stickler for the facts, as his Zanzibar exclusive had proved. More likely, the report was cobbled together from a tip-off. But the names of the hoaxers (although never published) quickly leaked out, and Horace's reputation for showing off was such that everyone simply assumed it was him.

Public response to news of the escapade was electric. Horace was inundated with letters from women: some offering to join him on his next exploit, others of a more suggestive nature. In an era before television, radio or cinema, the popular press created celebrity, making Horace known across the country. The *Express* even coined a catchphrase for the hoax. 'The "princes" were shown everything,' it narrated, 'and at every fresh sight they murmured in chorus *"Bunga Bunga"* which being interpreted, means "Isn't it lovely?"' None of the participants who published accounts or spoke later about the hoax remembered anyone actually saying 'Bunga bunga'. Yet it was seized upon by the press and public because it sounded right. It fitted Edwardian opinion of how Africans should speak, even if they didn't. Naval officers were taunted with the phrase in the street, while music-hall artists delivered it on stage (the Pavilion at Weymouth rushed out a song incorporating the phrase within a week). Fact and fantasy had finally merged.

It no longer mattered what was true and what was not. The hoax now belonged to the press, and the press made it what it is. All talk of lips, wigs and 'Bunga bunga' was superimposed

"ONCE BITTEN, TWICE SHY."

THE ABYSSINIAN PRINCES HOAX

WHAT WILL HAPPEN NEXT TIME SOME GENUINE EASTERN PRINCES VISIT A BRITISH MAN-O' WAR

Everybody has been talking of the practical joke played by some funny people who dressed up as Abyssinian princes and, in this disguise, were received with royal honours on H.M.S. Dreadnought a few days ago. Our cartoonist imagines that the next time Oriental personages, however genuine, visit a man-o'-war, their reception will be rather warm, and something of the sort shown here.

How Haselden in the *Daily Mirror* saw the hoax, 17 February 1910.

on the story by the newspapers to titillate their readers until no one, least of all the hoaxers themselves, really knew the truth. Like the Sultan of Zanzibar who never was, the *Dreadnought* hoax was so shaped by its retelling that even Adrian Stephen, in his supposedly definitive account, eventually thought he had been led by the Emperor of Abyssinia and not by some princely underling.

Far from discouraging the notoriety, the hoaxers initially seemed to encourage it. The first participant to talk was Virginia, who had the press camped outside her door in Fitzroy Square within hours of the story breaking. A week after the hoax, she gave an interview to the *Daily Mirror*, though she declined to be photographed, and certainly not in the evening dress the papers desired to impress its readers. Under the headline 'Lady Prince's Story', she twittered away about her adventure. 'The only really trying time I had,' she gushed, 'was when I had to shake hands with my cousin, who is an officer on the *Dreadnought*, and who saluted me as I went on deck. I thought I should burst out laughing, but happily I managed to preserve my Oriental stolidity of countenance.' Only this last vivid description gives any clue that the reporters were dealing with an accomplished writer and not with just another bored upper-class girl. She was having fun, and saw no reason to be ashamed or embarrassed. Indeed, for the rest of her life Virginia enjoyed telling the story, giving a talk about it to the Women's Institute as late as 1940. Fascinated by the questions of gender that the hoax threw up, she also wove the experience into her fiction. A fleet of Royal Navy battleships glides past the heroine of *The Voyage Out*, written at this period, while the plot of another novel, *Orlando*, rests on sexual ambivalence and cross-dressing. In a little-known 1921 short story, Virginia even went so far as to describe how a young woman 'had dressed herself as an Ethiopian prince and gone aboard one of His Majesty's ships'. As Virginia knew personally, this elaborate conceit was an intriguing way of exploring perceptions of honour and behaviour between men and women. Her impersonation of a man, and a black man at that, apparently poses more questions for Virginia Woolf's admirers than it ever did herself.

The *Mirror* followed up its scoop by splashing the Lafayette photograph of the hoaxers across its front page, fuelling a further firestorm of coverage. Editorial comment, like public opinion, was generally positive, admiring the boldness of the harmless enterprise and its skilful execution. However, praise was not entirely unanimous. A correspondent to the *Express* was not alone in decrying the joke. 'I see nothing to laugh at,' he harrumphed,

> but very much to be ashamed of, and I think that the perpetrators of the impudent and scandalous trick ought to be punished for playing a contemptuous fraud on His Majesty's authorities. If such tricks as these may be performed with impunity I can imagine that in the guise of a prank a more diabolical piece of mischief might be accomplished.

At West Woodhay, Horace's Uncle Alfred agreed. His sister Annie was said to be 'not at all inclined to be proud of her brother's exploit', summing up the Coles' attitude towards the prank, coming as it did so soon after the Pasolini fiasco.

Despite the wide coverage, there was little more to add to the story except for some juicy titbits such as the glorious suggestion that Admiral May had asked the King whether he could retrospectively accept the Abyssinian order. All eyes now turned to see how the navy would react. With the exception of the good-humoured Captain Richmond—who pretended to call a policeman when he bumped into Adrian and Horace in the street—the omens were not good. Admiral May in particular was irate. Enraged by the press coverage, he turned defence into attack, firing a broadside at Whitehall to demand action.

Can the law touch people who send false telegrams in the name of high officials? Will the Foreign Office or the Admiralty move in the matter and prosecute? Will the Admiralty take the opinion of the Law Officers of the Crown and let me know if it is against the law. Do the Admiralty wish me to report the matter officially?

The Admiral's fury was stoked by Willy Fisher. He idolised May and was bitterly angry that he may have been the cause of the Admiral's embarrassment. It didn't take him long to discover the truth, or to work out his cousins' aim. Shamefully, he offered up the names and addresses of Adrian, Virginia and Horace. He also stirred things up by reporting that the wardroom were calling Virginia a whore for participating in the hoax. He began orchestrating condemnation. Virginia and Adrian's aunt Dorothea called the hoax silly and 'vulgar', while their uncle Harry, who had rather enjoyed the Zanzibar joke, deplored the insult to the navy. 'His Majesty's ships are not suitable objects for practical jokes,' he huffed. 'For God's sake keep Virginia's name out of it.' One disgusted cousin of the Stephens, who maintained Virginia had been led into the hoax because she had not found Jesus, sent a religious tract to absolve her from her 'vulgar' actions.

Under mounting pressure and with rumours now circulating that *Dreadnought*'s duped officers would be disciplined for their stupidity, Adrian felt honour-bound to appeal to the Admiralty for clemency. Someone told him that by accepting full responsibility he would let Fisher and the other officers off the hook. So with Duncan by his side, and like Horace before him, Adrian headed to Whitehall to, in Virginia's words, 'make a clean breast of it'.

It was a spectacular misjudgement. From the start, the Admiralty had wanted to brush the incident aside as a nine-day wonder. Punishing the officers involved was never seriously considered. In private, the First Lord of the Admiralty, Reginald McKenna, even saw the funny side of the story. Consequently he was amazed, and not a little displeased, to find two of the hoaxers in his office pleading leniency not for themselves but for his officers. He accused them of impertinence, told them not to do it again, and bundled them out of the door. Adrian, who felt he was acting in the best interests of everyone, took umbrage at his treatment. Almost thirty years later, he still bridled at how he had been treated '*de haut en bas*', by the minister, as if 'he had rowed in the Cambridge boat before he was First Lord of the Admiralty'. In Adrian's world the first was far more impressive than the second.

At first the Foreign Office was as relaxed as the Admiralty about the hoax. Sir Charles Hardinge—who had more reason than most to feel aggrieved, as his forged signature was on the hoaxers' telegram—sensibly argued that taking matters further would simply prolong the joke. But the press coverage and Admiral May's loud protest now made that impossible. The Director of Public Prosecutions was consulted and the matter raised in the House of Commons. However, it soon became obvious that the only crime actually committed was the sending of a counterfeit telegram. Admiral May leapt on this legal lifeline. 'I would point out,' he wrote gravely, summoning up the remnants of his shattered dignity, 'the possible danger to the public service of fictitious telegrams…being sent to Officers in Command of H.M. Navy.'

Scotland Yard was now dragged into the mounting furore. The evidence against Horace rested on his own admission and on the testimony of others, neither of which was deemed admissible (this being 1910), as they had been given in confidence, and by gentlemen. Proof was needed that he had been personally responsible for the illegal telegram. The trouble was, his handwriting didn't match the text handed to the telegraph operator at the post office in St James's Street; nor did the handwriting of any of the Weymouth party. In any case, they had all been on a train at the time it was sent. Then the police had a lucky break. The Great Western Railway Company handed in a letter it had received from a Mr Tudor Castle requesting a refund for six unused train tickets from Weymouth on the day of the hoax (the Abyssinians had returned to London using a different rail company). It was a ludicrous error to make, but somehow typical of Horace's trusting friend. The expense was insignificant, but it proved a very costly mistake. With the help of a handwriting expert, the police were able to link Tudor's letter directly to the telegram. They had their man.

But what to do? A month had passed since the hoax and it had long before been pushed off the front pages. The Foreign Office had washed its hands of the matter, while over at the Admiralty McKenna was preoccupied by budgetary issues. Both departments gratefully left the decision to Admiral May whether to prosecute Tudor or not. May decided not. Reluctantly, he saw there was nothing to be gained by a conviction, except possibly a derisory fine and a slap on the wrist, and everything to lose in reputation. Despite his own acute embarrassment, he also sensed the official lack of appetite for prosecuting a minor accessory to the prank rather than its chief orchestrator. So for the good of the navy, and himself, May stepped back from the brink glad, at least, of having the opportunity to appear high-minded. 'After consideration,' he informed a relieved First Lord, 'I am of the opinion that it would be better on the whole not to proceed with the prosecution of the person who sent the forged telegram.'

As far as officialdom was concerned that was an end to the matter. The slim file of letters, telegrams and press clippings was closed, sealed and locked away under embargo. *Dreadnought's* log was doctored, and May left to enjoy the last years of a long and illustrious career. There would be no more mention of Abyssinian princes, real or otherwise. Horace acknowledged the navy's magnanimity. He recognised that in return for immunity from prosecution, the hoaxers should stay silent. Several of the hoaxers, himself included, had now spoken to the press, but he forbade any further comment in print. As he boasted twenty years later, 'I refused to write anything and would allow no one of my entourage to do so either!' He understood the pact they had entered into with the navy. This tacit agreement was broken when Horace died and Adrian published *The 'Dreadnought' Hoax*, encouraged by Virginia, whose press printed the book. None of the other participants ever wrote a word about it.

13

Only Willy Fisher was disappointed with the outcome. In fact, he was furious. He saw the lack of action over the hoax as a whitewash, and brooded angrily over what to do next. In the end he took matters into his own hands by assembling a posse of like-minded officers to exact violent revenge. The first Adrian and Virginia knew about their cousin's intentions was the vigorous pulling of their doorbell early one Sunday morning in April, two months after the hoax. From her bedroom window Virginia could see a cab outside the door. Then she heard raised voices in the hall. Willy had burst into the house and was yelling hysterically at Adrian.

> 'Do you realise that all the little boys ran after Admiral May in the street calling out 'Bunga Bunga'? Do you realise you owe your lives to the British Navy? Did you realise that you are impertinent, idiotic? Did you realise that you ought to be whipped through the streets? Did you realise that if you had been discovered you would have been stripped naked and thrown into the sea?'

On and on Willy went at his terrified cousin, who was convinced he was about to be beaten up or, worse, stabbed. Then Willy paused, breathless and red-faced to reveal, with obvious regret, that some obscure naval custom prevented him from punishing another member of his own family. However, this nicety did not extend to the other hoaxers. 'I know who the others are,' he shouted, 'and now you've got to tell me their addresses.' To Adrian's shame, he did. Virginia said it was a mistake, but she was displaying the loyalty her brother lacked towards his friends. In *The 'Dreadnought' Hoax* Adrian slides over the incident, claiming his cousin had cajoled or 'hoaxed' him into revealing the names and addresses, which 'innocent as a lamb' he had. Willy's triumph was ill-disguised. He snorted at Adrian's mumbled regrets, his superiority now restored. He insisted that Adrian apologise in person to Admiral May on the quarterdeck of *Dreadnought*—an offer Adrian dismissed as 'ridiculous'. The hoaxers were 'too wary to fall into any trap,' he retorted. Incensed, Willy brushed aside Adrian's proffered hand and, turning on his heel, strode out of the door. Moments later the cab sped out of the square, leaving Adrian shaken and dreading a return visit, though one never came.

The same day Duncan Grant was having breakfast with his parents in Hampstead when he heard the knock on the door. The maid announced that there was a friend to see him. Curious, and still in his pyjamas and slippers, Duncan followed her out. Through the window Mrs Grant saw her son tripped up by Willy Fisher before being bundled head-first into a waiting cab. Alarmed, she turned towards her husband, the imperturbable Major Bartle Grant.

'What on earth are we to do,' she shrieked. 'Someone's kidnapping Duncan.'

Major Grant barely looked up from his paper. 'I expect it's his friends from the *Dreadnought*,' he calmly replied. Indeed it was, but from Duncan's viewpoint on the floor of the cab they hardly seemed very friendly. All he could see were three burly men holding long canes. He looked so scared that Willy, with unusual consideration, enquired whether he felt ill. When Duncan plucked up the courage to ask what was going on and where he was going, Willy would only say menacingly that 'You'll see plenty of Dreadnoughts where you're going'.

The cab headed out of London towards a remote part of Hendon, where Duncan was unceremoniously tipped out on the ground. It was hopeless putting up any resistance. Duncan was facing three armed naval officers in his dressing gown (and, Virginia gravely noted, 'without a hat'). Bravely he waited for the inevitable onslaught, resigning himself to his fate. However, his gentle courage unnerved his assailants. Duncan's meekness was confusing to men used to receiving and exacting physical punishment. 'I can't make this chap out,' one said. 'He won't fight. You can't cane a chap like that.' But Willy ordered them to proceed; he would have blood. In a revealing phrase, Virginia noted later that her cousin 'was too high in the service to lend a hand himself'. Yet he was perfectly happy to stand by as his henchmen set to work. Fortunately, they still possessed a sense of fair play even if Willy did not. They merely tapped Duncan a couple of times on the behind and, honour satisfied, told him to go. They even offered him a lift home, but Duncan, his dignity intact, opted instead to return by tube. Anything was better than another terrifying ride in the cab.

Locating the other hoaxers was more difficult, especially as Willy could only satisfy his bloodlust on intermittent day leave from his posting at Portsmouth. Tony Buxton and Guy Ridley were unreachable in the country, so Willy sent them notes summoning them to Admiral May's residence in London. One—it is not known which but I suspect it was Tony—turned up intending to apologise, but was given very short shrift by the Admiral. May was clearly anxious to distance himself from the reprisals carried out in his name. Pressed later, he denied any knowledge of the beatings. With Virginia excused punishment because she was a woman (and Willy's cousin), this left only Horace to be dealt with. But matters were complicated by an illness which had confined him to bed. Indeed it took three trips to London before Willy and his cohort could gain access to Cadogan Place. What happened next was recalled by Horace in an interview for the *Daily Mirror*.

Late one night, two officers of high rank on the *Dreadnought* came to my house and were admitted to the drawing room, where I received them. They carried canes and their manner was very serious indeed. They said they had come to avenge the honour of the Admiral, but they admitted they had not informed him of their visit. After brandishing their canes in the air they demanded that I and the 'princes' should re-enact the hoax scene on board the *Dreadnought*, and that I, as the ring leader, should then apologise to the commander-in-chief on behalf of the whole party. Failing that, they had, they declared, decided to cane me.

I declined to accede to the suggestion and protested against the caning on the ground that I was ill and under medical treatment. My butler became so alarmed that he entered the room to protect me, and said he would send for the police. I told him not to do that, and he thereupon remained in the room. There then was a discussion as to what should be done. The naval officers said they had come to London for the sole purpose of avenging the honour of their chief and they could not possibly go back without having 'blood'. The butler again protested and threatened to go for the police, and finally, in order to salve the wounded feelings of the naval officers I suggested that the principal officer should meet me, either with boxing-gloves, sword or revolver, when I recovered.

He declined, and finally I said, jokingly, that if the principal officer would allow me to inflict on him six strokes with the cane, I would receive a corresponding number from him. To my astonishment he was so serious that he readily accepted the offer. We then retired to a neighbouring mews, and there we found a rubbish-box, which served as a sort of 'triangle', and here I gave the naval officer six strokes with the cane—not very hard ones, as I treated the matter as a joke, and did not want to hurt. Then I, in turn, received six strokes from the officer who, with his colleague, was very serious the whole time. Then we all shook hands, and the naval officers left, apparently satisfied, for they said they did not intend to cane other members of the hoaxing party.

What are we to make of all this? It is a bizarre tale laden with symbolism and with a strangely homoerotic schoolboyish element. Apparently Horace and Willy even tossed a coin to see who would 'bat' first. The earnest, tight-lipped way in which Willy Fisher embarks on the duel is in sharp contrast to Horace's easy-going approach. Willy's frustration and his deep resentment at how he was being treated is palpable. He can see that his naval rank means nothing in Horace's well-appointed drawing-room. The only status that matters is class, which his opponent (Eton, Cambridge) has in abundance and he (minor prep school, Dartmouth naval college) painfully lacks. The butler is a lovely detail, introducing an imperturbable Jeeves-like figure to the highly charged scene. His aloof, unruffled presence and the possible disgrace of being handed over to the civilian police merely add to Willy's growing discomfort.

The duel itself is ludicrous, made more so by its setting in a Chelsea alleyway. Had Horace fought Willy with gun or sword he would certainly have been prepared to kill him, without hesitation or regret. This way was more exquisite. It satisfied Willy's desire for revenge but humiliated him. As Duncan had also found out, Willy Fisher was a coward and a bully. Worse, he was one lacking a sense of humour. His behaviour had vindicated the hoax. Horace had no scruples over telling the press about the canings, though there is compelling evidence that he deliberately underplayed the punishment. After Horace's death, David Scott-Moncrieff recalled him revealing that he had taken 'an awful hiding' from the naval officers, who had been specially selected by Fisher to match his own impressive physique.

In the end, Willy's mission was entirely counterproductive, removing from Horace any possible discomfiture over his escapade. He could now enjoy his 'navy joke'. His friends gave him a gold-bound pocket book from Asprey to comme-morate the feat (subsequently pawned but recovered and still with his family). And as he had after the Sultan of Zanzibar adventure, Horace gave out framed photographs of the *Dreadnought* hoaxers, causing, according to the *Express*, 'much amused comment' when he gave one—still posing as 'Herbert Cholmondeley'—to his friend Lord Maidstone as a wedding present. Moreover, the ridiculous sequel to the hoax stirred up the press all over again, heaping fresh misery on Admiral May and the Royal Navy. Willy's fellow officers on *Dreadnought* distanced themselves from his actions. Stony-faced, the Admiral refused to comment. But the public loved it. Their appetite for more fun was satisfied by the Apollo Theatre's production of *The Islander*, a musical comedy set on an 'exact reproduction' of *Dreadnought*'s quarterdeck which featured a posse of sham princes in oriental costumes. Three years later interest was still undimmed when Cecil Raleigh's play *Sealed Orders* opened at Drury Lane. Apart from the introduction of an airship to proceedings—'the first to appear on a stage'—this comic drama faithfully recreated the hoax, and ended in spectacular fashion when a 'Lieutenant Willoughby' dived off the battleship. Having delighted in theatre since childhood, Horace could now see his own actions depicted on stage, and from 1918—when *Sealed Orders* was made into a silent film—at the infant cinema. He was at the height of his fame, at his happiest, with 'passionate dreams of the bright midday'.

14

Passionate dreams of the bright midday
The night descends, you fade away;
The morning glimmers, you come again
With your infinity of pain;
White-hot dreams of the midday hours
What is the toil of your secret powers?

You have raised up hopes that had no morrow,
Dreams still-born of a nameless sorrow,
Evoked the spectre of wild despair
At war with nought, in a vast nowhere,
When the temple of life seemed tumbling down,
Who could have known it was London town?

The *Dreadnought* hoax caught a wave of enthusiasm for dressing up which was all the rage before the First World War among the *beau monde*. Everyone from Bloomsbury to Belgravia wanted to join in. Virginia Woolf recalled she was inundated with invitations from 'Great ladies' to come to their parties dressed as an Abyssinian. A month after the prank, over four thousand party-goers crowded the Albert Hall in a kaleidoscope of colour for the Chelsea Arts Club Ball. It was the largest fancy-dress party ever held. There were plenty of Abyssinians; but also elephants, bears, harlequins, pirates—and Queen Victoria. Cowboys jostled with Indians; kings with queens. Forty female art students combined into an eighty-legged 'flu germ' with flashing electric eyes. The rest of the country looked on with amazement. It was surreal and liberating, and at the heart of it all was Horace, revelling in his notoriety. A photograph taken about this time, possibly ahead of this very ball, shows him with other revellers. He is dressed as an Arab and looking fierce beside a gawky-looking girl and black-faced and madly grinning 'African'. But his interest in oriental disguise—now that it was popular—was already waning. Soon his jokes would take on a less encumbered, more spontaneous look.

Other things were changing too. On 6 May the King died, bringing the curtain down on frivolity and ending a manner of raffish living which had defined the age. The twentieth century could finally begin, heralded appropriately by the passing that

Horace going to a ball with unidentified friends, circa 1910 (Valerie Crosia).

year of Halley's Comet. In November Roger Fry unveiled his ground-breaking exhibition of what he termed 'post-impressionist' paintings, signalling the dawn of modern art. The vivid colours and skewed perspectives of the Cézannes, van Goghs and Gauguins on the gallery walls reflected the changing world around them. The organising committee included Adrian Stephen's brother-in-law Clive Bell and Lady Ottoline Morrell, the exotic literary hostess whose Bedford Square soirees Horace occasionally attended. The exhibition was greeted with a 'post-impressionist' fancy-dress ball and the arrival in London of Sergei Diaghilev's sensational Ballets Russes with their striking costumes and avant garde performances. Only months after the *Dreadnought* hoax, Virginia, Adrian and Duncan Grant again donned native costumes and applied black make-up to attend the ball as savages from a Gauguin painting. For Virginia, the occasion marked her return to London following a further period of mental illness triggered, her sister Vanessa suspected, by her participation in Horace's prank.

The Gauguin natives were applauded at the ball, but opinion was sharply divided on the merits of the artist himself. Like many others at the time, it seems Horace failed fully to appreciate the post-impressionists, though he had considered some impressionist paintings shown him in Paris by Hugh Lane to be 'wonderful'. Unconventional in so many other ways, he instinctively preferred the more traditionally minded (in art not life) painters of the New English Art Club. People like Henry Lamb, Derwent Wood, James Dickson Innes and Augustus John, who showed in London at the same time as the post-impressionists. They rejected the stuffiness of the Royal Academy but stopped short of stepping fully into modern expressionism. Founded in 1886, the NEAC had modelled itself on the anti-establishment Salon des Refusés in Paris, though over time it became almost as stilted as the institution it sought to oppose.

Today Horace's family have every reason to regret his lack of artistic foresight. As a well-funded, well-connected and fully engaged art buyer, he could have built up a goldmine of works by Picasso, Matisse and others at a time when important work was affordable. But Horace was a true collector, buying from sentiment not for investment or display. He pictured himself as the noble patron of the indigent Innes. He valued art for art's sake—freely lending or even giving paintings away. Friends in hospital even received original artworks as 'get-well cards', as Horace believed utterly in the restorative power of beauty. 'When a man is ill what he wants is something beautiful to look at,' he would say. Horace was the complete antithesis of today's autograph-hunting contemporary art buyer who buys to impress his friends.

Edwardian London was turning into a modern metropolis and among Horace's friends the rebellious were becoming respectable. His collaborators in the Zanzibar and *Dreadnought* hoaxes were starting careers and getting married. Guy Ridley was at the Bar, Dummer Howard was working in the offices of the architect Sir Edwin Lutyens, Tony Buxton had returned to the family brewery, Leland Buxton was farming in South Africa and Robbie Bowen-Colthurst had been appointed (rather incongruously) Inspector of Irish Produce in Britain. After a spell in Australia, even Tudor Castle had settled down to work as a land agent and marry Dummer Howard's sister Muriel. Only Horace resolutely held out as a prankster.

Early in 1911, after rejecting writers Joseph Hone and Walter Lamb (who also optimistically proposed to Virginia Stephen), Horace's sister Annie married future prime minister Neville Chamberlain following an introduction managed by Uncle Alfred and Aunt Lillian at West Woodhay. Lillian was the widow of Neville's uncle Herbert, and she saw him as a safe antidote to Annie's more wilful side. Chamberlain considered Horace 'a little mad', and as his political career progressed he probably saw him as a slight embarrassment. Had Horace lived to see Neville into Downing Street he may have become a major one.

Not that Horace any longer really cared. He had fallen out with Annie over the Mildred Pasolini debacle, when she had sided with their stepfather in his disapproval. He now turned his back on her bourgeois world, as she had the fairyland they occupied as children. He wanted to immerse himself fully in the fast-living world of London's artistic *demi-monde*, where convention was flouted and class counted for little. He frequented the Café Royal, the unofficial headquarters of the bohemian world which catered for everyone from prince to penniless student. There were other places to drink. Edward VII's favourite hostess Rosa Lewis still presided magnificently over the Cavendish Hotel in Jermyn Street and Romano's in the Strand resolutely maintained a faded Edwardian feel long into the new reign. But the Café Royal was the place to be. Beneath the gilded caryatids of its famed Domino Room, you could gorge on oysters and champagne or simply linger over coffee; eat steak or stew, muse and gossip. Horace devoured the atmosphere and was soon a fixture of the place, as every memoir of the period testifies.

Here he mixed with aesthetes from the nineties like Arthur Symons, whose poetry celebrated the music halls, and Irishman George Moore. As a young man Moore had supped deeply in bohemian Paris and was an old friend of Horace's mother through his links to Yeats and the Irish literary movement. Both men feature in Horace's 'mixed bag of acquaintances' and both had an incalculable effect on him. Their belief in life for art's sake validated his fantasy world, giving it meaning and intellectual foundation. Of course the shade of Oscar Wilde also still lingered at the Café, and some ancient roués with dyed hair and rouged cheeks kept the flame alive. But a whole new army of Royalists now occupied the marble-topped tables where Oscar had once sat with Bosie. Slade School painters, would-be writers, Fleet Street hacks, officers on leave, and gaiety girls were all thrown together in a colourful hubbub of noise and laughter. To them Oscar was old school and hopelessly camp. They were pleasure-seekers in the vanguard of a new

Horace the dreamer and poet (Francis Chamberlain).

sexual revolution. No longer did men need to rely on the many prostitutes plying their wares outside and in the Café. Young women, many from entirely respectable households, were now willing, indeed wanting, to enjoy casual sex, aided by more widely available contraceptives and liberated morals. Men like writer and poet T.E. Hulme, last seen being sent down from Cambridge, took full advantage. He would pop out of the Café between rounds for a quick assignation against the railings of Piccadilly underground station nearby. Even such lubricious behaviour as this paled beside the carnal goings-on of the Café's lecher-in-chief, Augustus John.

In 1910, Augustus was thirty-two and already the leading British artist of his generation, known as much for his personal reputation as for his art. His tall, red-bearded figure struck fear and longing in those who crossed his path. He was desirable and detestable. Like his ego, everything he did was on a gargantuan scale. He painted, drank and screwed at a staggering rate, destroying all obstacles to his desires and instant self-gratification. Success had brought money, lots of it, which he sprayed around the grill room, fuelling the adulation. He had five known children, had buried his own wife and slept with countless others. What he wanted he got, and as quickly discarded. His will was irresistible, so no one resisted. Until Horace arrived.

Horace had met Augustus in Paris, but he had known of him for much longer. His mother Mary Studd had encountered the painter back in 1900 at his first show in London. Like every woman, she was struck by Augustus's mesmerising eyes and his steady, unnerving gaze. She told her son later that Augustus 'had made suggestions' to her at the preview, despite having only just met her and the twenty-year age difference. Mary was the first of a series of women connected to Horace that Augustus would try (usually successfully) to seduce. Horace had also seen Augustus's work in the Cambridge rooms of Louis Clarke, a noted connoisseur and later director of the Fitzwilliam Museum.

So Horace had been watching the developing cult of Augustus for some time now, and their paths had frequently crossed. Augustus, too, was aware of 'the Sultan of Zanzibar', as he called him, intrigued by a life force as great as his own. But it was only after the *Dreadnought* hoax that the two men became intimate, their lives entangled. They circled each other for the next twenty years, frequently clashing, often violently, but unable to draw away. For Augustus, Horace was a refreshing change to the sycophants and art-school groupies who usually mobbed him in the Café Royal. Like him, Horace was physically intimidating, confrontational and careless of opinion. He was also sufficiently rich and well connected to be useful to any artist, however famous. Above all, he was as celebrated as Augustus himself, and one of the few people in London that the painter could admire. Augustus might despise himself for wasting his talent on lucrative portraits of plutocrats and politicians—as he was already doing—but with Horace he could still pose as a provocateur. Each saw themselves in the other, by turns despising or admiring what they found there.

Evenings with Horace and Augustus, usually ending in a brawl, were legendary. Nicolette MacNamara, one of the ragbag of children attached to the court of Augustus, recalled going to a party and seeing them going hammer and tongs at each other beneath the kitchen table. Their relationship was a trial of strength: an old-fashioned test of virility which Augustus waged with his cock and Horace with his fists. On one thing the rivals were agreed: the primacy of art—be it painting or poetry—as an expression of love, and the only thing worth living and dying for.

No one embodied this essence of life more than the third member of a 'blood brotherhood' Augustus and Horace forged in the back of a cab by stabbing themselves with a knife. Like Augustus, James Dickson Innes had trained as a painter at the Slade under its inspirational principal Henry Tonks. Like him too he was Welsh by birth, although his French mother gave him his dark colouring and strong will. Physically, however, Dick Innes was very different to his larger-than-life, heavily built companions. When Augustus described his friend's 'slightly cadaverous cast with glittering eyes' he was seeing a man dying of consumption. Horace judged Dick one of the very few genuine artists of the age (Augustus, Spencer Gore, Wilson Steer and, with personal regret, Jacob Epstein were the others). He was dismissive of most of the rest. 'I hate bad artists, and semi-professional moneyed ones,' he declared. 'There's nothing more futile than the art talk of half-baked and educated amateur "artists" whose whole outlook is futile and a waste of time.' But Dick Innes was different. He had an exceptional talent for colour and composition, winning a prize at the Slade for a vivid and unsettling Sickert-like interior of a music hall. After art school he crafted a vision all of his own, painting landscapes of deceptive tranquillity bathed in iridescent light. His artistic debt to Constable and Turner was obvious and acknowledged: he carried Turner's *Liber Studiorum* everywhere he went, and visited the Tate almost every day to view his hero's work. But he injected something uniquely other and modern into his work, combining the verve of the post-impressionists with the English landscape tradition. Dick's shy manner and quiet voice matched his work. His friend John Fothergill thought there was 'something of the saint about him'. Yet beneath the frail exterior lay a fiercely romantic and passionate man driven by impulse and desire. He drank heavily, got involved in fights, and was arrested for hitting a policeman. 'He loved all things where beauty is most wild,' Horace wrote in an elegy after Dick died. 'His soul a poet, and his heart a child.'

15

Early in 1911 the brotherhood of Horace, Augustus and Dick decamped to North Wales, settling into lodgings beneath Mount Arenig. Dick began feverishly to paint the mountain, racing Augustus to complete oil sketches regardless of the weather. He endowed Arenig with sacred properties. His output was phenomenal, even though he burnt more paintings in frustration than he preserved for posterity. Though they painted in tandem, Augustus suspected that Dick resented his presence on the mountain. Dick was driven on by the relentless progress of his tuberculosis and by his hopeless love for Euphemia Lamb, the wilful wife of fellow artist Henry Lamb. Thwarted in his desire, he buried Euphemia's letters in a silver casket at the summit of Arenig in a dramatic gesture which Horace, the eternal romantic, understood. Dick cared

Dick Innes, who 'loved all things where beauty is most wild'. Pencil drawing by Ian Strang which Horace kept until his death. (National Portrait Gallery; © reserved).

little for his own appearance or his health, drinking heavily and wandering the moors alone after dark. When Horace then invited him to Ireland, he drank so much whiskey at the races that he almost died.

In a final search for a cure, Dick headed to the South of France with Horace and a one-legged Australian artist called Derwent Lees, whose work imitated his own. Horace was now almost entirely supporting Innes ('whom I consider a more original artist than John'). He paid over the odds for his paintings and encouraged him in the face of critical disregard. He pictured Dick as a visionary struggling heroically then dying for his art. He saw much of himself in the younger man, and envied his fate. But the manic dissipation continued. Dick was on his final descent, gathering comparisons with Keats and Chatterton, while Lees eventually went mad. When Dick died, aged just twenty-seven, Horace was heartbroken, and more affected than with any other bereavement he had had to endure. He cherished a portrait of his dead friend for the rest of his life, carrying it wherever he went. With Augustus, he arranged Dick's simple funeral ceremony, writing a poem 'which was buried with him'. The poem was published in the *New Age*, one of three poems by Horace accepted by this influential literary magazine.

J.D.I.

He loved the mountains, and the spaces
Where breakers curl along a desert shore,
Great suns, and women's magic-making faces
Aglow amidst some vineyard's trellised store,
He loved all things where beauty is most wild,
His soul a poet, and his heart a child.

The storm-girt summits of his native land
Made mountain music that to him was speech;
He learnt their secrets; and a flaming brand,

Born of their vapours, wisp-like out of reach,
Lured him to seek out beauty in the woods
That crown with purple those wild solitudes.

He found her in deep, amethystine caves,
He saw her form athwart the dawn-barred sky,
Followed her track across the dewy waves
That trembled at the sunbeams—soon to die!
He watched her clothed in all her midday spell,
But felt her nearest when the evening fell.

And through his vision and enchanted brain
He caught and held her for a moment's space,
And ever after she returned again
When from his soul he summoned her embrace,
And in his eyes, where once her kiss had stayed,
For ever after gentle lightnings played.

And now she lures him back to the unknown
Whence she came forth, and where her lovers go;
You were his friends, and knew his spirit's throne
How high it was, and bright as southern snow;
Then mourn him not; this is his wedding day;
His bride called to him, and he could not stay.

Horace observed that 'Not another line was printed about Innes for nine years', and little has been written since. He remains the 'lone star' of Modern British painting, as John Fothergill put it; a visionary in the artistic mould of William Blake or Samuel Palmer. His work is overshadowed by more famous, longer-lived Slade School students of his generation like Stanley Spencer, Paul Nash, David Bomberg, Mark Gertler and Richard Nevinson. But it has never been without value among the *cognoscenti*. Dick's best, jewel-like representations of Arenig can fetch over £30,000 at auction. Indeed, as Horace's financial situation deteriorated he lived off the proceeds of his friend's paintings, selling or pawning his large collection to family and friends.

He was more cavalier with his smaller collection of paintings by Augustus. Horace owned several important works, including 'The Blue Boy' (probably now known as 'A French Fisher Boy', and in the National Museum of Wales), which he sold for £525, a small oil of Aran and an epic work entitled 'Forze e Amore'. This had been specially commissioned by Hugh Lane for his sumptuous new property in Chelsea, but after a row Augustus had intemperately sold it to Horace. He then bought it back for £1200, overpainted it with 'The Flute of Pan' and resold it to American collector John Quinn. Lesser works and drawings by Augustus, Horace happily (when in funds) gave away. On one occasion, he even sold them cap-in-hand on the pavement, delighting in telling the painter afterwards how little they fetched. 'You call yourself a painter,' he said. 'Here I have been nearly two hours in the street exhibiting your paintings, and all I have earned is fourpence. Painter indeed!'

By March 1911 Horace was, as Virginia Woolf told Clive Bell, 'sampling human nature and spitting it out'. No longer young, he had crossed a line into degeneracy, occasional delinquency. The consequences were almost immediate. Having dodged the law so far, he finally made an appearance in court following an impulsive joke involving Oliver Locker-Lampson, his Old Etonian schoolfriend who was now a rising member of parliament. Locker-Lampson had foolishly boasted that as an MP he could not be tried for a criminal offence. Taking the bait, after dining in St James's Horace had slipped his watch into his friend's pocket. He then challenged him to a race up Bury Street. As Locker-Lampson pulled away, Horace flourished his stick and yelled 'Stop thief! He's got my watch!' When his friend was intercepted by a policeman, Horace triumphantly cried out 'It is only a practical joke.' According to the press reports, they were sent on their way by the policeman with a ticking off. However, Horace, obviously drunk, kept 'flourishing his stick and nearly struck a person who was walking by'. Both men were then promptly arrested and taken to Vine Street police station, that traditional clearing house for West End crime.

After disentangling the mess, Horace was charged with a breach of the peace and Locker-Lampson released. The next day, after a night in the cells, a suitably contrite Horace—described as 'Twenty eight, of independent means'—appeared at Marlborough Street Police Court. After pleading guilty, he was bound over and fined £5. He was horrified to see Locker-Lampson's name published in the press, forcing the Home Secretary, Winston Churchill—who called Horace 'a very dangerous man to his friends'—to defend him in the Commons. In a statement, Horace fumed 'that I pleaded guilty in this case, on the understanding given to me by the police that by doing so Mr Locker-Lampson's name would not be mentioned.'

He sent Locker-Lampson a telegram announcing his death. 'Mr Horace de Vere Cole,' it read, 'died at his residence this morning of lung trouble.' An elaborate funeral cortege appeared outside his house, replicating the student tradition at Cambridge for escorting rusticated students away from the university. The clumsy apology amused few and fooled no one. 'Why pretend only?' commented one newspaper correspondent. There was a widespread feeling that Horace was becoming a bore and a liability. 'His presence in a restaurant causes terror,' reported one paper, 'and although the prince of good fellows, some Bohemians, and not a few Belgravians, would have been glad if the telegrams sent out last month announcing his death had been true.' This touched on the irony of Horace. He was neither rich enough nor aristocratic enough to feel entirely comfortable in Belgravia. As Uncle Alfred painfully demonstrated as he rifled through the family tree, the Coles were still searching for pedigree. Yet Horace was also too well-off and educated to be fully bohemian. The gulf between the two worlds was wide, and Horace could never straddle both, however hard he tried. For his *Who's Who* entry, Uncle Alfred listed 'Shooting, Tennis and Golf' as his recreations. In an act of bohemian bravado, his nephew proposed 'Fucking'—and was excluded.

This rootlessness and ambiguity was reflected in Horace's physical world. He lived on the fringes of Chelsea and drank on the borders of respectability at the Café Royal. He frequented music halls at one end of Piccadilly before retiring to the gentlemen's clubs of the other. The thoroughfare between was his stage—quite literally on the occasion he drove a herd of cows up the street to picnic in Leicester Square. War and development has taken its toll, but the street is still recognisably his, with park and mansions at one end and the gaudy lights of Piccadilly Circus at the other.

Most of Horace's London pranks took place on or near Piccadilly, including his personal favourite, the string joke. In this famous gag, which he generously attributed to an eighteenth-century source, Horace posed as a surveyor: notebook in one hand and a ball of string in the other. A passer-by—usually the 'pompous sort of good citizen of the bowler hat and rolled umbrella sort,' according to David Scott-Moncrieff, who witnessed the gag—was then cajoled into helping Horace while he made some measurement. Leaving his victim holding

one end of the string, he walked around a corner to ask for similar assistance from 'another consequential ass'. As Scott-Moncrieff remembered,

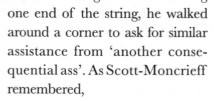

How the press saw Horace's string joke.

Both victims held their ends for fully ten minutes, each invisible to the other, while the perpetrator of the joke quietly slipped away and joined me in a pub commanding a full view of the fun. It succeeded far better than I had dared to hope, due to his brilliant selection of two absolutely perfect victims. Each blamed the other and they nearly came to blows.

This clever little gag gave Horace a thrill of private pleasure, but it had no crowd participation or wider effect. His most celebrated escapade on Piccadilly was entirely different. Taking place soon after the *Dreadnought* hoax this was, as Horace himself described it, his 'Pulling up Piccadilly' joke. Again he turned to Willy Clarkson for help, appearing in his shop one morning with a noisy crowd of friends.

'What is your problem this time,' enquired the wily costumier (as he recounted in *The People* years later).

'We want a change, I think' replied Horace, 'A few days ago we were aristocrats—sleek and silken. Now I feel that we need rebalancing. We'll be proletarians—horny-handed!'

'Make us up as navvies, will you. Daylight disguise. Real, burly or sinewy London navvies, as our figures suit you; ready to step out of your shop ravening to rip up roadways. Oh, and we'll need tools, of course,' he blithely continued, 'shovels, picks and measuring tapes. And let's see—some trestles, stout rope, and a piece of chalk. Ah, I forget—one of those red notices with a "Road Up" inscription.'

Three hours later Horace and his accomplices emerged from Clarkson's shop suitably attired. After lunching nearby at a 'workmen's steak-and-kidney eating house', they picked up their tools and strolled down Piccadilly. Opposite the Cavalry Club, at 127 Piccadilly, they recruited a guileless policeman to direct traffic while they energetically started to dig a trench from one side of the road to the other. 'For over half an hour they hacked with gusto at the crust of Piccadilly,' remembered Willy Clarkson, with the customary breaks to mop at perspiration, regard the sky, discuss politics and to compare opinions as to what they would do to a pint when they knocked off. In short they gave to proceedings a touch of burlesque which warmed their own hearts, but which was not sufficiently apparent to the knot of interested spectators to arouse suspicion. The public seemed greatly disappointed when, with one accord, the navvies broke off work, leisurely put on their jackets, picked up their tools and wandered off leaving behind as relics of their exploits the trestles, the rope and the board, a plot of havoc and a piece of chalk. Those citizens who remained behind for an encore were robbed of their expectation: but it was the unexpected which fell upon the police at point duty when a hurriedly summoned police inspector appeared on the scene two minutes later!

'Pulling up Piccadilly' was a very expensive operation to mount. Some people said Horace did it for a bet, others to take revenge on a society hostess who had barred him from a function on Piccadilly. Lord Grantley, who participated in the joke, recalled that a lot of people had to be bribed to get it done, and that he himself had put up £100 towards its cost. He also remembered retreating with Horace to a room at the Ritz Hotel to watch the unfolding mayhem with the same voyeuristic desire he had demonstrated in the string joke. The joke was typical of Horace at his best and worst. It

A newspaper cartoon strip inaccurately retelling 'Pulling up Piccadilly'.

was well conceived and planned, efficiently executed and had a clear, satisfying denouement. There was no obvious target and no real harm was done. But it also showed up his many contradictions. Here was a Fabian socialist and self-proclaimed champion of the poor taking pleasure impersonating the working classes before disappearing into a luxury hotel and leaving them, presumably, to tidy up his mess.

In his memoirs, Grantley recounted another occasion when Horace, to avenge some slight, went to every piano-maker in London and ordered a piano from each to be delivered at the same time on the same day to his victim's address. 'When the morning arrived,' Grantley wrote, 'the roadway was blocked by scores of grand pianos converging from all directions.' The story closely matches the famous Berners Street hoax perpetuated by Theodore Hook in 1809 when, in addition to furniture, the Lord Mayor of London, Governor of the Bank of England, chairman of the East India Company and the Duke of Gloucester also arrived unannounced at the victim's home. Like Horace, Hook earned notoriety as a hoaxer and prankster, though he was also a spirited satirist, publisher and writer. After the *Dreadnought* hoax, the press compared Horace to Hook, who was surely in his mind when he pulled off his piano joke. It is worth mentioning, however, that the Edwardian era was the heyday for practical joking and that Horace did not operate alone. Even the King's mistress Lily Langtry had joined in the fun by asking Willy Clarkson to disguise her as a flower girl for a stint in Piccadilly Circus. Another prankster was Jimmy White, a notorious property developer and speculator who would hire slapstick comedians to serve at dinner. Arthur Roberts, a famous music-hall star and founder member of the Eccentric Club, made a career from 'spoofing' his audience in a variety of elaborate disguises.

Nevertheless, Horace's drunken race with Locker-Lampson lacked the finesse and elegance of either his piano or Piccadilly pranks. It was crude, boorish and an omen of Horace's fading powers to amuse. Instead he now set out to shock. Old friends cast him off, and he became embroiled in what Virginia Woolf described as a 'sordid gas lit Piccadilly Circus affair' with a chorus girl called Lilian Shelley. He had decided the course his life would take.

16

I am an 'elpless female,
An unprotected female,
My husband's been and gone and run away,
My heart to wring.
He's gone to join the Mormons,
Those gay and festive Mormons.
And while he's getting married there
I'm left alone to sing
O my Popsy Wopsy's vanished
From my sight.
And we might have been happy,
So we might!
But now he's gone away
To be a Mormonite.
And I've no doubt but that
He has a dozen wives or more

song from Ernest C. Rolls's production of *Step this Way!*, 1913

*B*y all accounts, and there are many, Lilian Shelley—called variously 'Shelley', 'Billy' or 'The Bug'—was very, very sexy. She had coal-black hair bobbed in the modern way, shocking red lips (no respectable woman wore make-up) and, quipped Augustus, 'an American accent contracted in Soho'. Horace stoutly maintained that a woman's beauty can be judged by her nose, and Lilian's could not be faulted. Her stunning figure was compared to Poliare, the music-hall pin-up girl from Paris who was five foot three with a corseted waist size of 14 inches. Shelley was only sixteen or so in 1911 (Horace was developing a predilection for very young girls): not unusually youthful for a girl beginning her career on the stage but far too young for the life Shelley led.

She lived in a squat in Ormonde Terrace at the bottom of Primrose Hill with a group of other girls who hung around the Café Royal looking for theatrical and modelling work. Like them, she dreamt of stardom. But Shelley was also a true bohemian, keeping her clothes in a heap under her bed and reportedly killing with food poisoning another tenant who found and ate some rotting kippers she had secreted in her room. Yet despite her poverty she was wilfully generous, giving her things away to anyone who admired them—including her body—earning a reputation for picking up the dirtiest, poorest and most miserable down-and-outs in bohemia and taking them back to her dilapidated lodgings. Dick Innes developed a passion for Shelley, and plotted to elope with her in a gypsy caravan to save them both from the life they led. According to Augustus, they planned to 'take to the open road, and travel the world together in healing contact with Nature and the beneficent influences of the mountains'. As usual, reality failed to match the fantasy. Shelley did join Dick in Wales but preferred reading novels to gazing soulfully on Arenig. She also refused to budge from her whisky and soda at the local inn. Eventually they trooped back to London, abandoning the caravan in a field, where Augustus found it rusting away months later.

Horace's motives towards Shelley were ostensibly altruistic. Declaring she had a 'voice' and talent, he set about having her professionally trained for the stage. Eventually, Horace's influence, and possibly money, secured his beautiful protégé a minor role in *Step this Way!*, a vaudeville production which opened at the Oxford music hall in June 1913 before touring the provinces. Augustus thought Shelley's performance 'owed less to art than to impudence'. But her rendition of the song

'Popsy Wopsy' stole the show and was encored nightly. Shelley may have been a one-hit wonder but she made that hit pay for drinks in clubs for years to come. And if she occasionally acted foolishly, she was no fool. In 1923 she published a powerful, thinly-veiled autobiographical novel about an innocent young girl from the Bristol slums called Mary Bryant, drawn to the stage by her looks and voice.

'She was not beautiful in the strict sense of the word, yet there was that in her face that attracted most people. It was, to begin with, a perfect oval; her complexion was so white, and her eyes and hair so dark, that she was often thought to be a foreigner.' Mary's strongly romantic imagination sustains her through an abusive childhood. She reads Keats and Longfellow, and is mesmerised by an engraving of 'The Death of Chatterton' that she stumbles across in Bristol Art Gallery. 'For years afterwards Chatterton filled her dreaming hours and he became her one hero.' Mary works as an artist's

left Portrait of a girl by Adrian Allinson, 1912, found in Horace's collection and identified as Lilian Shelley (Tristan de Vere Cole).

above Newspaper advert by the publisher of 'Popsy Wopsy', the song Lilian Shelley made a hit.

model before being scouted for the London theatre. She goes on tour, avoids the heavy drinking of the other girls and falls in love with a charming, kind and rich young man called Frankie Carew. But then Frankie is taken away to New York on business, leaving Mary in the hands of a corrupt and lascivious theatre manager. After the show one night, he introduces her to the sinister Seymour Cavendish, for whom he had clearly procured girls in the past.

Cavendish's first words to Mary are 'Come to Italy with me by the noon train from Charing Cross tomorrow. I want you. I promise you you won't forget it.' She 'was entirely hypnotised by his baffling personality'. 'In utter amazement Mary stared at the cold grey eyes which seemed to have no pupil. She at once felt like an animal trapped in some terrifying device.' Reluctantly, she goes with him to a fancy-dress ball at the Opera House, where men and women in 'red or black dominoes with black masks' (Willy Clarkson gifted Horace just such a suit) whirl about in a 'mad, joyous throng'. But she is appalled and frightened by Cavendish's drinking and his unsettling attention. "'I believe you are all the fascinating women in the world rolled into one beloved body," murmured Cavendish, leaning towards her. "Shall I ever know you absolutely? Do you realise your own power? Or are you still so blind that you cannot see that I am yours body and soul?"' He bombards her with diamond jewellery, fine clothes and scent. He sends money to her alcoholic parents. His car and chauffeur is placed at her disposal. Urged by her friends not to look a gift horse in the mouth, Mary accepts the gifts and eventually agrees to go with him to Paris as his mistress. Cavendish takes a luxurious suite at the Hotel Meurice. She starts drinking, and night after night is dragged around the Place Pigalle and the seediest nightspots of Paris. Cavendish grows violent and insanely jealous.

From café to café they wandered: at every one champagne appeared on the table. Coming out of one café finally, Mary implored Cavendish to take her home. He walked up the street to get a taxi; their way, however, lay past the 'Capitol' a famous Paris night-café. With a cruel smile Cavendish changed his mind, and insisted on entering. Weakly Mary tried to resist, but he dragged her in.

Cavendish's behaviour becomes increasingly erratic. He jumps up on Mary without warning or just sits for hours watching her in silence. Finally, after a particularly debauched evening among the 'lowest haunts of Montmartre', Cavendish picks up a 'vile-looking man and woman' and takes them back with Mary to the hotel to continue drinking. He demands that Mary join the drunken party. When, horrified, she refuses

he rushed at her and caught her by the hair: throwing her to the floor he dragged her to the bedroom. 'Now then I'll make you speak,' he raved. He held the point of the revolver to her head. At the contact of the cold steel she shivered slightly...

'Why don't you shoot, madman?' she cried. 'I'm not afraid of you.'

With a clatter the revolver fell to the floor. The next moment he was on his knees beside her crying brokenly: imploring her to forgive him...

'Oh! Mary, Mary forgive me,' he cried. 'I was mad with jealousy—and the brandy. I ought never to drink brandy...I can't live without you. I'll be different, I'll be different. Marry me, Mary, and then I'll know you've forgiven me.'

Salvation for Mary arrives with the return of Frankie, who has been searching for her for weeks. He rescues her from Cavendish and they marry. Finally, as she heads towards a new life in America, Mary hears that Cavendish has shot himself outside the Varieties theatre. "'Poor Seymour,'" she sighed. "How unhappy he must have been. Hold me tightly, Frankie— never let me go. I'm so frightened of life, and the world. I've only you now. Love me always, always, always.'"

Mary Bryant is all but forgotten now. It's similarities to *Tess of the d'Urbervilles*—with the dastardly Cavendish as Alec d'Urberville and Frankie as Angel—were surely intended and in Shelley's mind. The seduction then redemption of an innocent girl from the provinces is a timeless plot device. But reading the novel demoralised me. Details of Horace's relationship with Shelley are sketchy, but they ominously echo Mary's story. Were elements of Cavendish based on him? From Virginia Woolf's gossip, gleaned from her brother Adrian, it appears that early in 1911 Shelley got pregnant, had an abortion and ran away to Paris. Virginia was scathing at this turn of events. 'Killing an illegitimate child would surely be a slight crime,' she told Clive Bell, 'and she can't care for her character.' (In Shelley's novel, Mary's unmarried aunt has a baby which is put out for adoption through the columns of the *Western Mail.*) Damningly, Virginia goes on to say that Shelley 'has got no money out of Cole, so that it does not seem politic to bolt just yet'.

As he had with Mildred, Horace sent Adrian to fetch Shelley back. Adrian scoured the brothels of Montmartre until he eventually found her. 'The poor creature is in love with Cole, who treats her shockingly,' he told Duncan Grant. A sinister Jew was also involved in this murky affair, perhaps as a lover, abortionist or blackmailer. A few months later John Quinn spied Shelley in the Café Royal. Shelley, Quinn noted, was with her lover, 'young Valentine'. Was Frankie Carew a fictionalised memory of this Valentine? We will never know. The details of the affair are too sparse, but those we have differ considerably from the plot of *Mary Bryant.* Mary never loved Seymour Cavendish as Adrian claimed Shelley loved Horace. But Adrian's comment that he treated Shelley 'shockingly' leaves a terrible doubt. In the novel Cavendish acts like Horace: the violence, the irrational, frenetic behaviour; the drinking, the brandishing of a revolver. We know Horace was prone to terrible jealousy. Nina Hamnett recalled him breaking into her studio on one occasion brandishing a dagger and shouting 'Where is she? You know where she is!' (She later commented that 'this dagger did not cut. It is the kind made for tourists, although it is a frightening looking weapon.' Horace's family still have it.)

Cavendish even sounds like Horace. During his seduction of Mary, Cavendish writes her such a melodramatic letter that it could have been penned by Horace.

> Come to me when you get this, or in a week or a year. I shall be waiting, dear lady, always waiting. I warn you it is dangerous keeping me waiting too long. When you have spent your money, write for some more. My fortune is yours. Take the car where you will—the chauffeur has his orders. Ah! Mary, why not come now? You are already mine, although you don't believe it. There is no escape. I love you madly, madly. Seymour.

Little of Horace's correspondence survives from this period, and none concerning Shelley. But compare Cavendish's impassioned appeal to Mary with a letter Horace would write nineteen-year-old Mavis Wright in 1928:

> I don't apologise for writing to you again. I write because I must and because I am so deeply fond of you with a fondness of love that runs through my blood and permeates my whole being. No man can be mistaken about such a feeling for it comes from his immortal part, his soul. With all my soul I love you. I should not have driven you back last night for you did not wish me to. I was very tired from want of sleep and very unhappy, but you were wrong in thinking I wanted to argue with you; there was nothing to argue with you about. You have told me how you feel and I accept it and I hate and loathe myself for it. I think all might have been different if I had not been such an unutterable fool. Truly I would rather have killed myself than have killed your love, for I do think you did love me, although you say now that you only thought you did…As for my not allowing you all liberty, that would be impossible now. That jealous madness has passed, my love is more serene and embraces and soars above

passion. You could do as you chose if only I felt that all the while a part of your heart was mine and that you were fond of me and looked to me as your husband and friend and companion in life…I know now that I was unkind to you because you loved me and I loved you and tortured myself. This could never have been again for I understand now that real suffering is the only way to get an insight and a cleansing of oneself.

Cavendish's appeal in the novel is so similar to the tone of this letter, with its pleading, self-pity and remorse, that Shelley may have based it on a letter she herself had from Horace. I suspect Shelley used characteristics of Horace in the creation of both Frankie and Cavendish. But they were also based on the good and bad she had found, often to her cost, in other men. Fact and fiction did part in one tragic way. In the novel, Mary Bryant marries Frankie and sails to a bright, new future in America. In reality, there would be no such happy ending for Shelley. She killed herself.

17

Cloudily, grey-green, from the tumbler's depth she whirleth;
So to my brain's innermost chamber she whirleth,
Grey-green, cloudily

Ivar Campbell, from *Absinthe*

The Café Royal closed its doors for the final time in January 2009 to be converted into a luxury hotel. Happily, its famous rococo Grill Room, the scene of so many literary, artistic and sexual assignations, will be preserved. However, most of its fixtures were dispersed at auction. Some of the items for sale, like the curtains and wall lights, were mundane. Others, such as the vast oak barrels used to store brandy in the cellar, were evocative. There was also a large selection of prints, photographs and paintings which had adorned the Café walls over the years. Among them was a striking depiction of the Café interior painted by Adrian Allinson in 1915. Allinson was a regular at the Café, and even for a venue renowned for eccentricity was a highly distinctive one, with his wide-brimmed hat, velvet coat, black stock and long hair. He had studied at the Slade with Dick Innes and exhibited at the New English Art Club with Augustus. Horace knew Adrian well, and owned at least one of his paintings, a portrait of a young girl, identified as Lilian Shelley.

In his panorama of the Café Royal, Adrian 'tried to embody...the glamour of this rendezvous for the great ones of my little world'. He sketched at night, often returning by day

Inside the Café Royal by Adrian Allinson, 1915; an all-too-familiar scene to Horace. Key (above):
1. Alan Odle;
2. Horace de Vere Cole; 3. Iris Tree;
4. Evan Morgan;
5. Nancy Cunard;
6. David Sampson;
7. P.G. Konody;
8. Dorelia John;
9. Augustus John;
10. Adrian Allinson; the waiter in the background is Mario (kind courtesy of the Court Gallery, Somerset).

when the tobacco smoke had cleared to add the architectural features. He populated his painting with the 'most inveterate habitués' of the Café, including Horace, 'famous for his elaborate practical jokes', and Augustus. The other people crowding around the marble-topped tables are less familiar to us today, but they were all friends of Horace and formed the hub of his pre-war world. There was the artist Alan Odle, who 'dressed like a dustman and carried himself like a duke', the critic Paul Konody and the Hon. Evan Morgan, later Lord Tredegar, whose 'insanity', according to Horace, 'takes the form of building Catholic chapels, giving gifts to Rome, and seducing working-class boys'. Between them all circulated Mario, the Café's waiter, distributing the fuel necessary to stimulate the arguments on aesthetics which raged around him.

So picture the scene. It is a winter's evening before the First World War and you come into the warmth of the Café Royal from the chill of Regent Street. The doorman in his cap nods as you pass beneath the colonnaded entrance. The fog melts away behind you; the sound of horse-drawn traffic is replaced by the buzz of talk and the clinking of glasses. The air is heavy with cigar smoke and the mingled scents of people in heavy clothes packed closely together. Waiters in long white aprons glide between the tables expertly balancing bottles on silver trays. The low gaslight throws shadows across the room. The plush crimson interior and sinuous gilt decoration looks organic. It feels as if you are entering the belly of some fantastic beast. Over there you see Dick Innes playing chess with Daviel, the renowned engraver. Near them, Irishman George Moore is discussing art and artists with an elegantly-dressed German critic and the fiery young sculptor Jacob Epstein. The door opens behind you. Heads turn, the hubbub pauses then resumes at a higher pitch. Augustus John has arrived with Shelley on his arm. Space is made, they sit. People come over, but Augustus just stares at the girl, trying to hypnotise her. Moore leaves. He is replaced by Euphemia Lamb and Dummer Howard, who is very drunk. Euphemia is carrying a Pekingese—it's all the craze. She kisses Shelley on the lips. The men flirt with the girls. Giggling, the girls agree to join them on a trip to the South of France they know they will never make. Augustus tells you about his affair with Frida Strindberg, the fervent former wife of the Swedish playwright. He says she forced herself on him and that she is now plaguing him. Everyone laughs. You are swept up into the party, and around midnight you follow the crowd as it moves to Augustus's studio. You all collapse onto divans, drink Chablis and encourage your host as he wildly sings, dances and performs pantomime. In the morning you remember little, except to return again to the Café that evening. And every evening after that.

This account is based on John Quinn's diary entries for September 1911. It portrays the life Horace was leading night after night before the war. Of course the cast varied, but very few English artists and writers of the early twentieth century, many now household names, failed to make it through the doors of the Café Royal or to become entranced with what they found there (an exception was D.H. Lawrence, who hated the place and was sick on a tablecloth). As Augustus put it, they had also entered 'the dangerous neighbourhood of a whooping Anglo-Irish practical-joker', for Horace was unmistakable by his presence. Many stories of his antics swirl around the memoirs of other Café regulars, most of them ending in a brawl, this being an era of simmering rivalries, artistic cliques and gangs. One of the best known recalls an evening Horace spent at the Café with Augustus and fellow-painters Richard Nevinson, Mark Gertler and Irishman John Currie. The younger artists were members of a Slade School-based group of male students called the 'Coster Gang', as they wore black jerseys, scarlet scarfs and black caps like the costermongers selling fruit on the street. This grouping existed for no other reason than to provoke fights with the other gangs roaming Soho, or with medical students from the hospitals in Bloomsbury. It was a deliberate statement of modern artistic machismo in reaction to the delicate aesthetes of the nineties. Rivals included the 'Camden Town Lads' a group of older artists clustered around Walter Sickert and Spencer Gore. Unencumbered by artistic integrity, Horace tried to keep a foot in both camps.

That particular evening Horace was immaculately turned out as usual. But the Coster Gang artists were dressed in their trademark medley of scruffy clothing. When some bookmakers drinking nearby made loud, derogatory remarks about their appearance, Horace launched a soda siphon in their direction, sparking a full-scale riot which took an hour to clear. The fight typified the simmering conflict between bourgeois and bohemian. The police were called to break it up, and everyone was hauled off to Vine Street. In those days, the authorities generally took a tolerant view of student high spirits. However, a fight on such a scale in such a well-known venue could not be ignored. Typically, the wealthier rioters were reprimanded and released while the poorer ones were locked up until they sobered up. For example, Mark Gertler was charged with affray while Horace was let off scot free. After all, Uncle Alfred was now Governor of the Bank of England. But there were more serious repercussions. After the waiters had swept up the broken glass, righted upturned tables and wiped the blood from the walls, the management barred all artists from the Café Royal. They never paid their bills and were more trouble than they were worth.

Naturally Horace was exempted from the ban. He had incited the fight, but he was not an artist and he was rich. Notwithstanding his rowdiness, he was the perfect client: an Old Etonian with connections to the sort of polite society the Café so assiduously courted. The Café certainly prided itself on its cosmopolitan and respectable clientele. However, in truth it was very different. As the poet Roy Campbell observed, 'you met everybody there except Royalty, the General Staff and Bishops. Bankers, financiers, bookies, statesmen, prostitutes, pickpockets, millionaires, jockeys, boxers, painters, sculptors, poets and musicians all rubbed shoulders together in that one tiny room.' (In his biography of the Café Keith Waterhouse colourfully described its customers as 'kiteflyers, ear-biters, bounders, layabouts, friskers, prossers, four flushers and double dealers'.) It was a place for misfits and for people running from themselves or others. Nevertheless, the Café still looked respectable enough for Horace to justify his going there to his increasingly sceptical and disillusioned family. They still harboured hopes he might settle down. Indeed, while Horace was chasing artist models and chorus girls around the West End, the Coles were trying to marry him off to Lady Isabel Wodehouse, the daughter of his father's old flame Lady Kimberley.

Horace's artist friends were not as lucky or well connected. Nevinson in particular was deeply offended when he was subsequently turned away by the Café's doorman. Furious, he vowed to return to complain to the manager. He did so, dressed in a suit and bowler hat and not his usual paint-spattered garb. Only after he had been warmly welcomed back into the Café did it occur to him that it was not how you behaved that mattered, but how you looked. It was not a lesson this notoriously dishevelled artist was prepared to heed. On a later occasion, Horace turned this maxim gloriously on its head when someone in the Café teased him for his, by then, luxurious mane of white hair and whiskers. 'How ill white hairs become a fool and jester,' the drinker jeered. Horace bowed and disappeared. He returned with his hair and moustache dyed bright red. 'Better?' he queried.

The story of the bookmakers' brawl has a tragic epitaph. In October 1914, just weeks after Dick Innes died, Horace joined John Currie, Augustus and Ivar Campbell, a nephew the Duke of Argyll, for a drink in the Café. Ivar was a fresh-eyed, loose-limbed idealistic young poet who had tramped the lanes of England with Guy Ridley and, for a wager, had travelled from London to Hampshire with the writer Arthur Ransome in a cart pulled by a donkey (he also had an aborted affair with Ransome's wife). Ivar had recently returned from America, where he had worked in the British Embassy in Washington, to sign up for the war. Bitterly disappointed at failing the medical examination, he now planned to go out to France as an ambulance driver. After the war, he wanted to open a gallery/bookshop in Chelsea dedicated to the work of young artists.

The son of an Irish navvy, John Currie had arrived in London after working as a decorator in the Staffordshire potteries. He was a rugged and impassioned man determined to overcome his impoverished beginnings to carve out a career as a painter. Though married and with a son, Currie was locked in a turbulent relationship with a tempestuous red-haired Irish model called Dolly Henry. The affair had a violent edge to it, each urging the other into acts of brutality and self-degradation. Currie drank heavily, shamelessly stole from friends and shops, and was prone to raucous recitals of poetry by Yeats or Synge. His behaviour notwithstanding, no one doubted he was a hugely talented painter. With Nevinson and Gertler, Currie formed the 'Neo-Primitives' in tribute to the artistic techniques of the Italian Renaissance though most contemporaries praised his work more highly than that of his friends. Despite his depraved personal habits, that evening Currie was on the verge of fame and looking forward to a solo exhibition at the Chenil Galleries.

Unusually, however, he refused a cigar, 'something he never did,' as Horace recalled, then 'left us so early we remarked on it—for he was a late bird'. They heard in the morning that Currie had gone straight from the Café to his Chelsea studio, where he had shot Dolly Henry in a fit of jealousy before turning the gun on himself. The incident caused 'quite a sensation in spite of the declaration of war for artists don't commit murders. He died of the wound he had given himself or we would have been called, as we were the last to see him alive. He had a wife in Cornwall but he had kept her a secret from everyone.' Speaking for many in the artistic community, Augustus blamed Dolly, 'a deceitful little bitch', for causing the tragedy and depriving the world of a great talent. It was an ugly attitude which encapsulated the selfishness and destructive egotism of the painter and his friends.

Adrian Allinson's painting captures the essence of all of this perfectly. It is a dark work, and the portraits of the drinkers are indistinguishable and strangely indistinct, as if reflecting the insecurity of the lives they represent. The painting can only be deciphered by Allinson's words and a key which identifies the sitters. So we learn that sitting beside Horace in the left background of the painting, almost hidden by Evan Morgan, is seventeen-year-old Iris Tree, the daughter of the actor–impresario Herbert Beerbohm Tree. She is there because, for a few months in 1914, Horace assiduously courted her. In his own way, of course, by taking her on moonlit jaunts through London and breaking into pubs to get her breakfast. The relationship was serious enough for Horace to briefly consider marrying Iris. His Studd stepsisters Dorothy and Mary even bought the couple a bonsai trees as a wedding present. Horace was bowled over by Iris's startling and careless beauty, her cropped auburn hair, girlish figure and exotic modern dress. Like Shelley, she was painted by Augustus, sculpted by Epstein and seduced by both. Her first entrance to the Café Royal with her friend and flatmate Nancy Cunard (also featured in Allinson's work) is one of the defining moments of modernity. How this teenage girl from a wealthy and respectable family sauntered into a public bar without a chaperone to smoke and drink. Only prostitutes, models or actresses did such a thing. But Iris's reputation was unimpeachable, making this simple act a momentous blow for emancipation. Yet it was entirely in keeping with the girls' determination to flout convention and resist the social shackles of their class. Iris was helped by theatrical parents who encouraged creativity and courted a bohemian way of life. She painted and wrote poems, declaring in one:

I am fat.
I am a soul.
I am an artist.
I am a wanton.
I am a hypocrite.

Nancy's background equally fed a rebellious imagination. She was the daughter of a baronet and a headstrong American heiress who hosted a literary salon and had a well-publicised affair with the conductor Thomas Beecham. From a young age Nancy had been surrounded by radical writers

Iris Tree, who became the 'oath on Horace de Vere Cole's lips' (private collection).

and thinkers. This had emboldened her, and gave her courage to pursue her goals. 'I wanted to run away and be a vagabond,' she confided to George Moore, a family friend and long-time admirer of her mother.

The two girls had met at school, but grew close after they took a secret flat together to avoid the attention of their parents. Here they kept a store of make-up and fancy-dress costumes for forays into London's avant-garde nightlife before returning to their parents before dawn. Each evening would begin at the Roebuck pub near the Slade, where Iris was studying. Surrounded by students, prostitutes and labourers they sat giggling and drinking port and lemon. Iris recalled, 'We were bandits escaping environment by tunnelling deceptions to emerge in forbidden artifice, chalk white face powder, scarlet lip rouge, cigarette smoke, among roisterers of our own choosing.' This was how, in her own words, Iris 'became the oath on Horace de Vere Cole's lips'. The physical attraction for Horace was strong, but he was also drawn by Iris's theatrical background and her free spirit, which matched his own youthful self. In return, he offered Iris a route into the life of rebellion she craved. He was handsome, dangerous, unpredictable and careless of opinion. Sitting beside him in the Café Royal she could bask in his notoriety and earn her own.

18

His blood was boiling, all his frame
Did quiver with a fierce delight,
His eyes twin sockets were of flame
Instinct with ancient battle-light,
He bended o'er his love to kiss,
And from his tongue a viper leapt,
It pierced her with its venomed hiss,
And left her dying where she slept.

The only trouble with the Café Royal was that it sometimes closed. Soho was full of small restaurants—the Armenian Café was a favourite venue where late-night revellers could have coffee and eat Turkish delight—but what you really wanted was another drink. The pubs shut at eleven and there were no nightclubs. So why not open one? Which is what Augustus John did. He was tired of having his Mallard Street premises wrecked by his friends, so he set up the Crab-Tree club in Greek Street. The club was funded by the artist William Orpen, gallery owner William Marchant and wealthy collector Lord Howard de Walden. Yet despite this well-heeled committee, it was little more than a bare room with a few tables and chairs. There were no waiters, evening dress was banned as being too bourgeois, and drinks were charged only on an erratic basis. Nevertheless, the club briefly flourished under the light of its leading patron and chief subsidiser. Augustus envisaged a cultural rendezvous for artists, poets and musicians. Instead, the Crab-Tree became little more than a hangout for his own groupies, led by Shelley, who danced on the tabletops singing 'Popsy Wopsy'. Besides dancing, there were boxing matches—planned and impromptu—and wild bouts of drunken singing. It was chaotic, shambolic and undoubtedly seedy, but it was also revolutionary and undeniably good fun.

Most of the regulars of the Crab-Tree are long forgotten. A few, like the exotic dancers 'Dolores' and Betty 'Tiger Woman' May, painter Alvaro 'Chile' Guevara and guitarist Carlo 'Norway' (foreigners were nicknamed by their country of origin), are sketchily recalled in memoirs. Together these people and their rackety lives made up the vibrant chorus to Horace's existence. They were the flotsam and jetsam of bohemia, drifting wherever the prospect of cheap money, drink or sex took them. There is something heroic in the way these people battled hunger, extreme poverty and social opprobrium to lead the lives they did. They existed for the moment, and with the hindsight of a war which would shortly kill millions, who could blame them? Through them all stalked the demonic figure of Aleister Crowley, self-styled Beast from the book of Revelations. Crowley's heavy, black-caped figure, with his mad, staring eyes, bald head and wild proclamations about sex-magic and occultism amused and bemused the bohemians. All they wanted was a good time, although some, like Betty May, were led disastrously into drugs by Crowley. Augustus was intrigued by Crowley but Horace loathed him (and drugs). Crowley was a fake whose posturings were no better than a bishop's or admiral's, and a great deal more sinister.

The Crab-Tree was only one of many clubs springing up in the West End immediately before the First World War. London was in a strange, manic mood. There was a feeling of living on the edge of a precipice, and the clubs satisfied a need to induce oblivion by drink, drugs or crazed dancing. They came and went with dizzying speed, with names such as the Ham

Bone, Harlequin and Bullfrog. Like the evenings spent in them, few are remembered today. One name does shine on. This is the Cave of the Golden Calf, established as a cabaret club in Heddon Street in 1912 but now seen as the spiritual home of the Modernist movement. The club was founded by the indefatigable Frida Strindberg, and like its owner it immediately had a sophisticated, cosmopolitan and exotic feel. The club was an intoxicating mixture of unbridled hedonism and high culture. A string quartet played Schoenberg and there were stagings of plays by Dostoevsky, Aristophanes and, naturally, the owner's former husband August Strindberg. In between the guests maniacally danced the 'Bunny Hop', the 'Turkey Trot' and the 'Grizzly Bear'. The decor of the club was even more radical, and in absolute, shocking contrast to the faded grandeur of the Café Royal. Under the direction of Spencer Gore, it became a monument to modern art, a celebration of the avant-garde, a work of conceptual art in itself.

So after passing through the club's nondescript street entrance, you were immediately struck by Eric Gill's bas-relief of a golden calf, its huge phallus warning the faint-hearted of the illicit pleasures ahead. Above the stairs was a vast abstract engine by Wyndham Lewis depicting a carnival, but unlike any ever seen. Descending to the cave's throbbing, smoky interior, you were confronted with pillars wreathed in painted plaster gargoyles by Jacob Epstein: in mocking tribute to the peeling gilt caryatids of the Café Royal. Around the walls were jungle scenes by Gore and Charles Ginner suggestive of the predatory nature of the mad, gyrating dancers and the lawlessness of the world they represented. Through it all pulsed the ragtime beat of a Negro orchestra, the first in London, who played against a stage backdrop by Wyndham Lewis depicting raw meat. This bestial element of the club caught the untamed nature of the times. Iris Tree and Nancy Cunard were club regulars; so was

Shelley, who, adorned with golden embroidered headband, sang there nightly. (Every evening, Frida Strindberg sent Shelley to the Savoy to fetch food for her pet monkey.) In February 1914, the club advertised a 'Babies Night' beginning at 11 p.m., with Shelley as the cabaret and all members required to dress 'as babies or toys'. Three nights later came 'Pyjama Night' with 'pyjama, nightdress, or dressing gown costume de rigueur'.

But it was, as Augustus scathingly put it, the 'Cubists, Voo-dooists, Futurists and other Boomists' who made the place their own. He was referring to the loose confederation of cultural movements which had sprung up across Europe unified only by their violent rejection of all things old: in art, politics, literature and music. The earliest and most influential of these was Futurism, led by the wealthy Italian poet Filippo Marinetti. Marinetti specialised in absurdist performance art as a means of shaking the establishment. Based on the music-hall tradition, and accompanied by discordant music, his productions were violent, scatological and anarchic. Futurist performers were encouraged by an early manifesto to 'go out into the street, launch assaults from theatres and introduce the fisticuff into the artistic battle'. Tricks aimed at infuriating the audience included double-booking theatres and putting glue on seats.

Marinetti's muse was the flamboyant Marchesa Casati, the wife of a Roman nobleman who spun dreams or caused nightmares in all those who gazed stunned upon her. Supported on towering heels, plastered in mascara and sporting a leopardskin top-hat above flame-red dyed hair, the Marchesa crazily inspired poets and painters. Her very presence was a performance in itself. Like Futurism, she was impossible to define. Horace called his poetic tribute 'An impression of La Marchesa Casati', as if she was some ephemeral being like the spirits of Irish folklore:

Strange as the background of some remembered dream
The half-forged links of memory arise,
As through her enigmatic eyes
You catch a light of slumber's undergleam!

A child at heart, and sad as children she,
With memories of life within the womb,
For from that universal tomb
Came forth the spirits known as you and me

One English faction of Futurism were the Vorticists, a hard core group of painters, sculptors and writers, led by *enfants terribles* Epstein and Lewis. The Vorticists rejected all the other multifarious strands of the London art scene. They took their name from American Ezra Pound's striking description of pre-war London as a vortex of art. They were sneering, provocative and perplexing to painters of the old school. Their like was not seen again in London until Damian Hirst and the Young British Art movement of the 1990s. The Vorticists were small in number, and the movement shortlived, but they were noisily influential. From the bowels of the Golden Calf they plotted the overthrow of progressive rivals like the New English Art Club, Roger Fry's Omega Workshops and Walter Sickert's Camden Town group.

Augustus did his utmost to avoid the Golden Calf (and his old nemesis Frida Strindberg), but Horace tried to understand the labyrinthine politics of the Modernists. There was much to admire in the Vorticists. After all they blessed the Pope and praised friends such as Howard de Walden and Paul Konody as key influences on modern art. Rather sweetly, Horace invited Ezra Pound, who thought him 'mad', to see his collection of paintings by Innes. 'Rather interesting, I think, for his school' was the American's faint praise. 'Perhaps a little too suited to all the Mayfair drawing room.' However, Pound did pay Horace the compliment of referencing him in his epic *Pisan Cantos*:

Horace C. started
buying someone else's paintings
whose name, be it not Innes, escapes me
But impersonated a sultan
of was it Zanzibar and took up the paving in Bond St.
to compensate for a partial deafness
which, he felt, lost him part of life's fun

Canto 80/310–15

Horace may have admired the aims of the Vorticists, Imagists and Futurists, but he was baffled by their art. He blamed the artists' wives for the perversity of their work.

Mrs Epstein and Mrs Frank Dobson are not noticeable examples of feminine beauty, which may account for their husbands' love of the ugly and the pleasure they appear to take in distorting the human form. Their distortions, and occasional abominations, are skilfully done, for they are masters of their craft but being otherwise, stupid and unimaginative men, and overweeningly conceited, their finished work is too apt to reproduce their ideal of female beauty as shown in their chosen partners; and of male beauty, as seen in their looking-glass. Curves are the evidences of outward physical beauty—not lines. Wherefore we admire the leg, hip, breast, lip, instep and cheek of women, those self-lovers Epstein and Dobson cannot reproduce curves as we see them: they prefer planes, but the former sees himself stripped, and the latter sees himself daily in plus fours—and they have their wives.

The Vorticists retaliated by declaring, with Horace in mind, that 'the rich are bores without exception'. Wyndham Lewis later characterised this antagonism in his rambling Modernist novel *The Apes of God*. In the book, Horace is caricatured by Lewis as Horace Zagreus, a shallow observer of the art world and, it is insinuated, a corrupter of young men. Yet the Modernists, too, had a darker, authoritarian and antisemitic edge. Too often their anger tipped into extremism. Wyndham Lewis later expressed admiration for Hitler (though he retracted it before the Second World War) and Pound actively supported Mussolini by broadcasting for the Fascists.

Horace took more direct action against his enemies. After his death, the *Yorkshire Post* recalled his raid on a London nightclub—possibly the Cave of the Golden Calf—with Leeds-based artist Jacob Kramer. Like Richard Nevinson, Kramer was on the fringe of the Vorticists but an uneasy bedfellow with Epstein and Lewis. According to this report, Horace and Kramer recruited some friends and stormed a club posing as police officers. As Chief Inspector, Horace demanded the names and addresses of everyone in the club, causing 'wild consternation and several women [to become] hysterical'. The game was only up when someone slyly offered the inspector a drink, which he readily accepted. 'Great was the relief—So great that the raiders were freely forgiven.' The alarm caused by the fake raid was often experienced by Frida Strindberg for real, as she frequently fell foul of the licensing authorities. Eventually, she threw in the towel and headed to America, leaving a trail of debts and a mightily relieved Augustus.

Despite his aesthetic opposition to Modernist art, Horace did absorb the tumultuous energy it generated, converting it for his own act. It is not known whether he attended any of Marinetti's Futurist happenings in London or saw the showman's extravagant avant-garde performances at the Cave of the Golden Calf in November 1913. His insatiable love of theatre, poetry and Italy surely drew him. A typical routine entailed Marinetti declaiming random passages of poetry while hammering a table, scribbling madly on a blackboard and repeatedly slamming down a telephone. For one performance, Richard Nevinson accompanied the artist by banging a drum in the background. The act was influenced by the anarchic tradition of variety theatre, with a healthy dose of slapstick from the music halls. Marinetti did not set out to please his audience, but to shock them and shake them out of their complacency by direct action. He abhorred lazy applause, preferring the more liberating sound of energetic booing. So he threw rotten fruit and roundly abused his audience—as Horace had done in his 'general election' joke.

One infamous Futurist stunt was to send an actor onto an empty stage in front of a packed auditorium to pronounce solemnly the single word 'Merdre'. This was an unspeakable vulgarity at the time, the equivalent of a performer saying 'cunt' on television today. Horace cleverly adapted this outrage by recruiting four bald men to sit in the stalls of a theatre while attending some play or other he loathed. Each of their heads was emblazoned with a single letter. Seen from the more expensive seats of the dress circle these spelled out 'SHIT' (the word 'fuck' was unknown in Britain until the First World War). But this was one of the last occasions Horace used accomplices to achieve his aim. Carefully stage-managed jokes like the Sultan of Zanzibar and *Dreadnought* hoaxes seemed hopelessly dated in the face of the Modernist onslaught.

So Horace went solo, adapting his act to the changing times. Sudden collapses, playing dead, loud farting and scatological outbursts were his new method of provocation. They operated best in a private sphere against individual targets, like hated artists or boring fellow-drinkers. Horace was an inveterate attention-seeker, so the mixture of alarm, anger and disgust such events generated gave him instant gratification. Laughter was no longer the goal or the reward. He viewed it with the disdain Marinetti had for applause. Laughter was easy, mediocre and stultifyingly bourgeois. He needed a more physical reaction to satisfy his need. He wanted his audience to feel uncomfortable, unnerved and disorientated. Violent retaliation was sought and welcomed as the acknowledgement of his success.

Few of Horace's new-style absurdist performances—there is no other word for them—were ever recorded in print. They exist as anecdote, the stories gathering momentum as the years pass. Among his own notes, Horace mentions only kneeling to pray in Regent Street and hymn-singing in Leicester Square with the young painters Geoffrey Nelson and Chile Guevara. The gossip columns fill some gaps. They reported Horace's fit in a crowded ballroom, which caused a doctor to be summoned and the last rites administered before he miraculously recovered, or his going to sleep on a bed in the shop window of Maples furniture store. Some pranks invited death. Several times he threw himself down stairs at parties. He was even known to have stepped in front of a train to light his cigar off the engine after it screeched to a halt. Other acts betrayed a dark, sexual element. On one occasion he apparently walked down Piccadilly with a cow's teat hanging from his open flies, before cutting it off in front of a policeman and horrified bystanders. These were the chaotic demonstrations of a fractured imagination: as humiliating for him as they were disturbing to the onlooker.

Even Augustus could be unsettled by such antics. As he confessed in his memoirs,

> It was embarrassing to find myself, without warning, in charge of an epileptic in convulsions on the pavement and foaming at the mouth; or to be involved in a collision between a whooping lunatic, and some unknown and choleric gentleman who had been deprived suddenly of his headgear, and who had all my sympathy.

Yet these chaotic performances should be set in context. They were as much a product of that troubled age as Wyndham Lewis's paintings, Epstein's sculptures, Pound's poems or Duchamp's urinal. I think Horace saw his activities in these terms. He was fulfilling the Futurist mantra to 'introduce the fisticuff in the artistic battle'. This is precisely what Horace did, making himself the art object. He pictured his jokes 'like good works of art for succeeding generations!!'

The writer Shane Leslie, who had witnessed the Zanzibar hoax, told a story about Horace which captures all these elements. He related how they had once shared a taxi in Piccadilly with the dummy of a naked woman. As they passed a policeman, Horace stopped the taxi, opened the door and starting banging the dummy's head on the pavement shouting 'Ungrateful hussy!' This exhibition wasn't intended to be funny. It was absurdist and very modern in the sense that it abused all reason, convention and good manners. The shock of the sudden aggression, the sadistic, pornographic undertone of the violence, and the venom directed towards women made it a deeply unsettling experience for any unlucky passer-by. Yet there was still craft to the performance. With just two words, Horace offered his audience a plot and a narrative. Who was he thinking of as he assaulted the dummy? And what had she done to deserve such brutality? His audience felt confusion and alarm as their attention was grabbed and they were drawn into a world where the boundaries between the real and artificial are disordered.

Horace may have been inspired into these extreme, surreal gags by the German playwright and performer Frank Wedekind, a former lover of Frida Strindberg. Wedekind outraged public morality by urinating and even masturbating on stage. Like Horace, he also induced convulsions in public, throwing his audience into confusion and alarm. Extreme cabaret of this sort had its roots in the irreverent music-hall tradition. Much of it was still inchoate and childish, but it led to influential movements like Dadaism and the Theatre of the Absurd. Drama of this type had no manifesto, but its broad aim was to shake the bourgeoisie out of its complacency.

Like the revolution in art, many of the sources of Dadaism lay on the continent: in France, Germany and Italy. Horace was sufficiently well funded and fascinated by cabaret to have been exposed to these influences on his travels. In this light, he should be seen not simply as prankster-turned-agitator but as an innovator of performance art as a medium of artistic expression.

Jacob Epstein, in the forefront of the Modernist movement, would not have given Horace credit for anything. The feud between the two men was mysterious, bitter, long-running and hugely entertaining for anyone out of arms' reach. Epstein was chippy about class and Horace casually disdainful of Jews (though many of his good friends, like Kramer and Mark Gertler, were Jewish). Horace dismissed the suggestion that Epstein was 'the greatest English sculptor': not on grounds of the artist's proficiency—which he begrudgingly acknowledged—but because 'Epstein is a nationalised Chicago born Jew whose father came from Frankfurt'. Something about Epstein, his smug self-assurance perhaps, made Horace furious. Yet time and again the antagonists were thrown together by the company they shared. Their spats were famous and violent, with each provoking the other to furious outbursts. Sexual jealousy played its part. Shelley and Iris Tree both sat to Epstein, with casts of each being bought by John Quinn. Looking back in his autobiography, which ignores Horace altogether, Epstein said that Shelley was 'temperamental', though beautiful, and that her 'devotion to Art' ceased as soon as she stepped down from the model's stand. He vividly recalled meeting her at the Tate Gallery after unveiling a bronze of her head. Shelley was

leaning on the arm of a gentleman who turned to me and said self-righteously: 'Yes, I can see that you have depicted the vicious side of Lillian.' I answered that he 'knew her perhaps better than I did'…In truth I had made the head expressive of innocence and sweetness. A short time later the gentleman who had so offensively rebuked me was kicked to death in Cornwall by the miner-father of a girl he had attempted to seduce.

Was this man another possible source for the wicked Seymour Cavendish in Shelley's novel *Mary Bryant*?

In particular, Horace loved baiting Epstein at the Café Royal, where the sculptor's court of Modernist admirers had come to rival that of Augustus. Once he pinned the sculptor to the floor of a taxi, 'where I'd put him all the way from the Café Royal to Paddington and then had a Turkish bath'. On another, more threatening occasion witnessed by the composer Cecil Gray, Horace 'uninvited and unwelcome' joined Epstein's table in the Café and proceeded to 'pour forth a tirade of the wildest abuse against Epstein and myself, with the most outrageous implications'. This violent verbal assault quickly led, as Horace hoped, to a fight. He always relished physical challenge and the spilling of blood: it satisfied a deep lust. Strong men earned respect. Horace once swung Robbie Bowen-Colthurst round by his legs, breaking open his head—he did the same to Jack Yeats with a croquet mallet—and he always favoured men who used their fists in an argument. This time he underestimated his adversary, coming off worse, with two black eyes and a dangerously wounded pride. His revenge was swift: he hired a gang of thugs to attack Gray's house in a sinister escalation of his crazed and unfathomable hatred for Epstein.

19

Softly to the listening leaves
The nightwind whispered of its tale,
Dead men seen, like broken sheaves,
Underneath the moonlight pale,
And the poor leaves frightened were,
And trembled in the midnight air.

Then a breeze flew past and said
It had sped a cornfield by
Where the men were lying dead,
Distorted with death's agony,
And the poppy's fragrant red
Was mingled with a dreadful dye.

from 'War. September 1914'

*I*t was the war which brought the mysterious feud between Horace and Epstein into the public eye. The Café Royal emptied as even the most degenerate of artists, like sculptor Henri Gaudier-Brzeska (known as the dirtiest man in London) and writer T.E. Hulme (ditto, the randiest), volunteered for active service in the trenches. Others like Augustus, Richard Nevinson, Henry Lamb, John Lavery, William Orpen, Paul Nash and Dermot Wood joined up as ambulance drivers or were recruited as war artists. War had a strong romantic appeal for bohemians like these. In contrast, Bloomsbury, now an identifiable coterie of artists and intellectuals configured around the Woolfs and Bells, were placed in a quandary. A very few, like poet Rupert Brooke, went—and died—but most of Bloomsbury reacted strongly against the war for political reasons, and when conscription was introduced registered as conscientious objectors.

The attitudes of Horace's cohorts in the Zanzibar and *Dreadnought* hoaxes illustrated these contradictions. Dummer Howard, Tudor Castle, Guy Ridley, Robbie Bowen-Colthurst and Leland Buxton (who was posted to Cairo to assist T.E. Lawrence's exploits in the Middle East) all met the call to arms. Duncan Grant and Adrian Stephen registered as conscientious objectors, and after facing tribunals eventually worked on the land. Horace's reaction to events was ambiguous. En masse his Old Etonian schoolfriends departed for France, where 1157 of them were killed. Fifteen years earlier he would have leapt at the chance to join them. But deafness and his earlier wound ruled him out of volunteering, while his politics and outlook had shifted towards socialism. Adrian Stephen was an activist in the Union of Democratic Control, formed on the outbreak of war in opposition to British foreign policy and which grew to become a popular movement which lobbied against conscription. The UDC captured the reforming and liberating spirit of Horace's Cambridge years, bringing together radical liberals like Charles Trevelyan, brother of Horace's history tutor at Cambridge, and Leland Buxton's brother Charles. It quickly developed into a confederation of interests. Radical suffragettes, pacifists and supporters of the Labour Party like Ramsay MacDonald all rallied to its cause. Horace lent his ideological support to its aims. He raged against the 'force, cajolery and propaganda' used to whip up enthusiasm for the conflict. From Nina Hamnett we hear of him 'ragging' recruiting officers with Lilian Shelley, and in 1915 leading a boisterous march through Soho against Italy's entry into the war.

Unable to fight, Horace responded to the crisis in typical fashion—with jokes. Cecil Kent, a friend from Cambridge days, recalled one evening at the Four Hundred Club, 'where all the fellows back on their week's leave from the front used to go to dance and dine during the few days of their ephemeral existence at home. A real dance macabre it was in truth.' Then Horace entered in evening dress, flanked by two assistants in ecclesiastical garb. Each was carrying a large wicker basket filled with ping-pong balls, which Horace

> in a most pontifical manner, and without a smile, proceeded to benedict about the room. This was thought great fun, and people began to throw balls at one another. In a while it was found that the whole floor was absolutely covered with the balls, and no one could either walk or dance, nor could the waiters operate.

Horace then as silently disappeared, leaving the club in happy chaos. It was a small but characteristic contribution to the war effort. An even bolder suggestion was put to Horace by 'Gooseberry', his old schoolfriend Viscount Bury. As Horace recalled,

> It was in early spring 1915 and my mother and I were getting waterproof things to send to my brother in France when Bury came in. He was on Lord French's staff and he said to my mother that he and his comrades (in the Scots Guards) had kept themselves warm during the winter in the trenches by telling each other jokes of mine—real and imaginary. I'd known most of the men. Most are dead of that lot. Lord Bury then offered me a press, compositor etc, *everything*, and a post (as officer of course) at G.H.Q. I was to bring out and distribute a paper weekly in the trenches and tell all my jokes. It *would* have been the first war paper. For many reasons, I refused.

This proposition was stillborn, but a year later, in February 1916, a similar idea spontaneously emerged with the publication amid the mud of Flanders of the popular *Wipers Times*, a morale-boosting newspaper produced by the troops themselves.

But humour couldn't mask the unfolding tragedy, or pacifism stall it. As the conflict ground on, Horace's attitude towards it hardened. He no longer took refuge in political idealism, the reality was too stark. As he said with bitter regret, 'The war has cheapened the lives of men everywhere, and the world has grown callous.' The jokes started to fail: friends and family began to fall. His brother Jim was badly wounded; Arthur Hay, Teddy Mulholland and Ivar Campbell (who had made it to the war) were killed, and Hugh Lane lost when *Lusitania* was torpedoed off Ireland. The war cut a swath through the *Dreadnought* and Zanzibar hoaxers. Within a year of the outbreak of war, three of the five who signed up were dead. Robbie Bowen-Colthurst was the first to die, shot through the head in March 1915, leaving four young children. Six months later Dummer Howard was destroyed by a shell near Arras. Finally, in September 1915, Tudor Castle, who had fought alongside Dummer in the Royal West Surrey Regiment, was gassed at Delville Wood. Three tragedies out of millions. Yet the deaths of the hoaxers symbolised the bloody end of a world of friendship and laughter. The war produced a concentrated poetic response from Horace, as if he could only phrase his despair in verse.

> Old friends of mine, new friends and old,
> With strong blood surging in your veins,
> The heedless bullet swift and cold,
> Has mixed your blood with vintage plains;
>
> Whene'er in times to come I raise
> My glass to pledge, with living friend,
> I will recall those gallant days,
> And drink to your unconquered end.

Another strangely affecting death was of Peter Willoughby, the charming young lieutenant in *Dreadnought* who had greeted the hoaxers at Weymouth Station. He was lost at Coronel. Against this bleak register, the refusal to fight became unconscionable to Horace. To his mother, he complained of feeling a failure 'at being so hopelessly out of the war, and of my friend's lives—alive or dead'. So when he heard of Jacob Epstein's success in June 1917 in gaining exemption from the call-up as an 'irreplaceable artist' he was sent into paroxysms of fury. He whipped up a vociferous chorus of opposition to the decision, engaging Sir Philip Burne-Jones, son of the eminent Victorian painter and an establishment figure, to lead a vituperative campaign. In an interview with the *Evening Standard*, probably arranged by Horace, Burne-Jones deplored the decision to exempt Epstein.

> Some of our most gifted native artists have, without protest... gone quietly and ungrudgingly out to the Front to make the supreme sacrifice. It should not be a hole-in-the-wall affair, and many distinguished artists...question the propriety of British Museum officials, of the Art Collections Fund subscribers, arrogating to themselves the task of placing this or that artist upon the pinnacle of fame.

Burne-Jones concluded with a carefully aimed dig at modern art. 'What of the artists,' he said, 'who, though pre-eminently talented and possibly among the world's immortals, do not happen to be the vogue of the moment, with a fashionable clientele.'

A co-ordinated flurry of letters greeted the interview in the press. Writing anonymously as 'Artist, now Lieutenant', Horace's friend Derwent Wood (who cast the memorial to the Machine Gun Corps standing on Hyde Park Corner) summed up the generally expressed view. 'Why should one who poses as a genius be exempted from military service? He should have come forward long ago, like many more of us who sacrificed our art to our country.' Wood was forcefully backed up by G.K. Chesterton and Epstein's fellow American expatriate Walter Winans, who wittily commented,

> If the Futurists, Cubists and Vorticists, who want to hide behind their 'Creations', would only go into the trenches with their 'artistic' productions and pop them up into the faces of the enemy, the latter would fall down, thinking they had overdone things and got an attack of 'D.T.'

To Horace's delight, his dirty campaign succeeded—exceptionally—in overturning Epstein's exemption. He had his victory. Epstein was devastated. He ranted against this 'sycophant of John's' who had tormented him for years and now threatened to cause his death. Having failed in a final desperate attempt to escape the trenches by becoming an official war artist, Epstein was conscripted as a private in the Jewish 38th battalion of the Royal Fusiliers. Ironically, Horace's vendetta probably eventually saved the artist, as it contributed to the nervous breakdown which led to his early discharge from the army before he even sailed for France. But it was never forgotten nor forgiven, with Epstein's Modernist friends combining in their condemnation of Horace. Unlike the burly Cecil Gray, most were unable to take physical revenge. They preferred to exact more subtle retribution through their art by lampooning him in print.

With his friends dying at the front, Horace kept up the frenzied partying. Before Christmas 1916, the artist Dora Carrington, a Slade School friend of Iris Tree, spotted him at a rave-up hosted by the novelist Dorothy Richardson, a former lover of H.G. Wells who had married Alan Odle. She told Lytton Strachey (with whom she was besotted),

> Seldom have I seen such a debauche of white arms and bosoms. It was indeed a sight to see, everyone trying to outrival their companions in viciousness. Beauty was absent. It was no wonder that the female element turned to their own species for embrasures when the males consisted of Horace Cole, Boris, the Armenian, Rodker and even more degraded specimens.

Boris was the mosaicist Boris Anrep, 'the Armenian' was the writer Michael Arlen (real name Dikran Kouyoumdjian), and Rodker the Modernist poet John Rodker. When conscription was introduced in January 1917, Rodker went on the run as a conscientious objector, sheltering with Robert Trevelyan (George's brother) before his arrest and imprisonment. Like Arlen and Horace, he contributed to *New Age* magazine.

After Christmas Horace took to his bed with a heavy cold and lung infection, a legacy of his childhood diphtheria. Before the war he had moved from Cadogan Place deeper into bohemian Chelsea, to 34 Cheyne Walk, only a stone's throw from the Chelsea Arts Club, a favourite wartime haunt. Here his feverish brow was mopped by Deborah Webber, a twenty-five-year-old married woman with a seven-year-old daughter. She had recently escaped her aristocratic Danish husband, had an affair with an English flying officer and trodden the boards of the Vaudeville Theatre, where Horace spotted her. 'She has looks and ability,' Horace told his mother, 'and has had offers to be "starred" but always refused because the stage was only a momentary pastime.' 'She is only a chorus girl by a fluke,' he hastily added. 'She is very well educated, with good taste and well brought up. She says her greatest fault is "too great a capacity for loving".'

Horace and Deborah thought they were in love, though she had no intention of marrying him, only to be 'free'. By now, this was a familiar story, with all the ingredients of the Pasolini affair ten years before. Here was Horace again hurtling headlong to the rescue of a damsel in distress, careless of opinion and regardless of consequence. Deborah moved into Cheyne Walk during Horace's illness, causing local tongues to wag. A maid in the house opposite even sent Mary Studd a long account of the 'disgraceful conduct happening in 34'. 'And the rowdiness,' she added, 'at two and three o'clock in the morning has roused the *respectable neighbourhood*.' It was not a good omen, and the relationship quickly foundered. Mary was untroubled by her son's behaviour (she was used to it). Instead of a reprimand, she invited him to Ireland to recover his health and heart. But Horace was furious. He suspected that his former housekeeper—dismissed for stealing cocoa and 'eating off my china with my silver and eating my precious strawberry jam'—had colluded with his neighbour's 'evil faced' maid in the accusations. With his unreliable temper, his irregular hours and destructive friends, Horace was not an easy man to work for.

20

She came and asked me for a flower,
I gave her one the wind had blown,
She wore next her heart an hour
When all its gentle life had flown;

Its wings lie folded as a cowl
Like sheets upon some formless thing,
And from its petals comes a foul
Smell of decay, and burying.

Horace sought the peace and his 'native air' of Ireland to recover his health and spirits after his shortlived but intense liaison with Deborah Webber. Instead he found himself pitched into a country at war with itself and into another passionate love affair which finally led to his marriage. It was exhilarating to be back in Ireland after the dreariness of wartime London, with its recalcitrant servants and vengeful artists. The origins of Irish rebellion lay far beyond Horace's childhood, but he had grown up under its looming threat, and its terrible possibility had fixated and agitated Anglo-Irish minds for decades. Before the war the prospect of home rule for Ireland had confused loyalties, forcing the opposing unionist and nationalist movements into extreme and then armed positions. The picture was not a straightforward one, nor was it entirely drawn along lines of religion, family or friendship. Horace's friend Shane Leslie, a Catholic convert, was a very committed nationalist, whereas Shane's father was an equally fiery unionist. The divide was even more bitter at Mount Trenchard in County Limerick, where Horace's idealistic young cousin Mary Spring-Rice, daughter of Earl Monteagle, had rebelled against her father's staunchly loyal stance by gun-running for the newly formed Irish Volunteers. Occasionally these bitter arguments spilled over into England, causing a scene. Horace recalled lunching with Sir George and Lady Colthurst, owners of Blarney Castle and parents of his close friend George, at Brown's Hotel when Sir George 'began damning the English in the crowded room...in the most violent way'.

Like most Anglo-Irish, Horace was in favour of home rule but ambivalent about full independence for Ireland. He was his mother's son, and Mary Studd had close ties to the Irish literary revival with its strong nationalist yearnings. But unlike her, his romantic vision of Ireland was tempered by pride in his English blood. He could be close friends with republican activists like writers Darrell Figgis (who had helped Mary Spring-Rice smuggle arms) and James Stephens, who contributed to the nationalist paper the *Irish Citizen*; yet still enjoy all the benefits of the Ascendancy. The contradiction of this position was illustrated by a dangerous prank he had played at Dublin Castle before the war while staying with Robbie Bowen-Colthurst, who was then vice-chamberlain to the Viceroy, Lord Aberdeen. One afternoon, Horace had jumped out from behind a bush and pierced the Viceroy's coat-tails with his swordstick. He claimed to be testing the Viceroy's security. 'You are twenty seconds too late,' he calmly informed the bodyguards when they rushed up. 'The Viceroy is already dead.' In fact, he had come closer than the republicans ever did to assassinating the hated symbol of British rule, and was deported back to England for his trouble.

Robbie, a veteran of the Zanzibar hoax, was dead now, killed in the trenches. But his elder brother John, a captain in the Irish Rifles, had earned terrible notoriety for going on the rampage during the republican rising of Easter 1916. He had ordered the summary execution of the pacifist editor of the *Irish Citizen*, Francis Sheehy-Skeffington, and personally shot down an innocent man and two boys in the street. Writing to Maud Gonne, W.B. Yeats described John Bowen-Colthurst as a 'friend of Horace Cole, the practical joker who is hardly sane. As the mad attract their like one can measure him.' Controversially, Bowen-Colthurst was indeed adjudged insane at his court martial, sparing him prosecution for murder. 'It's a terrible thing,' he had commented, 'to shoot one's own countrymen, isn't it?' The killings summed up Horace's dilemma and the tragedy of Ireland. Here was one close friend shooting down in cold blood the colleague of another.

The centre of Dublin was still burnt out, many of its buildings in ruins, when Horace returned to Ireland in 1917. The Kildare Street Club, a favourite retreat, had been in the midst of the fighting and still bore its scars. But there was a sense among its Ascendancy members that the boil of violent republicanism had been lanced by the brutal execution of the insurgency's ringleaders. The inexorable rise in popularity of Sinn Fein after the failed revolt and the ominous emergence of the IRA, a hardline splinter group of the Irish Volunteers, went largely unheeded. Instead, ordered progress towards home rule, so long delayed by parliament then derailed by the war and uprising, was renewed. Attention drifted back to more mundane issues, like racing and hunting. For Horace, this meant coming to terms with his surprising feelings for Denise Daly, a headstrong seventeen-year-old from Galway who had run away from home and thrown herself on the mercy of his Aunt Eily, now Lady Shaw. Holed up at the Shaws' mansion near Dublin, Denise was an irresistible draw to his romantic imagination.

Her pedigree was as impressive as her spirit. As a sole surviving twin, Denise had been heiress since infancy to no fewer than three estates in the west of Ireland. Two, at Raford and Furbough, came through her father, Denis Daly, who had died before she was born. The third, Petersburg, would come to her on the death of her mother, Kathleen, whose family, the Lynchs, had run Galway for centuries. But such riches came at a price. The eccentric Kathleen Daly now travelled the world under the *nom de plume* Daly de Sedruol (Lourdes spelt backwards) and Denise was made a ward of Chancery to protect her fortune. This prevented her from marrying or touching her inheritance until she was twenty-one. Now in her application to the Lord Chancellor of Ireland to have the wardship lifted, Denise complained that she had 'lived in constant terror since I was eleven'. She claimed that her drunken grandfather Lynch (living up to the family tradition for 'Lynch law') had attacked her with a knife and beaten her with a hunting whip, and that her own mother had threatened to kill her or have her committed for lunacy. An embittered Horace later dismissed such allegations as

Denise Daly, the beautiful heiress who woke Horace from his 'endless, uncomfortable dream' (Mrs Pat Davies).

'*all* fabrication and lies'. But at the time he fell for them, and for Denise, completely. They played powerfully on his susceptibility for girls in distress. Denise's wardship, like Mildred's unhappy marriage, was simply another obstacle to overcome, a great challenge in the quest for happiness.

In her large childish hand, Denise wrote Horace's mother, whom she affectionately called 'Mus', a series of helpless-sounding, conspiratorial and highly manipulative letters. 'This child is so longing to be with you,' Denise implored, seeking Mary's protection. 'I do do love you and worship you mus and you know it and I only wish wish wish I could be with you and of some use to you.' Horace ignored all the signs of Denise's mental instability—her manic outbursts, sudden collapses and hysterical behaviour—as he shared many of them. Unfortunately, these characteristics were all they had in common, so were not a sound foundation for a long-term relationship. Horace was indulgent in his care. He hunted for fairies with Denise in the hills of Kildare, wrote her poetry and attended her endless meetings with lawyers, doctors and psychiatrists. Just weeks after leaving Deborah behind in London, he proposed marriage, sweeping aside any misgivings about Denise's fragile state. The strength of his feelings for Denise was a revelation. 'I had believed that I could feel like I do, but had begun to think I never would,' he told his mother. 'She and I will always understand one another and I know we can be truly happy. I feel I have woken up and shaken off a heavy weight—not a nightmare—but an endless, uncomfortable dream.' Beneath a barrage of emotional and highly charged appeals, the Lord Chancellor of Ireland—described by Horace as a 'fat old man with a curling lip'—caved in and freed Denise from Chancery. Horace had opened the cage door, but could he tame the bird?

21

orace and Denise were married in a Roman Catholic ceremony at the University Church in Dublin on 30 September 1918. Horace, who was Protestant, was given special dispensation to proceed with the service, though he toyed with becoming a Catholic beforehand. The theatrical features and arcane rituals of the Catholic faith and its strange, otherworldliness had always strongly appealed to him. They played on his need for magic and mystery. Irreverent comparisons with the music hall were irresistible. He had probably been considering such a move since his mock conversion on a coffin at Cambridge. He even went so far as to consult Denise's priest, Father Sherwin, on the matter. Both his mother and great uncle Aubrey de Vere had converted, believing Catholicism the true religion of Ireland, but Horace never took the final step. Those drops of English blood held him back, and the fear that it would anger the Protestant Lord Chancellor of Ireland at a delicate time. He was a spiritual but never very religious man, and after stripping away the glamour of Catholicism he lacked the necessary conviction, energy and commitment to pursue it.

George Colthurst was best man at the wedding. Briefly reconciled to her daughter, and hoping perhaps for a payout, Mrs Daly (or Daly de Sedruol) returned from her travels to give the bride away. Denise looked radiant, losing for a time that awkward self-consciousness that so many people commented on. Oliver St John Gogarty, who had been embroiled in the successful manoeuvrings to secure Denise's release from Chancery, sent Augustus John an entertaining account of proceedings.

Before the champagne, there was a boring hour in the chapel—a
Byzantine structure with a living mystic tree painted in the hollow
of the half-dome above the altar. The place was filled. Nothing
for a while, and then an acolyte with short legs genuflected in
front of the altar, exposing sturdy buttocks. The omens were so
far favourable. I found my Lincoln Bennett [top-hat] bristling
like a tom cat because Mrs Studd (a name propitious) had seated
herself hard by. Then came Cole pale beyond porch and portal
with a shouting soldier and a white haired priest...Then the
bride far off between the pillars like Antigone...She went into
the vestry (divestry) on her mother's arm, Cole and all, followed
by an odd fellow with a fine name Monteagle and two sticks to
limp with, one shod with rubber like a phallus! But one's mind is
full of symbols on such occasions. The procession out was fine.
Two lovely symbolic babes held the train. Twins do run in the
Daly family—the bride was half one. Good luck to Cole!

The occasion wasn't universally greeted with joy. The Earl
of Westmeath, who was Denise's cousin, boycotted the event,
believing, like many, that Horace, at thirty-six, was too old and
too unreliable to marry a girl half his age. The Earl may also
have doubted the bridegroom's motives, correctly suspecting
that Horace's finances were on the wane. No Coles attended
the wedding. Jim Cole (who Horace accused of having designs
on Denise himself) was back from the war but stationed with
his regiment in Yorkshire. Their sister Annie also made her
excuses, though she and her husband sent a generous present.
It was no surprise that Uncle Alfred failed to make the journey,
and nor did any of Horace's ageing English aunts. There were
legitimate reasons for all their absences: wartime restrictions
made travelling to Ireland difficult. However, there is a suspicion
of a breach between the English and Irish sides of Horace's
family. By marrying an Irish girl, Horace had demonstrated his
loyalty to Ireland at a fraught time between the two countries.

Horace was more concerned about the effect his marriage
would have on his devoted mother than on the Coles. It broke

the prism of their self-absorbing love. He sensed her pain matched his when she married Herbert Studd. With that special understanding they reserved for each other, Horace wrote to her of 'feeling jealous that you had felt you might feel so for I had always felt that too...You and I will go off somewhere, perhaps to that coast by the Spanish frontier where Innes painted, or to Italy, just as if I wasn't married!' Mary had been physically usurped by Denise, but she had not lost that spiritual hold which bound Horace at the core.

Together with Issercleran, Mary's estate in Galway, the newly-weds were heirs to no less than four substantial properties in Ireland. By the terms of the settlement releasing Denise from Chancery and allowing her to marry, the Daly properties were hers but her fortune (estimated at around £50,000 in cash and shares, or around £1 million today) would be administered by the Bank of Ireland for her use and the future use of her children only. Horace had no rights over it. Likewise, Horace's property investments in Canada to a value of £30,000 were placed in trust for the children of the marriage. He remained entitled to the investment income and any sum over £30,000 arising from their sale. On paper, this made Horace and Denise look comfortably off, but their income was heavily circumscribed and very vulnerable to a property slump or, as in Ireland, civil unrest and war. Moreover, it was being rapidly whittled away by steeply rising taxes and the wartime slump in trade.

The marriage began brightly enough. After a short honeymoon the Coles settled into Raford, a handsome Georgian mansion at Athenry, County Galway which had been in the Daly family for generations. Within a year, Denise had a baby girl she christened Valerie, a fashionable name at the time and one definitely not among her loathed Irish forebears. Horace pictured himself settling down to a quiet life in the country with his new wife and daughter, to cultivate, as Dora Carrington, scarcely concealing her surprise, informed Lytton Strachey, the air of 'a respectable landed gentleman'. After years of leading a dissolute, peripatetic existence, Horace craved a quieter one. Or thought he did. It was more role playing, only this time he was fooling himself. There were already warning signs that it could never work. Horace and Denise were temperamentally unsuited for such a life. Each had their own demons to fight. Denise, in particular, having struggled so hard for her freedom, was not prepared to moulder away in the remote west of Ireland looking after a baby and hosting meets of the Galway Blazers on her lawn. She needed excitement.

Many men nearer to her in age than her husband, and a great deal more dashing, paid her close attention, and she thrilled at their suggestions. Nor was Horace an easy man to live with. Lady Glenarvy recalled lunching with the newly-weds at a hotel in Kingstown shortly before they all sailed for England. Horace was in the bath when they arrived (he was a notoriously late riser) and refused to appear even after Denise sent her guests upstairs to knock on the bathroom door. Instead, wearing only a towel and in complete silence, he began throwing anything he could find—'housemaid's mops, buckets, ornaments, other people's shoes'—out of the window. 'I think Denise had a difficult time with him,' mused Lady Glenarvy with admirable understatement, 'but as she was rather a handful herself it probably evened things out.'

Events in Ireland also conspired against their happiness. The early days of the marriage played out against rising tension in Ireland. Horace was amazed at the number of British troops garrisoned in the country 'when one always hears of our men facing superior odds in France'. The unexpected success of Sinn Fein in the 1918 general election (the result of the vicious British retaliation after the rising) led to the formation of an Irish parliament, the Dáil, in defiance of Westminster. The

Dáil chose Eamonn de Valera as its president and began setting up all the legal and financial arrangements of a fully independent state. Simultaneously, an emboldened IRA, led by the charismatic Michael Collins, launched a guerrilla war against the British army and a campaign of violence in the country. Houses occupied by the Ascendancy were targeted, with many robbed of arms and other valuables.

In a document he entitled 'Facts and their consequences (an answer to Mr Lloyd George)', Horace blamed the unrest in Ireland wholly on the 'unsympathetic treatment' of Britain and on the British Prime Minister. He cited the failure to achieve home rule before the war for stoking bitterness, and although he had not sympathised with the rising in 1916 he condemned the 'callowness and lack of imagination' of its aftermath, when dozens of nationalists had been brutally executed in reprisals. 'England does not care so long as one Irishman is killing his fellow countryman,' he stormed. 'Therefore murder thrives, through immunity under English government.' 'Martial law, repression, reprisal and murder, shall indefinitely complete the serpent circle,' he concluded with terrible foresight. 'Ireland should be allowed complete self-government, whatever the consequences to England; since England, in her blundering and her amazing stupidity, is the *fons et origo* of all these possible consequences.'

Ranting against England failed to save the Coles from the attentions of the IRA. Its men raided Raford and 'helped themselves to all my best Scholte clothes and best shoe leather!' They also took Denise's jewels—many of them recent wedding presents—Horace's gold hunting pin and, especially upsetting, a handful of semi-precious stones he had gathered up in the Pyrenees with Dick Innes. Broadly sympathetic to the aims, if not methods, of the IRA, Horace was stoic in his reaction, refusing (unlike Denise) to claim compensation for his losses.

The government then compounded the crisis in the country by raising an irregular force of auxiliary troops drawn from the ranks of shell-shocked men back from the trenches. Branded 'Black and Tans' after their hastily improvised uniform of half-and-half police black and army khaki, the auxiliaries quickly acquired a terrible reputation for brutality: burning villages, plundering houses and killing people in revenge for IRA attacks. The focus of their activities was to locate Michael Collins, the almost mythical leader of the IRA and a republican hero. In response to the provocation of the Black and Tans, IRA units began appearing at the dead of night on the doorsteps of the Anglo-Irish, giving the occupants a few minutes' leave before burning down the house. Over two hundred Irish country houses were lost in this way. Among the first to be torched was Oakgrove in County Cork, the childhood home of Robbie Bowen-Colthurst and his hated brother John.

Raford was spared the flames, but, remote and isolated, living there with a young child was terrifying for Denise, unsettling her fragile mind still further. The west of Ireland emptied of Anglo-Irish families as they sought refuge in England. Meanwhile her husband was reverting to former bad habits, staying at the Shelbourne Hotel in Dublin (outside which he once overturned a hansom cab in a trial of strength) to drink long into the night with friends like Joe Hone, James Stephens, painter Jack Yeats and republican activist Darrell Figgis. These Irishmen were united by idealism and a fabulist view of the world. Horace's description of Yeats as 'slightly fantastic, a realist who is always looking round the corner for a fairy tale' could have applied to any one of them. Yet the bonhomie could not hide Horace's deterioration or his worsening drinking. A British officer, a friend of Denise, remembered being invited to dinner at the Shelbourne by Horace around this time.

'Meet me in the bar at 6.30,' he said. After a few Irish whiskies which I never enjoyed (in his case a few more) it was plain to me that any idea of my getting a dinner out of him wasn't on. I became more and more embarrassed by his wild behaviour so I left the scene as the staff, who would know his ways well, took charge.

It is a troubling image of a man in denial and decline.

The Shelbourne was the location for another bizarre incident, when Horace claimed to have apprehended an English spy 'for his good, otherwise he would have been shot'. Horace sent the man packing back to London with the message that he had been caught by the legendary Michael Collins. Speaking to the *Irish Times* in 1931, Horace recalled what happened next.

He returned to England and two days later in my hotel room in Dublin I was suddenly confronted by two Black and Tans armed with huge Webley Service revolvers. The taller of the two, who was 6ft 6in, told me that they knew I was Michael Collins, and that there was a reward of £5000 for my capture dead or alive, they proposed to shoot me on the spot. I realised what had happened and denied that I was Michael Collins. They were not impressed. Then I produced some whiskey, and succeeded by lavish hospitality in reducing the men to a helpless state. They staggered away, saying that I was a jolly good fellow if I was Michael Collins, and anyway what was £5000 to them. That was touch-and-go. Yes, a very close shave indeed.

Eventually the government in London bowed to the inevitable and invited Sinn Fein to talks in London. The upshot was the Anglo-Irish Treaty and the founding in 1921 of the Irish Free State, putting Ireland on a similar constitutional footing with Britain as Canada or Australia. The real Michael Collins came out of hiding for the negotiations and became a minister in a new Provisional Government of Ireland headed by Arthur Griffiths, who Horace also knew. Other friends like Oliver St John Gogarty entered the Dáil, as Free State senators.

However, the treaty bitterly divided republicans. Concessions had been made to the unionists in the northern counties of Ireland, including the right to cede from the new state (which they promptly did). But principally the nationalists split over the granting of dominion status to Ireland rather than the establishment of the republic that so many had dreamt of and fought for. Furious debate in the Dáil soon descended into civil war, with the old IRA splitting into the pro-Treaty Free State army, led by Collins, and an anti-treaty 'Irregular' force which rallied to Collins's former ally de Valera. ('That man should be SHOT,' blasted Horace, voicing the opinion of many nationalist sympathisers who coalesced around the Free State cause.) De Valera vehemently argued that Collins, who had signed the Treaty, had lacked the authority to do so.

The war was short, brutal and terrifying. There was blood-letting on both sides. Even respected senators and long-term champions of Irish nationalism like Oliver Gogarty were kidnapped, tortured and their houses burned (Gogarty escaped death by jumping into the Liffey to evade his captors). In August 1922, Collins was killed in a fire-fight with anti-Treaty gunmen. Writing to his brother Jim, Horace, who had sought refuge with Denise at a hotel outside Dublin, painted a vivid picture of his forays into the city: of speeding dispatch riders and Free State soldiers cruising the streets in armoured cars 'out-aping' the once-hated Black and Tans.

> I had a letter from Father O'Farrell today. He says 'Tis a pity the late M. Collins was the chief means of creating turmoil in this country by his accepting unauthorised Mr Lloyd-George's terms.' It is impossible to convince a man holding such an opinion that Collins had the moral right and power on his side…Ireland is pro-treaty for she wanted peace and her leaders knew what England *could* do; but she is not pro-discipline in any direction, and if she does not quickly acquire the habit of discipline she will disintegrate.

The violence and anarchy which underpinned Horace's own behaviour now descended on his country at large. It scraped away his love of Ireland, with its assumed moral and aesthetic superiority to England, leaving him personally diminished. The rupture of Ireland mirrored the destruction of his marriage. Drink, war and mounting money problems had taken a terrible toll on his relationship with Denise. Uncle Alfred's well-intentioned financial advice back in 1912 was proving disastrous. Prices and taxes had risen, but Horace's rental income from his property investments in Saskatoon had fallen sharply. Above all, Horace and Denise's forceful, restless personalities never settled down comfortably together. Horace was now in his forties with fading fortunes while Denise was barely in her twenties and the centre of male attention. She told him he had had his life, now she wanted hers. He had been the key to her freedom, but once granted she, like the romance, had fled. Valerie, aged five, was dispatched to boarding school, leaving her mother to embark on a series of affairs. One was with a rich American called Morley Kennerley, the son of a New York art dealer, who Denise met in the liberated atmosphere of Augustus John's Dorset home. Morley was there having his portrait painted. Horace, in his self-pitying despair and a series of drunken, rambling letters, seemed almost to encourage the relationship, anxious perhaps for an excuse to escape the marriage. 'There is only one thing for you to do and you must do it,' he instructed his wife.

I don't think you would be very happy with me now, without any money I mean. So you must bag him now at all costs without fail. Besides you are in love with him, and apparently he is in love with you. So it's all damned simple. I have helped you as much as I possibly could. I can do no more now. I am very unhappy myself because I have lost you physically anyway. But I am very thankful that I have not lost you completely. Horace.

The circumstances of his affair with Mildred Pasolini had turned full circle. Now an attractive younger man was eyeing up *his* wife.

It was Morley—'a nice, rather ingenuous (for an American) young man', Horace judged dispassionately—who called off the affair with Denise. Horace told his mother that Morley 'was so worried about what he considered a breach of hospitality in having a love affair under his host's roof with another man's wife that he went and confessed to A.J., where I think he was told not to be an ass'. Denise was untroubled by scandal. In July 1925, months after her dalliance with Morley, she ran away with a young London waiter called James Stanley. They headed to Ireland, Denise no doubt seeing the newly independent country as a refuge from English law and her husband's rage. Something happened on the way. Denise must have suddenly feared her reception in Ireland, for she left the boat train at an isolated station high up in the Brecon Beacons near the village of Penywyllt in South Wales. Trailing Stanley and a large quantity of luggage behind her, Denise headed for the nearest house, which happened to be the local post office belonging to a Mrs Davies.

We can only imagine what Mrs Davies thought of the exotic couple who had landed on her doorstep, claiming to be man and wife. But she gave them lodgings, and there the runaways stayed for the next two years. Denise's appearance, heavily scented and wrapped in furs, caused a considerable stir in the close-knit rural community. Mrs Davies's young son David watched spellbound as Denise made up each morning, applying Bella Donna drops to enhance her eyes. Occasionally Denise slipped over to Ireland to attend to some mysterious business, but otherwise she and Stanley lived quietly in Penywyllt, lovingly cared for by their indulgent landlady and a local farm girl engaged as their maid. It was not long, however, before their whereabouts became known. First telegrams then unpaid bills started to arrive at the small post office. David Davies's widow still possesses a suitcase full of unpaid accounts from smart London dressmakers, furriers and perfumers. The bills were quickly followed by Augustus John, who sought out the couple in his native land.

Augustus always hungered after Horace's women. It was his way of bettering his friend through sexual prowess. Lilian Shelley and Iris Tree had already succumbed; now the ultimate prize of Horace's wife lay within his grasp, a trophy made easier by her unhappiness and vulnerability. Indeed, something may already have occurred between them during Denise's stay in Dorset. Certainly the artist, by then one of the most celebrated in the world, was sufficiently encouraged to leave his studio, travel to Penywyllt and offer his assistance. On this occasion

Denise hiding from her husband in Wales (Mrs Pat Davies).

(there would be others) I think Augustus was frustrated in his bid to cuckold Horace. Denise wanted a divorce, and may have suspected a trap laid by her husband. When the case was eventually heard at the High Court, in May 1928, she even vigorously denied adultery with James Stanley. Mrs Davies was summoned to London to testify loyally that she had never seen her lodgers in bed together (though she conceded they had shared a room for two years).

Despite Denise's protestations, and a lack of proof, the circumstantial evidence was overwhelming, and the court granted Horace divorce on the basis of his wife's infidelity. He was given custody of Valerie, who has no childhood memory of her mother at all, and the marriage settlement of 1918 was altered to secure Valerie's inheritance. Much diminished, Valerie eventually shared this with her mother, though it did little to save Denise from her reckless habits. Twice bankrupted, in 1944 she was imprisoned for obtaining credit under false pretences. In the words of her own counsel, Denise 'had been brought up to think that money would come to her like water, and that she could spend it like water' on her 'taste for astrology, fast cars and clothes'. Raford and Furbough were both sold, and shortly before she died Denise sought a buyer for her last property in Galway—Petersburg—but on condition she could remain living there. 'I need a man of vision and money who will enable me to restore the house to its former glory,' she informed the *Sunday Express*. 'The buyer will not be some bicycle-clipped character. This is a proposition for a gentleman. When I am gone he gets the lot.' She failed in her bid, and Petersburg, like Raford, was purchased for a nominal sum by the Irish Land Commission. It is now an outdoor activity centre.

Denise got through as many husbands as houses. After divorcing Horace she married (in a ceremony not recognised by the Catholic Church) a Mr Winterbotham. Her former husband celebrated in typical style by hosting a drinks party exclusively for people with names like his usurper's—Ramsbotham, Higginbotham, and Boddam-Whettam, for example—then leaving them all to introduce themselves. In 1948, Denise married again, this time to Antony Drew, who had also been bankrupted after squandering a family fortune. Horace was not shocked by Denise's erratic behaviour—which was not unusual in the circles he moved in—but he was furious at the destruction of his daughter's inheritance. Father Sherwin, who had married them in Dublin, told Horace that Denise's fault was 'moral weakness'. It was small consolation as the debris of his life continued to pile up.

22

Upon the hills of Esterel
The changing clouds reflect the sun,
And in the radiance where it fell
The orange twilight has begun

Like giant cliffs of Amethyst
Against the glow the mountains stand,
Their bases wrapt in dewy mist
That rises from a silent land;

from 'Sunset over the Esterel Hills, Provence'

*T*here was only one post-war joke on the scale and of the
sophistication of Zanzibar or *Dreadnought*. This was
the little-known 'Crown of Croatia' heist, in which
Horace attempted to sell the title of King of Croatia, complete with royal regalia, to an exceptionally vain, rich but unfortunately anonymous Englishman who had publicly boasted
of acquiring a foreign throne. Taking advantage of the constitutional chaos in the Balkans at the end of the war, Horace
promised the man the throne of Croatia (Leland Buxton,
veteran of the Zanzibar hoax with an avid interest in Balkan
politics, may have had a hand in the joke). After a series of
clandestine meetings with underlings (in reality two penniless
Russian émigrés hired by Horace for the occasion) the victim
was invited to a house in Eaton Place to discuss details with
the Croat Minister. Ushered into the house—presumably
the home of Horace's mother and stepfather, who owned a

property there—by powdered footmen, the 'mark' was greeted by Horace, brilliantly dressed and made up as the Minister by Willy Clarkson. Pleading conjunctivitis, the Minister apologised for the heavily shaded room. This was done obviously to protect Horace's disguise, as he knew the victim well, though he said later it was not really necessary as Clarkson had again excelled himself. Negotiations opened with Horace slyly making it known that an American was also after the new throne. After lengthy horse-trading, he agreed an astronomical price, accepted a cheque, and requested the man return at a later date to receive the crown and regalia from a delegation of Croatian bishops, generals and statesmen then on their way to England.

At noon on the appointed day, the victim duly appeared in white tie and tails for his 'coronation'. Again he was welcomed by footmen, who threw open the large double doors of the drawing-room to reveal Horace and some friends holding glasses of champagne and toasting the man's cheque, which was framed and hanging on the wall. (It seems post-war jokes about the Balkans were all the rage. One bright young thing of the day impersonated 'Prince Michael of Serbia' for a whole weekend at a country-house party, telling stories about his motoring feats and cheating at bridge.)

The joke was a swansong for a vanishing age. Never again would Horace muster the will or resources to carry out a prank on such a scale. It also prompts the interesting thought that in other circumstances Horace might have put his skills of deception to criminal purposes. He certainly needed the money. Into the twenties, with his wife holed up in Wales with her lover, his debts rising and his drinking escalating, Horace's jokes developed a desperate, vengeful edge. With stories in the press of gangsters on the loose in London, he pulled a menacing little trick on an innocent driver after dining with David Scott-Moncrieff in Charlotte Street (possibly at Elsa Lanchester's famed and slightly disreputable twenties nightspot the Cave of Harmony). With taxi after taxi passing them in the rain, Horace stepped in front of a car to stop it, then, grabbing his friend by the arm, jumped into the back seat. Pressing his fountain pen into the back of the driver's neck and assuming an American accent, 'which he managed to make incredibly sinister', Horace ordered him to drive them to the Piccadilly Hotel. At the hotel, the driver was told to wait. 'See that window up there?' said Horace. 'You are covered from there by a man with a repeating rifle. You will wait exactly ten minutes and then drive away and never tell a soul about tonight. If you attempt to move before your ten minutes are up, you will be as full of holes as a colander.' Horace and Scott-Moncrieff then entered the hotel, walked straight through it and exited by the Regent Street door, crossing the road for a drink in the Café Royal. 'By the look on that poor little man's face,' concluded Scott-Moncrieff, 'I am quite certain that he waited the full ten minutes.' He saw nothing cruel in the escapade, and enjoyed retelling how he then visited the Tower of London with Horace 'to see if there were any hoax, however elaborate, by which we could get away with the Crown Jewels'.

Other nights, accompanied by Chile Guevara and Roy Campbell, Horace would force his way into Belgravia mansions—targeted for some slight or other—to accuse the owners of kidnapping his wife. After turning every room upside down and emptying every drawer, the invaders would fulsomely apologise and leave. Or else he would accost punters in Piccadilly, claiming the prostitute they were with was his aunt, recently escaped from a lunatic asylum. Horace may have had his formidable Aunt Eily in mind. She had been appalled to hear how her nephew had haunted the house of a woman dying of cancer.

He took a house alongside where he started his curious ways and means of causing strange sounds etc in order to get all the servants to imagine it was so haunted that one by one they left. No one would go near and she the poor lady was in such anguish and pain and distress that I understand the police finally had to make enquiries.

Aunt Eily sought reassurance from Horace's brother Jim that the story was false—and it may have been—though she reminded him that Horace had done other haunting jokes in the past.

These were troubled, confused episodes: manifestations of a mind tilting towards madness. The physical effects of recent events were also marked. The audacity of youth was growing wearisome in middle age, the once admired physique flabby and dissolute. Even Horace's distinctive mane of hair, prematurely turned white, was thinning.

There's no obvious decrease in its quantity, but the amount that falls out every day makes me think of the miracle of the loaves and fishes. There always seem to be more hairs lying about that were once on my head than are apparent on my head now...I hope it does not portend a real storm wherein all my flakes will fall to the ground and leave my occiput as barren as an Easter egg.

Moreover Valerie now had to be considered. He told his mother,

I do not believe a small girl can need an elderly father, such a thing would be entirely unnatural. She would need a mother maybe, or a woman. Later on and for a short time a father might come on the scene! And I am no heroic father for a little girl's hero worship and for her friends' admiration. No V.C. No military tank. Not even a Rolls-Royce or Ford!

For the time being, Valerie was shuffled between relatives, her father appearing only occasionally with conscience-salving gifts. Her memory of him is pained and clouded by later events.

Horace was proud of Valerie—telling Augustus that she was going 'to be a lovely girl: brunette, creamy skin and speedwell blue eyes and small nose'—but he was unable to show her the affection she wanted after her mother left.

More pressing for Horace than the love of his daughter was the urgent need for money. What was left of his library in Ireland after the IRA raid was auctioned off and his house in Cheyne Walk let go. The library included first editions of works by Yeats, George Moore, T.E. Lawrence and J.M. Synge. Horace also planned a selling exhibition of his Innes paintings, which numbered over forty and had been on loan to the Tate since the war. In return for £50, Augustus generously offered to write the catalogue preface, as 'it would make *all* the difference to sales', he claimed. Sadly such stop-gap measures could never fill the gaping hole in Horace's finances. What he needed was a job. His sister Annie helpfully suggested he write a poem every month for a magazine. Instead, he fancied going 'on the films', where he had lots of good contacts. Strangely, for one so supremely confident when playing a role in a joke, he lacked the self-belief to pursue either course. All he really had to sell was wit and a fraying reputation.

After winning a competition at his club for making up the best gossip column in the style of a Sunday newspaper, he toyed with becoming a journalist, as 'I know I can amuse people [and] I have a good memory'. The difficulty was that his upbringing had demanded discretion and good manners, and though he knew plenty of juicy stories, 'I'd never journalise them'. He never even answered an invitation from the *Sunday Express* to tell his own story. Being deaf reduced his ability for picking up stories and his ability to tell them. 'I have no idea how people talk at all, and dialogue is 90% of the business of *saleable* writing nowadays.' Turning the handle of a barrel organ in Piccadilly was the only thing he felt qualified to do.

'It's an idea!' he bitterly told Jim, 'I would put my balance sheet on the organ: the amounts I owed, and the amount I was taxed in Canada; and advise no one to be fool enough to invest in that country while the politicians protected and favoured the dagos of the Argentine and their Jew backers in England.' After years of pestering from publishers, he did finally resolve to write his autobiography, encouraged by Lady Gregory, who told him that 'all the de Veres could write like ducks could swim'. One positive step he took was to return to the East End to volunteer his services as a teacher of English literature and poetry at the Central Foundation School in Shoreditch. His career in the classroom was shortlived, but still memorable enough for one old boy, the late Sidney Carr, to quote fondly his unconventional teacher's paradoxical favourite saying—'All men are fishermen and liars and I'm a great fisherman'—for the next seventy years. Late in the day Horace was trying, the only way he knew how, to mend his ways. But it was energy-sapping.

The drinking, which had spiralled out of hand long ago, looked easier to fix. Horace made a pact with the equally inebriate Augustus—on pain of a £100 forfeit—to drink only (only!) wine, cider, sherry and aperitifs like Dubonnet. Spirits were banned, 'an exception only to be made in case of severe illness and on such an occasion that a doctor should prescribe brandy, rum or whisky'. (One imagines the doctor was called for almost immediately.) More realistically, Horace planned a marathon walk through France, similar to his Italian exploits at another moment of personal crisis back in 1909. The lonely rhythm of walking had always restored his equilibrium, while the sun and air might rejuvenate his damaged spirit. More than ever, he needed to escape on the open road, as if every step would take him away from the creeping reality of his situation. Somewhat to Horace's surprise, Augustus, who was between painting commissions and had a house in Provence, agreed to join him, with unfortunate consequences. Designed to be therapeutic, the walking holiday quickly descended into competition then farce as each man vied to outdo the other physically and in their ability to attract girls in the villages they passed through. Horace was initially scathing of Augustus's fitness, noting how hard he sweated, got blisters and was sick from all the exertion (and cheap wine). But slowly his rival earned his grudging respect for his stamina and determination. Eventually Augustus almost seemed to enjoy the challenge, having 'fallen against his preconceived ideas into the line of swinging along the road'.

The artist A.R. Thomson, who caught up with the pair for part of the journey, called them 'John' and 'Super-John' as they strode determinedly along the dusty lanes of Southern

Horace and Augustus in a rare moment of harmony on their walking tour of the South of France (Tristan de Vere Cole).

France, often by moonlight and under 'great flocks of stars'. Horace's main worry was being run over,

> owing to the way French drivers try and see how near to you they can go. Luckily I always jump the right way for I rarely hear a hoot till its owner is just on me, and *then* it sounds like the last trumpet, which it may well be one day: the Almighty, some great machine, speaking with a million million power Claxton throat.

In rare moments of companionship the two men discussed art, poetry and literature. Augustus walked along reciting aloud *Mireille* by the Provençal poet Frédéric Mistral, and near Aix pointed out Mont St Victoire, which Cézanne 'never grew tired of painting'. Horace recalled seeing Cézanne's card-players on exhibition in London and sensing 'something intensely realised'. Comparisons with their dead friend Innes, with his feverish renditions of Arenig, were unavoidable. Then Augustus lectured Horace about Rembrandt, his claim that the painter was 'cut by all his friends and wife's relations on account of the company he kept', striking uncomfortably close to home. Like many old friends, they enjoyed sparring in this way. In the case of Augustus and Horace there was also an undercurrent of deep jealousy as two inflated egos clashed. Each considered the other vain and conceited. Augustus resented Horace's 'excessive vanity', while Horace always thought Augustus got 'too much flattery'. On one thing they openly disagreed. Augustus viewed gypsies as romantic and inspiring, whereas Horace saw them as dirty and stupid.

After a week and a hundred and fifty miles of hard walking the friends sailed across the Étang de Berre to Augustus's villa at Martigues. Horace was scathing about the adulation afforded to Augustus by his neighbours, many of them amateur artists (the worst sort). 'They fawn too much and he flies them,' he told

The only known portrait of Horace, drawn by Augustus in France, 1926
(Tristan de Vere Cole).

his mother. Here they parted: Augustus to paint and Horace to continue alone to Corsica, Algeria and Tunis. Perhaps he hoped by retracing his youthful steps that he might recover his zest and vigour. He certainly landed himself in some familiar fixes. After spending some days alone in the desert, he lost his money and papers in a bizarre accident on a train. His bag 'went off the rack and through the carriage window (which was shut). Holy Hell, I had 22 francs 50 centimes on me! Great scene. French officer unnecessarily officious. Explained to him he was so. Inspector came.' Poor man, he had no idea who he was facing. Horace blustered and bluffed his way out of trouble before catching the first boat back to Marseilles with barely a franc to his name. Then, reluctantly and with a heavy heart, he turned north for home.

23

Apart from sex
There's life beyond:
Below, you'll find
The demi-monde.

Horace was back in London. But it was no longer *his* London, nor he the centre of attention. 'Vulgarity is received everywhere if it has financial backing!' he exclaimed in horror. Talent, wit, class and manners no longer seemed to matter. In short, everything was more democratic. Clubs he didn't recognise were full of 'bright young things' he didn't know. To them, Edwardian London was as stuffy and irrelevant as Victorian London had once seemed to him. Even the fabled Café Royal had been given an art deco makeover, stripping away its odour, colour and character. Horace preferred Oddenino's restaurant nearby, founded by a former manager of the Café Royal, though his budget barely stretched to supper nearby at a Lyon's corner house. Fancy-dress balls and practical joking were as popular as ever, but now the focus was entirely on pleasure-seeking not provocative demonstration. Everyone seemed to be at it. The war had knocked out half a generation and the will to take anything seriously ever again. The edginess, purpose and flair of the pre-war years had gone. At sophisticated clubs like the Cave of Harmony, the Embassy and the 43, people drank and danced simply to forget. Many of these, often shortlived, clubs were managed by the indefatigable Kate Meyrick, who had grown up in a house in Ireland called Fairyland. Meyrick played cat and mouse with the licensing authorities throughout the twenties. Not always successfully, for she was imprisoned several times, sometimes with hard labour.

When Cecil Beaton and friends—attired in flowery waist-coats, full-bottomed skirts and powdered wigs—tipped out into Piccadilly after attending a Mozart-themed fancy-dress ball and started to dig up the road as Horace once had, they did so in mock homage to a bygone era and to a man they had heard their parents talking about. Horace was a relic, a has-been, famed for once being famous. He had even lost a little of the old spirit of rebellion. Seeing Richard Nevinson at the Café Royal now only reminded him to have a hair cut. He was a curio-sity, an upper-class eccentric who could still catch the eye of the gossip columns, but only when he fell down the stairs drunk at a party. Horace, once the brightest spark of his generation, had dimmed. Duller contemporaries now attracted the praise and garnered the accolades. Augustus bragged that 'I go from triumph to triumph. In addition to being regarded as a sort of Old Master, I have now been publicly accepted as a modern!' Even the ludicrous Willy Fisher (or 'the Lord High Admiral Sir William Wilberforce Fisher B.O.W.-W.O.W. etc', as Horace labelled him) now occupied high office at the Admiralty. Were the hoaxes and fights at the Café Royal all in vain? In short, everyone seemed to agree, Horace had had his day.

Looking back, Horace appears to be invisible for much of the twenties as if his light went out. The paper trail, already thin, runs out and the anecdotes dry up. But he was not quite finished. Not yet. If no longer young, he was at least free again, and single, and determined still to enjoy himself. He could still teach the young a thing or two. The *Sunday Express* loyally backed him. 'Despite the "Bright Young Things",' pronounced

Postcard of Horace in the late twenties: still enjoying his fame but not his fortune (Tristan de Vere Cole).

its gossip columnist Lord Castlerosse (an Anglo-Irish peer and friend of Horace), 'it is a long time since there was a really big rag in London, as in the days of Horace Cole.' He joined the Gargoyle Club—David Tennant's chic establishment in Dean Street, Soho—to maintain a presence. The club self-consciously played on pre-war bohemianism, encouraging ageing artists like Augustus to mingle with the rising stars such as Ed Burra and Noel Coward. In reality it was a bit of a freak show, where interlopers from the suburbs could come and gawp at the wrinkled specimens from a distant age. Commercially, they added stature and curiosity-value to the place. Horace soon grew tired of all this. He needed one last, great passion and adventure away from the surface gloss of twenties London. 'I'd like to clear off and see the Pacific for two or three years. I don't feel too old, and feel quite interested enough,' he confided to Augustus. But always he was pulled back by lack of money and Valerie.

He had no home, and having resigned his club was forced to stay in a series of lodgings culminating in a room at the Royal Court Hotel, Sloane Square. He was phlegmatic about the decline in his circumstances. He had always led an itinerant existence on the fringes of other people's more settled lives. There was even some romance in it. Many of the painters, poets and writers he most admired led irregular lives. It felt decadent and real. For a time it seems his situation steadied. Debts were cleared and he was able to survive on a greatly reduced but still sufficient income of £150 a month (perhaps £1000 in today's terms). He tried to live up to his responsibilities, sending Valerie to school in Cambridge and posing as a good father. He started playing squash and real tennis again, and took up his seat in the pavilion at Lord's, where he winked at the King, met old Etonian cronies like Reggie Bastard and sampled again a life he had long ago rejected.

Then came the death of his mother, the only person, Horace told Aunt Eily, he had ever really loved. With her loss, he lost his bearings again. The bond between Mary and her eldest son had been so much deeper than with her other children. Perhaps it was his early illness, his distress at his father's death or his vulnerable romantic nature which drew her sympathy and the focus of her greatest love. She believed in his poetry, telling Horace his poems were better than her own. When she said this, he knew she was being kind, as her own talent was so obvious and real. Only modesty, he thought, had prevented her becoming a truly great writer on a par with Yeats. Her death broke his tie to Ireland. He had no desire ever to return to the blood-soaked and treacherous country of his birth, nor did he. Issercleran was taken on by Jim Cole who, unlike Horace, had the wherewithal to look after the house and estate. 'Imagination and memory is enough for me,' Horace said sadly.

With his mother's death, the old demons and the urgent need for dangerous company returned. Horace had always sought, sometimes fought, to be the centre of attention, as if he only felt alive in the company of others. Unfortunately, even in the 1920s his divorced status locked him out of many of the drawing-rooms of Mayfair, while evenings playing billiards at the Chelsea Arts Club with friends like painter Arnold

Horace's mother Mary Studd, said to be the only woman he had ever loved (John Cole).

Mason seemed too staid. A kindly European aristocrat called Prince Maximilian Lobkowitz latched onto him and gave an introduction to the rackety world of post-war exiled nobility (with lands and a castle in Czechoslovakia, the Prince could also claim to be genuinely Bohemian).

There was one place where he need not feel old or passé or excluded. This was the Eiffel Tower restaurant in Percy Street: the beating heart of what became known as Fitzrovia. Here pre-war *demi-mondaines* like Nina Hamnett gathered to console themselves alongside new blood like Tallulah Bankhead, Cecil Beaton and 'It' girl Brenda Dean Paul. The Eiffel Tower had been going for years under the benevolent eye of its oleaginous and increasingly decrepit Austrian proprietor Rudolph Stulik. But it was only now, with its fading aspidistras and crimson velour seats rubbed bare by a thousand bohemian bottoms that it had finally attained a certain nostalgic chic. Its reassuringly steep prices kept the riff-raff out (if Augustus was there you could always cadge off him), and if you were really lucky you could disappear to one of the bedrooms upstairs with your dining partner—or someone else's. No restaurant has been more widely written about. In a rare moment of harmony, the Vorticists were painted in it; Nancy Cunard composed a poem about it, and Michael Arlen, who drove a canary-yellow Rolls Royce and warmed to Horace, based his bestselling novel *Piracy* around it. With longing for lost youth, Horace made his own contribution to this niche genre:

> 'Neath the palms and ferny bowers
> Gathered here are mighty powers;
> Monde artistic; monde that's stagey;
> Monde at the moment all the ragey;
> Dobson's nose; and Dobson's grin
> All, at the appointed hour,
> Eating at the Eiffel Tower!

Here you'll see Augustus John,
Like a shade from Erewhon
Piercing eye and forehead lofty
Here is no artistic softy
Forged his way to drink and fame
By the grandeur of his name,
By his craftsmanship and power
Lofty as the Eiffel Tower!

Here are Ministers and Princes,
Artichokes and juicy quinces,
Underneath lights alabaster
And a ceiling made of plaster
Guests of Rudolph, all are they,
Those who do, or do not, pay;
For the grapes are never sour
At the sign of Eiffel Tower!

The Vorticists at the Restaurant de la Tour Eiffel: Spring 1915 by William
Roberts. Ezra Pound is seated second from the left, Wyndham Lewis in
the centre, and Rudolph Stulik is standing right (© Tate, London, 2010).

Who is it you wish to gaze on?
Artist with the latest craze on?
Exile king or royal suckling
Slopping peas, or Stulik duckling
Birkenhead or Freddy Guest?
Rudolph always has the best:
Britain's beauty, Britain's flower,
Always at the Eiffel Tower.

Over there Tallulah Bankhead
Sups, before she seeks her lank-bed,
With a pretty girl beside her;
But as red wine is to cider
Is Tallulah's girl to me;
Were I young, and rich, and free,
I could never her deflower
Even at the Eiffel Tower.

The restaurant hosted an affecting scene one evening in the late twenties when Iris Tree invited Adrian Stephen—who Horace hadn't seen since the war—to join her, Horace and Viva King for supper. Horace could not resist playing the fool, and when his old comrade-in-arms arrived he pretended to be a German professor, adopting an accent in imitation of the hastily improvised one used by Adrian on the *Dreadnought*. 'He hasn't changed much in ten years!' Adrian remarked, poignantly. Yet everything else had.

24

*J*t was not at the Eiffel Tower that Horace had his epiphany but back at the scene of his greatest triumphs: the Café Royal. Dropping into the Café one June evening in 1928 for a drink with Arnold Mason, Horace noticed a young girl. With 'absolute clearness and certainty' he knew instantly that she was destined for him and him alone. 'It seemed wrong and it was wrong,' he told himself, that she was with another man. She was nineteen, wide-eyed and beautiful with, according to Reggie Bastard (a shrewd judge of the female form), 'The finest figure I ever saw in my life' (later she won a competition at the Eiffel Tower for the 'finest concealed charms'). She was called Mavis Wright, having—like many girls up from the sticks and on the make in those days—changed her first name from the less salubrious Mabel. She worked over the road from the Café Royal at Veeraswamy's Indian restaurant. Though still young, it was by no means her first employment. After a straightened childhood in Cambridgeshire, where her feckless father had relocated his family from the East End, Mavis had worked in a factory printing labels for jam jars, then as a scullery maid and latterly as nurse to the children of a vicar in Wimbledon who had tried to seduce her.

In time-honoured fashion, she had gravitated to the West End, where her looks and disarming manner had secured the job at Veeraswamy's and the attention of many men. Mavis knew the value of her looks. She told Horace 'she was going to get money value for her physical charms' and that she was often 'offered alluring sums in cash in return for her favours'.

Some of which she may have accepted. And who could blame her? All she had in the world was a cotton coat and skirt, a few odds and ends wrapped in paper parcels and 'a very smart pair of shoes—given her'. Poverty made her respect money in a way Horace never had, or could.

I doubt Mavis had heard of Horace. She was an infant at the time of the *Dreadnought* hoax, and he did not feature in the picture magazines she liked to flick through. On the face of it, there was not much to recommend Horace, with his 'grey hairs and descending bulges'. Strangely, however, this was part of his appeal. For a girl adrift in London, preyed on by untrustworthy men, Horace's age was reassuring, his maturity comforting. He was also celebrated and commanding, with

a winning aristocratic manner (class mattered a lot to a girl like Mavis). Moreover, unlike the cluster of men around her, he seemed to be interested in more than simply sex. He actually appeared fascinated by her, intrigued by her past and encouraging of her future.

The attraction of Mavis for Horace was irresistible. '*You never seemed a stranger to me,*' he would write. Mavis reminded him of the girls he had known in the slums around Toynbee Hall.

Mabel Wright, the waitress at Veeraswamy's who 'never seemed a stranger' to Horace (Tristan de Vere Cole).

They had aroused him then, but he had been unable to pursue them for reasons of social position and his own once-glittering prospects, both factors no longer in his way. Unlike the disapproving waiters at the Café Royal, he was charmed when she put sugar into her claret to sweeten it, or tried to mask her accent, or sat in eager but ignorant silence as the men droned on about art and aesthetic, absorbing everything. And when she looked at him and toasted 'Horatio Mio' or playfully tugged his coat-tails, he felt his heart splinter with love and pity. After Denise, he thought he would never fall in love again. He had told Augustus as much. With Mavis, life could begin again, and from now until his death there is a welter of surviving correspondence; a sudden late blooming of feeling and emotion.

It would be easy to see Horace simply as Henry Higgins and Mavis as Eliza Doolittle. Perhaps he cast the two of them in these roles himself, recalling his own childish performances of Gilbert's *Pygmalion* at West Woodhay. This early adaptation of a Greek myth portrayed an artist falling in love with his sculpture after it comes to life as an innocent and untutored young woman. There was an illicit thrill in the sexual union between high- and low-born. Horace undoubtedly strove to 'improve' Mavis's poorly educated but highly intelligent mind.

> You write delightful if slightly ungrammatical letteroos and you should never begin a sentence with 'well'. You can see in the 'News of the World' scores of letters in breach of promise or slander or murder or suicide cases written with 'Well's starred about them. I firmly believe that all elementary and secondary (and tertiary if there are any) schoolmasters and schoolmistresses dote on this word and tell their wretched pupils it is good English. It is not!

Yet he vigorously defended her looks and unaffected manner against the snide comments of friends and family. Jim Cole's suggestion that Mavis was 'common', looked 'improper' and wouldn't be 'received' in polite society provoked a furious response, made worse as Horace struggled to suppress the snob deep within himself. He told his brother,

> I know her accent is common, though not her voice. She acquired a wrong accent when young as some children acquire a brogue (which was considered common for an Irish lady) and it is very hard to get rid of. The pronunciation is bad, but not the voice. But even then it is only bad from the point of hearing of the upper middle and middle middle classes.

He liked her long fingernails, use of make-up 'to amuse herself' and hair loosely piled up rather than primly crimped and curled, as was the fashion. He took a great interest in her clothes, down to the colour of her stockings (mauve being his favourite). Grace was a product of nature not class, he stoutly maintained. Witness, he said, the society darlings Alison and Margaret Hore-Ruthven, twin daughters of Lord Ruthven, who he had recently seen at a dinner looking 'improper AND common, though they are "ladies"'. In contrast, the daughters of the infamous and much-reviled Kate Meyrick both married into the peerage and were highly respected.

Notwithstanding the fictional comparisons, the relationship which developed between Horace and Mavis was more complicated and ultimately destructive than the one portrayed in *Pygmalion*. It was founded not on exploitation but on their different yet complementary needs, meeting in genuine affection. Nor was the gulf in years as disconcerting to a generation decimated by war than it may appear to us; despite Horace's calculation, which he shared with Augustus, that 'when I am sixty, she'll be but thirty three' (he never reached that landmark). The speed with which their lives became fatally entangled was breathtaking. Headstrong as ever, Horace whisked Mavis away to Cambridge to woo her. They carved their initials on a tree like love-struck teenagers and, as is obvious from Horace's letters, they slept together. She was his Mavista; he her Horatio Bunganoosie, or Bungo for short (presumably an echo of the catchphrase for the *Dreadnought* hoax). She wrote him sexually charged love letters submitting herself to the erotic fantasy he wove of her enslavement to him. '*My* breasts *love* the Ouse,' she wrote from her parent's home in St Ives, 'after a dip therein they are as hard as bullets and raise their nipples to the sun and cry or rather scream for their mistress's Lord to come and caress them.'

Horace gave the affair a heroic flavour, a struggle against the odds from some medieval romance. They were Abelard and Heloise, fighting for an impossible love. On Mavis's behalf, he even drafted a mock appeal for mercy. 'Ever since my eyes first beheld thee I have been under the spell of that handsome mien and noble mind. I have not looked at another man nor could I ever again gaily flirt with others as I used to do, and as for my lips touching those of any man but thee— ah! Slay me first!' (Surely only Horace could have used the expression 'handsome mien' in the 1920s.) The lovers were building 'grand memories'. Horace pictured them living in a cottage with books and art and each other. They would make a life away from London and nightclubs and temptation. They would turn their back on the glossy and superficial, and when Canada recovered, Horace would give Mavis the life she deserved. Everything was falling into place, according to this fantasy, the same one he had played out with Denise. He proposed marriage even though he was still waiting to be granted the decree absolute in his divorce.

Mavis said no. Or she might have said yes, then no. She found Horace very different in London to the caring and gentle lover of the country. When among his drinking companions, Horace would ponder aloud his future within earshot of Mavis. 'What d'ye think? Ought I to marry this gal? I know she's totally amoral and totally ignorant and as sure as eggs she'll be unfaithful the first chance she gets...Should I take her on, eh? What d'ye think?' The anecdote typifies the glaring inconsistency between Horace's bullying public and his reflective private personas. Even facing ruin and the loss of future happiness, he still felt the need to live up to a role he had cast for himself long before Mavis was even born. He felt unable to stop himself, but it must have hurt and humiliated Mavis. Even Augustus complained. After bumping into Horace and Mavis at a Southampton hotel—triggering a late-night drinking session—he moaned about his friend's 'exaggerated stories and LIES that made him sick not the drink'. Dora Carrington, also present that evening, was more amused than shocked. 'There is no pleasing this younger generation,' she retorted briskly. 'After all an evening with Cole is an experience.' There would not be many more for the friends to share.

Worse still, Horace became insanely jealous of Mavis, and violently disposed towards any man who threatened to take her away, or even looked at her. 'The admiring and even questioning glances of men more of her age,' he confessed to Augustus, 'ignore them as she may, must make my grey hairs crinkle and sparkle with indignation.' It was the usual problem of insecurity that had seen him burst into houses and cause fights for years. Mavis had hesitated over the age difference, asking her family for advice, but it was Horace's behaviour and his legal status as a married man that made his proposal impossible to accept. She began an affair with another man and pushed Horace and his dream away. Horace was confused and distraught. The pain was amplified by the realisation of his culpability. He sent Mavis a plaintive letter, full of remorse. It is instructive on how he courted women and how pitifully he reacted to rejection, so I quote it at length.

I write because I must and because I am so deeply fond of you with a fondness of love that runs through my blood and permeates my whole being. No man can be mistaken about such a feeling for it comes from his immortal part, his soul. With all my soul I love you…You have told me how you feel and I accept it and I hate and loathe myself for it. I think all might have been different if I had not been such an unutterable fool. Truly I would rather have killed myself than have killed your love, for I do think you did love me, although you say now that you only thought you did. This can't be so with a girl of your fine character and sensibility, you must have loved me; the only wonder is that it stood the shocks I gave it…Fondness without passion is not enough; is impossible if one of the two feels passion as well, and my whole body is most passionately yours, as it always has been without a single back thought since we met in June. If I had been free we should now be married, for you would have married me. The difficulties of the position have mastered and beaten us and have led to our quarrels. You said once, and truly said, that if we were living together we would not quarrel. You were right, but I was blind and could not see the truth you saw when you did love me.

Our marriage would have meant an end to the life we led and its surroundings for we would have had a home and things to build our lives on. You would have met all sorts of pleasant people and made all sorts of new friends amongst those who are worthwhile. I hate to feel you are at a loose end. You have such beauty and such character and you will grow up into a splendid woman. But since you are untrained there is so little for you. With your beauty you can easily find a job but will it be a job that is worthwhile? I have broken the thing I loved…Again and again you have told me that you love the country and early hours. And so do I. You have only seen me in the wrong setting. You and I have a very great deal in common, but I always took you the wrong way. Plenty of leisure, books, a garden and a home and all one's own things is my desire but I cannot do it alone. I am a lonely man. You are lonely too. And we neither of us crave for excitement really. We could both have been happy with the same things. As for my not allowing you all liberty, that would be impossible now. That jealous madness has passed, my love is more serene and embraces and soars above passion. You could do as you chose if only I felt that all the while a part of your heart was mine and that you were fond of me and looked to me as your husband and friend and companion in life. I had hoped against hope that there was no one else…I thought you had given me your heart and that you were not one who would easily change, and not anyway change back. I know now that I was unkind to you because you loved me and I loved you and tortured myself. This could never have been again for I understand now that real suffering is the only way to get an insight and a cleansing of oneself.

Believe me, your loving Horatio B.

Mavis resisted this pathetic clamour. She left Horace to slip back into his old ways, miserably marking time in nightclubs until he was free to marry and his fortunes improved. Night after night he sought solace at the Eiffel Tower before moving on to the Gargoyle, where he could regale the mocking young with tales of his former antics. That life had long since gone, with his fame. Irène Dean Paul, the polish wife of a baronet whose wayward, drug-addicted daughter Brenda transfixed the gossip columnists, caught Horace's mood in a poem:

Horace sat a-dreaming beside a simple stream
Of wedding bells and maidens,
It was such a pretty dream!
Of life 'à deux' in Devon, upon some jolly farm

Where every day was heaven
And nought could do no harm,
Of simple little lambkins, a browsing in the Spring
And a pretty wife, doing such a pretty thing

The only thing that matters,
like making cottage pie
In a dainty dress in tatters
And the love light in her eye

The simple life he needed
When all might play and sing
And no-one ever heeded
If you did the simplest thing

And simple little children
In simple little draws
Or, simpler still, without them
Simply messing on the floors!

Then Horace shed a single tear
Which fell into a stream
Which babbled off to tell the wood
About his simple dream

But though the wood quite understood
How simple were his dreams
It answered back, Alas! Alack!
Life *is not* what it seems.

While Horace moped about in London, his money was fast draining away in Canada on falling rents and the refurbishment costs. 'Saskatoon buildings,' as Horace ruefully remarked, 'are not built to last forever like dear old Issercleran.' One building had been destroyed by fire in 1925 and the others were still uncompleted and not fully let. Bills were going unpaid, Valerie's school fees were in arrears, he risked being sued by his Irish creditors, and he was racking up large personal debts to friends like Jasper Ridley and George Colthurst. He was bankrupt in all but name. 'How dreadful are money worries,' he forlornly commented, 'and once on a time I never had them! Lucky me those days!' The family solicitor Sir Bernard Bircham assumed power of attorney in a desperate bid to get Horace's chaotic affairs in order, as he appeared powerless to help himself. He knew he was in a 'gorgeous fix', but he had no idea how to get out of it. Living his whole life on private means, he had never considered the possibility of one day having to earn money, or even of saving it. In similar straits his cousin Freddy Shaw, son of Aunt Eily, who had enjoyed an equally pampered life before the war, had swallowed his pride and started work as a travelling salesman for Crosse and Blackwell. It never occurred to Horace (or, to be fair, most of the hard-pressed British upper classes) to do the same. He pinned all his hopes on matters improving in Canada (which they never did) and on the goodwill of others. His last remaining assets were his paintings, though these were difficult to sell in the midst of the financial depression. 'It's the devil and all his black legion of angels!' he exclaimed in a despairing letter to his brother Jim.

This period of doleful reflection did bring some benefits. It allowed time for Horace's mad passion for Mavis to soften and gather meaning. She too, disappointed by a failed love affair, was drawn back to the cosy image of marital bliss that Horace had conjured up. They started to see each other again. This time Horace was more cautious and conciliatory, and unusually sensitive to her feelings. Aware it was his last chance, he was anxious to do the right thing. He shared his thoughts with Augustus:

> Mavis is, I think, truly in love. I think she really cares, surprising as it may seem, and it might last...I believe part of my attraction for her is my grey waviness of scalp fungae. Anyway I have to find a home sometime for Valerie and can no more disappear irresponsibly into Corsica or the Café Royal. So why not lay two birds in the same nest? Also I am getting poorer and should have to support two wardrobes of two young females intensely interested in dress. Mavis makes most of her garments now and does it marvellous well and enjoys doing it. But as a wife she might desist and I doubt if a husband could then insist. And there might be long-clothes. I have never had your once insatiable desire for self-reproduction. I don't want or need it. Maybe you thought that a genius should do his best to raise the race standard. Are you satisfied? Beethoven was not the

son of a genius though music seems to be inherited more than any other form of art. Mavis would never be satisfied without a son or even two, and Valerie is too old for little brothers. The class muddle of uncle, aunts and grandmothers I consider least of all.

If I was thirty six and free, I'd marry Mavis. But I'm forty eight and in sole charge of one very Irish and very alive child who loves me in her own way. But maybe I mean more to Mavis. I may be *dans sa peau*...Send me some words of consolation and advice when you have time off from work; from flower painting, and fruit eating. I need them. I'D LIKE AND VALUE some sober and considered advice from you, but I doubt if I'll get it. I do not really care what happens. One big thing has happened and dwarfs all other happenings. But I know some things are of importance and that I have a responsibility towards Valerie and, in a way, also towards Mavis...So why not get Mavis and Valerie together and a house in France and enjoy boredom and happiness and quarrellings and infidelities and all the other ingredients of the family pie?'

Referring to the pederast habits of his aristocratic acquaintance Lord Tredegar, Horace confessed to feeling 'Evan Morganed if I know what to do'. His family were unanimously against any suggestion of marriage, yet they also feared the social opprobrium of Horace and Mavis living together unmarried, even though, as Horace retorted, 'many people did live together in secret and in open adultery and it made no difference socially.' His half-sister Mary spent a whole day trying to talk him out of marriage, but gave up in despair when Horace loudly asked a passing waiter for his opinion on the matter. His family's disapproval—and a malicious anonymous letter from St Ives warning of Mavis's reputation—simply hardened Horace's resolve. Jim's highly critical comments about Mavis's class and her looks only 'reminded me of Uncle Alfred'. As soon as he got his decree absolute—'and so am FREE! Which sounds like "Wilhemina Sketch" of the "Daily Stitch"'—he proposed again to Mavis. This time she accepted. He was ecstatic and bewildered at the turn in his fortunes.

> Marriage seems lunacy even to such a nice and simple girl as my Woffly Wooff, for you should have a lovely trousseau and some jewels and various nice and expensive odds and ends and an expensive honeymoon in Sicily or Capri or Naples (under Vesuvius) instead of linking yourself to an old man who is sitting on a financial Vesuvius, is old enough to be your father and deaf enough to be your bed-post. You are, I believe, making a mistake, but Heaven help me from giving advice to girls!

Only time would tell.

25

'OAXER "KING" TO WED', blazed the *Daily Express* on 28 January 1931 above a lengthy piece on Horace and Mavis's nuptials. The item was trailed on the front page of the newspaper with a photo of Mavis, 'a tall, graceful girl with golden hair and brown eyes'. However, readers anxious to know the day of the ceremony were disappointed. '"No, I'll not tell you the date of my wedding," said Mr Horace de Vere Cole, King of Practical Jokers to a "Daily Express" representative yesterday, "There are too many friends of mine waiting to get their own back".' He was right to fear revenge. As the *Express* reminded its readers, in one of his celebrated jokes Horace had arranged for a dozen pretty girls to gather outside a church. When the bridegroom arrived, they had flung their arms around him screaming, 'Don't leave me, Eddy,' causing the bride's relations to plead a cancellation of the wedding.

The date did slip out, forcing Horace to arrive at Chelsea Registry Office three days later wearing a large false beard. He had almost made it past the waiting crowd when he was spotted and pursued inside. There he met Mavis, who had forgotten to remove her hair-curlers and was carrying a bouquet of daffodils. Her brown dress was topped by a jacket crafted out of the 'snorter' of a fur coat Horace had worn in his prime (Denise had already removed its collar to make a stole). After all the pre-nuptial excitement the ceremony itself was short and impersonal, lacking the glamour, colour and humour of Horace's first marriage. If it was not entirely the sort of wedding Mavis had dreamed of as a child—or the husband she had envisaged—she gamely entered into the spirit of the occasion. 'In future we shall joke in double harness,' she told journalists outside. 'He must do at least five more jokes to reach his century and I don't intend to stop him.' Afterwards, a small hastily assembled reception was hosted by Max Lobkowitz at his apartment in Sloane Square. None of Horace's family attended. His sister Annie pleaded the press of her husband's political business in Birmingham, though she sent her love and congratulations. Jim was now farming in Ireland, while Valerie languished at school in Cambridge.

Horace's financial downfall was almost complete. So why did Mavis marry him? Even Horace was mystified. 'What can you want with a rather decrepit, rather poor and rather sad middle aged man?' he asked her. She had her reasons. He had been a very persuasive suitor and a needy one too, playing on her natural sympathies. Most of all, he had created a vision of herself entirely different from the one she saw reflected in the opinions of other people. He offered romance and poetry

Mrs Mavis de Vere Cole: 'in future we shall joke in double harness' (Tristan de Vere Cole).

and boundless, unbridled love. These were things no one else in the Café Royal, or indeed anywhere else, had ever shown her. Horace was not perfect, but he offered her a world she had only glimpsed in books and on film. Her new name resonated class and breeding, and when the money returned she might be propelled to the forefront of society. This is why she married Horace. And why, as her son Tristan remembers, Mavis always fiercely defended Horace's behaviour against the ill-mannered jibes of Augustus. So she willingly joined him on his flight from reality.

This meant running from his debts. The world of make-believe Horace had spun in his mind for so long had finally collided with the brutal truth of his situation. He could no longer afford even a room at the Royal Court Hotel. Believing they would soon return to England, but perhaps knowing somehow he never would, Horace dumped his last few remaining possessions into storage and spirited his young wife away to France, where they could live for a third of the cost of London. He felt no shame at his escape, failing to see the abyss opening up before him. Exile in France had exciting (but also ominous) echoes of Oscar Wilde's fate. And was not the Côte d'Azur already crowded with honest Englishmen down on their luck? The casinos were packed with sons of the nobility gambling the proceeds of the sale of estates taken from them by the taxman. Had he gone to Paris he could have encountered any number of friendly faces at his old bohemian haunts. He decided to enjoy his freedom from the grime and worry of London, with its disapproving glances, unpaid bills and petty rules. This was his great test of moral courage, a life-defining moment to realise principles he had expressed in a poem years before:

Virtues are a sorry crew
Of make-believe and sham
Though we grow old, 'tis nothing new
We're wicked from our pram
Virtues 'on principle' drive me mad,
By instinct we are good or bad;
Man's nature cannot altered be,
He's chained to his heredity!
Still if you really want to know
What virtue I would most desire,
'Tis that which faces Fortune's blow
With mien proud and head held higher.

Buoyed up by the prospect of starting afresh with a new wife, and inspired by the epic qualities of his situation, Horace took Mavis to Ascain, the small village in the Pays Basque where he had holidayed as a child. It was 'a place of memories' and a refuge. The rugged, untamed landscape matched his temperament, while the sea over the horizon met a deep-seated need. 'I have NEVER been contented in any country that is *flat*, or out of sight or sound of the *sea*,' he told Mavis. 'That it's *there* is all that matters. Like some people one loves and knows well. One cannot be with them, but one knows they are in the world.' They checked in to the hotel beside the village square where the de Veres had always stayed. Horace liked the 'Soft footed Basque maidens, ox-eyed' who attended him there. The Hotel Etchola was still under the same management, and he was warmly welcomed back by *la Patronne*, Madame Freville. To her, he was still a man of substance. She waved aside the age difference between him and Mavis. "'What of it? That's no matter, has she money for hats and dresses for herself? Is she *aimable*? Does she really love you? Well if this is so, you have, Monsieur Cole, ten years of happiness before you become old.'"

The newly-weds settled into a comfortable double bedroom at the top of the house, with their own bathroom and view of

La Rhune. By turn bleak or bathed in sunlight, this mountain became his mirror on the world. Below their window was the village square, with its Pelota court and benches where silent old men sat and smoked in the evenings. Horace treated their stay as an extended honeymoon. They ate well and often. A typical lunch consisted of 'soup (a gallon bowl) hors d'oeuvres, black sausage in apple sauce, veal (that melted in the mouth) salads, spinach, camembert, apples and chocolate cake'. He walked Mavis up La Rhune and down to the coast. He gave her books to read and poetry to learn, as he said he would. But not much happened in Ascain, and there was a nagging sense, acutely apparent to Mavis but not her worldlier husband, that life was going on elsewhere: down the hill at St Jean de Luz, perhaps, or along the coast at Biarritz. She hated the wagging tongues and stares in the street from people who had known Horace for years. Speaking no French, she was forced into the company of middle-aged female expatriates. Far from the glamour she had expected, St Jean was full of seedy retired majors and wife-swopping Americans. The writer Cyril

The Hotel Etchola, beside the Pelota court, in Ascain, where Horace took Mavis (Tristan de Vere Cole).

Connolly caught the sordid existence of these social refugees perfectly in his 1936 novel *The Rock Pool*. When Valerie—the fees for her English schooling hopelessly in arrears—then joined them in exile the difficulties only escalated. Horace was torn between the demands of his wife and the needs of his bewildered daughter, who had been told she was going to France for a short holiday. Balancing both on diminishing resources was beyond him.

Valerie's arrival shattered the illusion of a honeymoon and the intimacy of Horace and Mavis's situation. It also made it impossible to remain any longer at the Hotel Etchola. In October 1932, leaving their hotel bill unpaid, the unhappy trio moved over the road into an apartment in a wooden-framed villa called Hiriartia. To give a semblance of normal family life, Horace acquired a cat, took out a subscription to the local library and settled down to write his autobiography. But husband and wife slept in separate rooms, and the rows soon started up again, sharpened now by drink and bitterness. Mavis cried most nights, and on one occasion, while out shopping with Valerie, she apparently threatened to throw herself in front of a car. In a letter to Horace a concerned Ascain resident, an American artist called Ferdinand Earle, praised his neighbour's 'charming and seductive personality, brainy and brilliant'. Yet he also complained of Horace's 'quixotic (and somewhat monotonous and boring) mannerisms' and his 'tragic habit of celebrating daily to the appointed saint of the hour'. ('I presume he thinks I am a confirmed drunkard,' snorted Horace.)

Earle continued,

> When you start making personal remarks, which you will admit can easily become tiresome, one must either ignore what you say, or yell a reply, owing to your infirmity. And for that reason, if for no other, you should refrain from over-exercising that (rather doubtful) wittiness. I should like to see you with

as many real friends as possible, and enjoying the esteem you could command...By alienating the affections of the majority of people, do you not tend to hold your wife in isolation? Were your conduct such that nice people would not refrain from entering into your daily life, would not Mrs Cole already feel less lonely and more content? And if you had friends of your own, would not Mrs Cole breathe more freely? A woman will seem to endure. Under the surface she may be contemplating separation or suicide or elopement, or some other quite cold-blooded manoeuvre, which should be evident and apparent to the otherwise-not-blind Lord of Creation. But the poor idiot, the fond idiot, who may be a captain among men, is apt to be blind as a bat about his own affairs.

Horace ignored the hint of his wife's infidelity—'there is a type of mentality that writes this sort of letter, known to police and doctors, and the writers don't always remain anonymous'— and blithely continued as usual. 'What a cess-pool the man's mind must be!' he mused.

He reminds me of that other American artist near Ajaccio who also built a fantastic villa and had a non-American wife he never could keep to himself: wanted his wife openly admired, and also wanted to see his male friends, well, you can guess what I mean (I think I told you)...There's some sort of *repression* in the nature of Americans in Europe that drives them to do outrageous things. They have such very mixed blood. Very few can claim real exact knowledge of a great grandfather or great grandmother and they have no real breeding or tradition, and a culture that is superimposed on very thin soil.

Mavis could stand none of this any longer. Pleading a desire to see her brother, who was on leave from the navy, she returned home to St Ives. She accused her husband of 'flinging' her back on her parents. Unable or unwilling to face the real reasons behind his wife's departure—the hopelessness of their situation and their incompatibility—Horace expected to see her back in a month or two. He warned her about the 'flu in England and the danger of mixing with his old friends: 'you can't afford it, and it is not right to go about and not be able to pay or to return hospitality. Probably you'll think this very stuffy advice, but it's sound.' Strangely, he seemed almost happier and more content without Mavis than with her, as if the burden of unfulfilled expectation had been lifted from his shoulders. He tried to mend some of the things that had damaged their marriage. He gave up brandy—'even beer is forbidden!'—ate lemons and broke the habit of a lifetime by rising before midday, 'but have not yet arrived at the 9 a.m. coffee and boiled egg I am aiming at!' This burst of energy spurred him on to finishing his long-awaited book. He wrote 10,000 words in 48 hours (how?), then translated 15 of its chapters into French (why?). A couple of the chapters were devoted to no less than 24 long-forgotten pranks involving 'cardinals, archbishops, bishops, priests, curies'. Others would deal with the Zanzibar and *Dreadnought* jokes, Eton, Cambridge, Oxford, Paris, Morocco and Spain. He aimed for 28 chapters, 75,000 words in total: very similar to this book, in fact.

Between frantic sessions of writing, Horace tried house-keeping: lugging meat up from St Jean in his haversack to make casseroles and pies for himself and Valerie. A favourite dish was Irish stew, but that required a separate journey in search of onions, as 'Irish stew without onions would be like a cocktail without gin'. Above all, he was forced to take notice of Valerie, who had been pushed to the margin of her father's collapsing life. What he really wanted to do, he confided to Mavis, was to send Valerie away to school then dump her on someone else in the family 'who could "bring her out" and take her to houses and dances etc. when she is eighteen…The whole object, of course, is to chance meeting a future husband, with enough to marry on, and her social equal.' It seems the lower he sank the more susceptible Horace was to the instincts of class prejudice he had once so loudly derided. What Valerie really needed, despite the occasional kindness of Mavis, was the love and attention of her father.

As he couldn't afford to send Valerie to school, as she so much desired, Horace tried to educate her himself. Her ignorance astonished him. He was still more taken aback by his daughter's spirited responses, as he reported to Mavis.

> She writes that the total population of England, Wales and Scotland is 50,000! Of Ireland 10,000 and of France 80,000!!!! That Cromwell lived 100 years before Queen Elizabeth, that Daniel O'Connell died recently and General Gordon (she had had an article to read on him) died the other day and was a soldier in the Great War! I had told her he was a friend of my grandfather Horatio de Vere and served with him in the trenches of the Crimean War! And also of my uncle Sir Howard Elphinstone V.C. who was his (Gordon's) senior officer. Valerie seemed to pay attention but she couldn't have done so. She writes that *Lord Haig* was well-known for '*inventing Haig's Whisky*'!! And this isn't meant as a joke! She had never heard, so she says, of Marconi (or Edison, or Grace Darling or Marlborough), or of your namesakes the Wright brothers who made their first flight near here at Pau where there is a monument to them. She says railway trains go at 150 miles an hour, and only looked at me suspiciously when I explained that if this was so she'd have arrived at Cambridge twenty minutes after leaving London! Sailing ships she says go at 30 miles an hour! All these questions need only common-sense answers: answers that 99 out of 100 children in their 14th year could give far more accurately. 'India has 500,000 people' (there are 360 millions and more), 'foxes and stoats are of the same family as dogs'; but why go on?!? 'Malta is a town in Africa' and the 'Americas' a great range of mountains in South America are other howlers. She even tried to prove she was right over the latter, and over a town called 'Egypt' 'where the kings of Egypt were buried'. She *is* conceited!! And she got 90 out of 100 marks for geography at that Cambridge school. What bunk!

Valerie is over ninety at the time of writing and living alone in an apartment in Toulouse. The 'speedwell' blue eyes of her father are unmistakable and still beautiful. Her small sitting-room is lined with books, many on painters, poets and writers. The door of her fridge is decorated with postcards of Ireland; images of a life denied her by self-indulgent parents. By the mirror in the bathroom is a reproduction of the famous *Dreadnought* photograph, showing her father before he set off on his greatest adventure. Until I met her, she had never seen a photograph of her mother, Denise. We agreed that she had been a startlingly attractive woman, but Valerie's opinion is clouded by her abandonment as a child and, later on, by her mother's begging then abusive phone calls. In more than seventy years since his death, Valerie has hardly spoken of her father or of her life with him in France. She remembers only the fights, the tears and the drinking. There was little else.

26

I had one to dine and one to dance,
The purple check which I kept for France,
One for Church, and two for wear,
One for the river and now I'm bare.

For there came a war, and trade went wrong,
And I had to live, and they sold for a song,
I let them go, though I felt it sore;
For now I'm a gentleman no more.

Tudor Castle, from 'Sartorial Studies' in *The Gentle Shepherd*, 1908

With Mavis in England, Horace fretted over her health and how she would survive without money. Reports that she had lunched at the Spats Club were unsettling. 'Whom did you meet?' he enquired, with as much calm as he could muster.

I could have belonged to that club but, alas, all this is another world for me now. It is all a matter of money! No one would enjoy an amusing life in London more than I would. I still know heaps of people. It isn't that I've 'had my day'. Not at all, I can't afford it. Surely you must realise this, Mavista? Quite possibly it is worse for me than for you not being able to go about amongst people I've known and use the ropes I've known!

As the weeks, then months passed, it became apparent, even to Horace, that Mavis would not be returning to France any day soon. If, indeed, ever. The tone of his letters changed to bitter regret, recrimination and self-pity. 'I'm an old man, and you are young and should have much happiness before you,' he wrote on her twenty-fourth birthday in December 1932.

> I know I'll never be happy again and that alone would prevent me making you happy…I don't ever remember feeling so gloomy, lonely and lost…I fear Bunga and Bungo were not made for one another after all. Darling I love you and wish I could have, or could make you happy. Someone else will.

He wrote Mavis rambling letters every day, he had little else to do. Her replies are lost but Horace complained of her 'nervy' writing. She did not want to return to that 'awful flat', nor did she want to end the marriage. Her suggestion of seeking work in London to ease their situation was swiftly crushed. 'What sort of job? What are you trained for?' Horace retorted.

> It's not right that my wife should look for a job if I don't want her to do so, and you'd have a perfect right to refuse if I did want you to do so! I am not refusing to support you, am I? You said you only wanted to go home for a month or so. You often said this. You can't be married and not married. If you are aiming at a separation, you must say so. If you are it only shows that you cannot forgive and that it is no use my writing anymore.
>
> *I* do not wish for a separation. I think it would be entirely wrong. You write that 'I hope something will happen and we'll be together again'. It's all so hopeless to write about. You can come back. What can happen? Why wait on vaguenesses like this? I can't come to London or England. If you've met someone, or think you know of someone who will give you an attractive job, it would account for what you've written. Do you mean you want to live alone? I simply can't make your letter out. It just hurts badly.
>
> And, of course, as you are clear headed enough to realize, if you leave me you put yourself in the way of temptation! Are you going to live alone, and never go about with any man? The idea is absurd. You said you wanted to 'live your own life'. You can't ask me to help you do this, it only means other men and I love you. You say you love me and want to be in my arms. If you

really mean this, we could clearly still be very happy, even here, and later we could move somewhere else, when and if I can get money from Canada or my book.

But I never said I'd live in England. I don't like England! What's the use of sending you any poetry? I feel too upset to think at all. I think I'll start brandy and sodas again and chuck my book and just write and read for my amusement and send Valerie into St Jean five times a week for French lessons.

Underlying Horace's reaction was his fear that Mavis had already met someone else in London. The agonies of jealousy, briefly suppressed by marriage, were bubbling up again to poison their relationship and challenge the fragile trust between them. Reports that Mavis had been to Cambridge late at night were met with dismay, then anger.

If we stay apart for a long time we will destroy all chance of ever coming together happily again. If you are thinking of divorce (as your mother suggested to you) you should tell me so. It is quite useless our continuing to write to one another unless we are candid. I've been completely candid with you. I want neither separation nor divorce. I do not wish you to look for a job or to get one (a fat lot of good a husband saying he wishes anything nowadays!) I am supporting you now, have all along supported you, and am ready to support you! I want you to come back soon, to fix an approximate date and stick to it! I am longing to hold you in my arms. You say, in almost the same breath, that you want to 'feel my whiskers' on your face and that you intend to leave me, for that's what your letter amounts to (after reading it three times)...You ask me to write and tell you you are a 'thoughtless heartless Woffles'. I can't, I don't think you are. Because I've been unkind is no reason you should be now. You may, of course, mean it to destroy the chances of being happy together I thought we still possessed (you have been very unkind to me in the past I remember). But two wrongs don't make a right. Oh heavens, what can I say?! Your letter doesn't make sense and doesn't face the realities of the position. It reads as if you were keeping something back from me. You write absolutely contradictory and cancellating (one another) statements. If you truly love me and miss me and want to be with me again (as I do you with all my heart) you will have to decide to be with me wherever I am, poor darling. Of course, one won't always be here! Heaven forbid. Will you write me an answer when you get this? I must bolt. My hands are quite frozen.

Horace kept himself to himself in Ascain: as far as was possible for a man of such glaring idiosyncrasy. He pictured himself as Waring, the absent hero of Robert Browning's poem:

What's become of Waring
Since he gave us all the slip,
Chose land-travel or seafaring,
Boots and chest or staff and scrip,
Rather than pace up and down
Any longer London town?

His mood fluctuated wildly: from periods of mad elation to deep depression, when he felt 'quite ready to get off this mad and uncomfortable globe'. 'Maybe my mind goes higher and reaches lower than yours! As a poet's should,' he told Mavis, partly in jest yet touching upon the nature of his curiosity for experience. Light and shade had always existed within Horace, making him by turns brilliant and bleakly despairing. Despite the posturing, Horace was never a religious man, but he clearly shared the voguish interest of his generation in the philosophy of Friedrich Nietzsche, so much of which chimed with his own poetic musings. Now in extremis he was swept by a nihilistic sense of the hopelessness of life.

What chance the whole damn business of life is. I wonder who you will be meeting and falling in love with next; and does it really matter?! Ants on dunghills engaged in futile comings and goings imagining we have immortal souls, and are of importance to the Great Architect of the Universe. How insane!

Horace considered his neighbours in Ascain a 'pretty foul lot', and deeply resented the suggestion that they viewed him as an 'eccentric rich man'. He had never seen himself as eccentric. Eccentricity was for people like Uncle Alfred, who trampled on other people to get rich. Not for poets like him, who dwelt on a higher plain of existence. Occasionally he ventured out. The visit of a circus to the village proved irresistible. Since he was a boy, Horace had loved the spectacle, thrill, earthy scents and colour of the circus. It offered that distorted version of reality he felt most comfortable in. So he was bitterly disappointed when the evening failed to live up to expectation.

> I never saw anything worse. It was advertised as being 'great equestrian feats by noble Russians in Cossack dress'. A good part of Ascain turned up but many didn't pay 5f entrance but got under the mangy canvas enclosing the field, for there was a gale blowing. Such sorry-looking nags (not Cossack ponies!) and a damp field, and four unhealthy looking men in clothes Willy Clarkson wouldn't have allowed in his wardrobe!

An invitation to a fancy-dress party at the Hotel Etchola was also impossible to refuse, if very poignant. Twenty years before, Horace was rumoured to have spent £500 preparing the costumes for the *Dreadnought* hoax. Now he simply donned a black hat and fraying tail coat, turned his collar back to front and went as a parson. The Sultan of Zanzibar as Father Brown. Valerie accompanied her father, dressed as a pirate, her face blackened with burnt cork.

In exile Horace still took an interest in current affairs, as he had since Cambridge days. Indeed he was obsessed by the press, particularly his own. Mavis sent him cuttings from London, other pieces he requested from journalists, and he read the continental *Daily Mail* avidly for the test-match scores and the 'fine rhetoric' of Churchill's articles. He reacted with horror to the rise of Mussolini 'and his parasites' in Italy, predicting war in Europe by 1936. The Italian invasion of Abyssinia, pretend home of the *Dreadnought* hoaxers, pitched one much-beloved country of experience against one cherished in the imagination. Unlike many of his embittered upper-class friends, he was not persuaded by the Fascist politics espoused by Oswald Mosley, whom he had met in London, and other extreme right-wing groups in Britain. Unlike Oliver Locker-Lampson, the MP victim of several of Horace's pranks, whose blue-shirted 'Sentinels of Europe' vowed to 'clear out the Reds', but achieved little except to undermine its founder's political reputation.

Horace was more agitated by the economic consequences of thirties politics on himself than their wider social impact. He was angered by what he saw as the failures of politicians in London, who allowed cheap wheat imports from Argentina at the expense of imperially-grown corn and the Canadian economy. Reading the newspaper, he was amazed at the number of his acquaintances who had risen to prominence. He marvelled at his sister Annie's public role alongside her husband, now Chancellor of the Exchequer (though he doubted his brother-in-law would ever be Prime Minister, as he was too old to be the 'coming man' while also being 'incurably modest and un-self-assertive'). Horace was entertained to read an interview with Annie in the *Daily Express*—previously the preserve of his own activities—and to see her described at court wearing a tiara and pearls. 'A contrast to her revered and eldest brother!!' he remarked ruefully. Mention of Augustus John in *The Times*, like some 'minor royalty', produced a snort of derision.

Despite dwindling funds, Horace remained a voracious reader. His subscription to the small library at St Jean, well stocked with English books for the many expatriates in the region, was one of his last luxuries to be culled. Seeing a 'wizened old English lady' there requesting Radclyffe Hall's Lesbian novel *The Well of Loneliness* amused him greatly. 'She could find first hand study in a certain set at Biarritz!' he told Mavis. The library offered an essential link to his former life back in England. Believing he was only going to be in France for a few weeks—months at most—he had brought only a handful of his remaining books out with him. He begged Mavis to send more. He told his brother Jim, 'It's awful to be without books, when you are longing to read and your mind is starving for nourishment.' His literary appetite, like his mind, was eclectic, often surprising and wide-ranging. Biography jostled with astronomy, physics, biology and history. A favourite book, read and re-read, was *The Story of San Michele*, an idiosyncratic and bestselling collection of memoirs by the Swedish physician Axel Munthe. It was the model for his own book, for which Horace requested *Who's Who*, *Philip's World Atlas* and *The Daily Mail Year Book for 1933* from his wife back in England as research material. For Valerie, he ordered *Alice in Wonderland* and *Alice through the Looking Glass*, insisting on the edition with Tenniel's famous illustrations. Populated with ducks, dodos, duchesses and bread-and-butterflies, the stories were a metaphor for his own world. 'I feel in some way like Alice through the Looking Glass,' he had once confessed to Jim. 'Everything seems topsy-turvy.'

Although he read widely and deeply, Horace avoided most fiction, especially Dickens. The writing was too real, and Dickens's moralising and mawkish sentimentalism grated on him. Conrad was 'worth reading', and he admired *Mrs Dalloway* by his *Dreadnought* accomplice Virginia Woolf; it 'makes me think it possible that V.W. has been twice in a private asylum, as I was told. She is Thackeray's grand-niece and has genius.' One book he was interested to see was *The Laughing Torso*, a recently published account of pre-war bohemian life by the painter Nina Hamnett, 'a rather poisonous, always drunk, person'. In fact, Horace did not figure among its many lewd anecdotes although in her second volume of reminiscences, *Is She a Lady?* Hamnett recalled walking with Horace through a narrow passageway off Piccadilly in the 1920s when he put his arms out to block the pedestrian traffic. 'In a few minutes an angry crowd of about fifty people had collected and I said "For heaven's sake, stop this or we will get locked up!" Horace shouted "That will be all right, Augustus will bail us out." I called a taxi and pushed Horace in and took him to the Eiffel Tower.'

Books gave respite from Horace's 'hole in the corner existence', but they could not disguise his approaching ruin. Back in London, Sir Bernard Bircham had gone ominously quiet. Endless requests for funds went unanswered, with Horace suspecting that his solicitor was no longer prepared to forward him money against future prosperity. The Georgia Investment Company in Saskatoon continued to rack up enormous debts. Local taxes alone accounted for about £265 a month, far more than the buildings' rents, decimated by the depression, were bringing in. Worse still, another £50 was being charged each month by his agents in Canada for unspecified expenses. 'They have got very cocky and seem to consider the property as belonging to themselves and the City councillors. I'd like to yell! I've just done so! And feel no better. I'd like to take a gun to my agents, robbers, all those incidental expenses, perhaps it's really cigars and fizz!'

Even the news that Bircham had received a repayment of £332 from the Inland Revenue for Horace's collapsed income was greeted with alarm. 'I am so afraid he'll bag it all! Then there'll be a shindy and I fear *that* will do no good.' Marooned in France, there was little he could do except madly fulminate against his misfortune.

Let no one say that *I* do not know, from personal experience, what robbery, bolshevism and confiscation means! After Ireland: Canada! A robbed landlord, a ruined capitalist! But, let us take heart: the British Empire still remains a happy hunting ground for almost every species of Jew and dago.

Too late, he had learned that 'money is everything (or almost, there *is* the imagination)'. He was the schoolboy at Eton again turning the image of liberalism against the wall. Prosperity had made him a socialist; now poverty returned him to conservatism. Uncle Alfred would have approved.

27

My thoughts are whirling round
Like Devils on a drum
Dancing a mad tattoo;
Oh! that my brain were numb!
Like feline in a zoo,
I pace and pace the ground;
No liberty can come
For I am fettered, bound.
Instead of castanets
My devils dance with dice
Red-hot, in hand, and bets
Are thrown for my sad soul;
The devil's names are 'Fool'
'Too late' and 'might have been'.
The last one bears a coal—
Burning, yet ribbed with ice—
He dips into a pool
Which turns a gangrous green,
And on the pool a skiff
Is circling, lettered 'IF.'

Then a miracle. In 1933 Mavis came back, clutching shamrock. 'If I'm not at St Jean station look for me on the first fine night amongst the stars,' exclaimed Horace when he heard she was returning, scarcely hiding his surprise. Even his wife's request that he should not kiss her on arrival failed to dim his excitement. 'However it's news to me that you "hate kissing" for I've seen you kiss several men under my nose and rather wondered why you weren't a little

more sensitive to touch! Augustus for instance…' He fussed
over her journey, and when she reached Hiriartia tried hard
to behave well. That Mavis returned at all shows courage and
commitment. She acted out of pity and hopeful self-interest.
She was not yet ready to relinquish her status as Horace's wife.
One indication that she was still willing to join her husband
in his fantasy world was occasioned by the visit to Ascain that
summer of the Prince of Wales.

The last time Horace had seen the Prince he had been
a 'little pin headed naked boy shivering a-top' a swimming-
pool slide at the Bath Club in Dover Street. Horace was only
prevented from giving the boy a firm shove by Oliver Locker-
Lampson, who had yelled a warning that Horace would be
thrown out of the club if he did so. Now the Prince was the
leader of high society, a celebrity pin-up enjoying a playboy
lifestyle and globetrotting the world in pursuit of pleasure.
Horace convinced himself that the Prince was visiting Ascain
solely to gawp at the fabled Mavis. But all attempts to extract
his wife from her hiding-place in her bedroom failed. So
Horace was left chatting amiably to the Prince's aide-de-
camp—'whom I knew before the war at Sunday luncheons
chez the Abercorns'—while the Prince kicked his heels in
the garden of the Hotel Etchola. At 4.30 the Prince left and
Mavis emerged.

Twenty years later in a gossipy column she wrote (or had
ghosted) for the Sunday tabloid paper *Empire News*, Mavis
recalled the visit in quite different terms. 'It was at one of
our dinner parties at Ascaigne,' she wrote, 'that the Duke
of Windsor, then Prince of Wales, first met Mrs Simpson.'
This preposterous claim, completely at odds with the truth,
offers one reason why Mavis stuck by Horace for as long as
she did. Who else did she know, a working girl from the back
of beyond, who could even offer her the possibility of such

a thing happening? 'Horace was brilliant in most things,' she later told her son Tristan, 'and women fell for him like ninepins.' Despite all she had suffered, she would not let go of the dream just yet, not while her husband's rank and fortune might still be restored. Horace laughingly recalled how she even suggested to an acquaintance in St Jean that the 'de Vere' part of her married name came from her.

At Christmas, his romanticism undimmed, Horace gave Mavis a copy of *The Idylls of Theocritus.* But by now things were becoming desperate. Even with his economising, Horace had still managed to spend over £750 (perhaps around £35,000 today) of money he didn't have over the previous year. Apart from a long list of trade creditors—totalling £300 in Ascain alone—he also owed substantial amounts to his brother, sister, aunts and various friends. With income from Canada expected to be no more than £260 over the coming year (in fact, it was a lot less) Horace faced complete ruin. As a clearly exasperated

A happy day at Ascain: Mavis, second left, and Valerie, far right (Tristan de Vere Cole).

Sir Bernard Bircham had washed his hands of the matter, Jim Cole bravely stepped in to take charge of his brother's chaotic affairs. The English debts were secured against Horace's few remaining pictures; others in France he agreed under duress to repay at a rate of £5 a week from money sent to him by his family. In addition a further £5 would be made available for his weekly living expenses. The implications were obvious. Horace, one-time heir to the treasures of West Woodhay, would become a remittance man, living abroad at his family's expense.

There was no honour in this condition, and Horace knew it. Poverty was uncomfortable but noble: living off charity was not. He had played many roles in his life, from labourer to sultan, but he had never dreamt of being cast in such a sordid one. The spectre of the remittance man haunted English upper-class society as much as the banshees prowled the imagination of the Irish. He was depicted as a dissolute outcast who had wasted his good fortune pursuing his own selfish desires. In an era before benefits and social-security payments, the remittance man was an all too-familiar figure, cadging drinks and boasting of his conquests in sleazy bars across Europe. This was not the bohemian manner of living. This was demeaning, humiliating, petty and depressingly bourgeois. There was no beauty or poetry in it at all. In short, it was the fate of wastrels and failures. Horace had always treated money flippantly, now it had destroyed him. 'Am I right to continue on charity?' he implored his brother. 'Would you do so?' He sought solace in a saying of their mother's: 'Tout passé, tout lasse, tout casse'. Nothing really matters.

Jim had more bad news. The distinguished writer and art critic Paul Konody, who had long championed Horace's proposed book, had died. According to Horace, Konody had lined up a publisher for his long-awaited autobiography, and had even discussed serialisation with a national newspaper. Now with his death (and, I suspect, with the lengthy serialisation of Willy Clarkson's memoirs in *The People*) Horace lost heart in the ill-starred project. Jack Squire, the editor of the *Mercury* newspaper and a friend from Cambridge days, had already misplaced some early chapters. Others were later entrusted to Augustus, who lost or destroyed them. News that his old sparring-partner had been talking to Jonathan Cape about his own book had initially spurred Horace on in his endeavours, prompting him to pen this poetic tribute:

> Augustus John,
> My bearded söhn,
> Can it be really true,
> That you are writing,
> (Type-writing)
> (No quill-biting)
> Memories from the blue?
>
> Memories of the days when you
> Were some years younger (so was I)
> Ah! John I cannot really ken you,
> Putting pigs thus in their sty!
>
> Augustus John
> Great-bearded man
> I told you, I recall,
> That I was writing,
> (Quill a-biting)
> (No type-writing)
> Of jokes, called Practical
>
> And you told me not to do it,
> Clearly said that I would rue it,
> Said 'You've played 'em, why the hell
> Should you write those stunts as well?'
>
> Well, my John, you've painted pictures
> Which will certainly be fixtures,

(After buying, after sellings)
On the walls of splendid dwellings,
Until kingdom come brings down
All the walls of London Town

You'll have had your day, Augustus;
You'll have had your say, Augustus;
(If that book of yours appears)
You'll be P.R.A. Augustus:
Tout will be au fait, Augustus,
Numbered with the Celtic Peers.

But my John, if you'd not painted,
By the camel's hair been tainted,
Your memories had not been sung,
So with me; in humbler guise,
Just a joker, not too wise,
My book of jokes had been unhung!

In fact, Augustus's book *Chiaroscuro* would not appear until
1952, by which time Horace was long dead and Mavis was the
artist's mistress. *Chiaroscuro* is tainted with all the bitterness of
a jealous friend. In the book, Augustus describes Horace as

> a pseudo Anglo-Irish aristocrat impersonating the God of
> Mischief…his fine blue eyes blazed malice and self-assurance…
> when all went well he could be amiability itself; when it didn't,
> that is, when his excessive vanity had received a jar, he would
> manifest his resentment in language which any bargee would
> have envied. It was at such moments that he came near to
> achieving true expression, and it was a relief to be able to pay
> tribute to a genuine home-grown accomplishment.

Mavis—who was furious to see that Augustus had called her
husband 'Horace Cole' and not 'Horace de Vere Cole'—was
succinct in her disapproval of the tone of *Chiaroscuro*. 'I know
why Augustus is so vicious about some people,' she told Tristan,
'he's got a complex, poor old thing.' However, the painter may
not have been entirely responsible for the final loss of Horace's

book. Within weeks of Jim Cole's ultimatum, Horace destroyed 45,000 words of his manuscript himself. 'I am sure some people would be relieved if they knew,' he joked morosely. Only two or three chapters—considered the best and presumably covering the *Dreadnought* and Zanzibar hoaxes—remained intact. They had been written in England and stored at the Pantechnicon storage building in Fulham before Horace's hasty departure for France. In 1941 they too followed the rest of the book into the flames, courtesy of enemy action.

The steady obliteration of Horace's book by instalments was perhaps the greatest and saddest irony of all. All that survives is a few scribbled notes and a list of provisional titles. These not only give a tantalising taste of the sort of book he envisaged, but also reveal something of himself:

Why Not?
What's the harm?
The Joker
Let it go at that
Unpractical journey
Studies in Jokology

Like many authors, Horace planned the illustrations before writing his book. These included the famed Zanzibar and *Dreadnought* group photos (see pp. 53, 55, 110, 111) as well as the two postcards published after the Cambridge hoax (see p. 62), a cartoon which appeared in the *Daily Mirror* (see p. 127) and a pen-and-ink drawing of himself by Augustus as the frontispiece (see p. 223). (Strangely, for a man so closely linked to the art world, this is the only known portrait of Horace.)

Horace had other difficulties with his book, and I think it was these which ultimately defeated him, rather than the actions of his erstwhile friends. Principally he lacked the confidence and application to complete the task. He had read too much and known too many talented writers to consider his own efforts worthwhile. 'Book-making,' as he called it, was a young man's game, 'except for a few persons of genius'. He was no longer young or a literary genius. Finally there was the question of content. He knew he would have to write a 'pot-boiler' to make money, but did not know how, certainly without Konody to guide him. 'Practical jokes one after another are as cloying made up as a book as a book of jokes is,' he complained to Jim.

> I think I need something else as, for instance, tales about the happenings in Ireland, a story or two about Augustus Edwin John and a few other persons whose names are news (George Meredith, Sinclair Lewis, Henry James for instance). A celebrity said if I put on the duster that Annie said she wouldn't buy the book I'd make a great sale.

His sister had told him that she would boycott the book if Horace mentioned caning Willy Fisher, who since the *Dreadnought* hoax had been knighted and promoted Admiral and commander-in-chief of the Mediterranean Fleet. 'However I did cane him,' protested Horace, 'and I think I should say so, *and* I caned him before he caned me. I wrote the ballad "I'm one of His Majesty's Bottoms I am" about it, though I could hardly put *that* in.' I wish he had kept a copy for posterity though.

28

Go thou thy way—a blessing or a curse
What does it matter which I send with thee?
There were some things that well might have been worse.
Some things there were that never more can be;

Yes, go thy way, as I am going mine
No more to meet you; See! Our roads divide
Oh! One more kiss, full-bodied as this wine,
And one more dream to close our eventide!

*P*roblems for Horace were mounting faster than his
debts. Barely had he absorbed the ignominy of being
a remittance man than he clashed with the French
police. It was the latest episode in a long-running skirmish
with the authorities in France dating back to his former days
in Paris. The trouble was caused by Mavis's lack of a French
identity card, which prompted a visit to Hiriartia by two
police officers. The issue might have been resolved swiftly if
Horace—previously cautioned for calling the French police
'pigs and mackerel'—had not lost his temper and 'damned
all Frenchmen and especially the police'. He was immediately
arrested and threatened with deportation. Mavis believed the
police were simply looking for any excuse to apprehend this
foreign troublemaker in their midst.

Even Horace thought he was 'for it' this time. 'The police
have their knife into me and if they have a decent excuse to
go for me they will, and now one has been presented to them.'
With furious creditors calling on him every day, an illegally

resident wife and few friends, the prospect of prison loomed before him, 'and French goals are not nice I believe' (though he had some experience). Horace considered running to another bolthole. But Spain was even more expensive than France, and Canada—where he at least had somewhere to live—was too far away. Tirelessly patient and ever efficient, Jim repeatedly asked for a list of his brother's debts and engaged the assistance of the British Consul in Bayonne. The Consul resolved Horace's dispute with the police, but he could do little about his debts. Nor could he ease the escalating misery at Hiriartia, where Horace had piles, Valerie had scabies and Mavis was again near breaking-point. According to Horace, one morning in January 1934, she rushed at him shouting, 'How dare you leave the hot water tap running when I want a bath, you dirty old man.' ('Her usual term for me before Valerie is "dirty old man",' sighed Horace.)

Since Christmas and the crisis of the identity cards, their relationship had deteriorated and entered a new, more dangerous, phase. His wife blamed him for ruining her life and forcing her to marry him 'That is all I have to show for the money spent by you the last six years,' she would yell, striking at her gold wristwatch. In one row, Mavis bit Horace's finger down to the bone then threatened to throw herself downstairs so that she could accuse her husband of assault. 'It is part of her declared policy of manufacturing evidence,' Horace told Jim. But he was surely not blameless himself, despite his plaintive letters to his brother. Horace had a long history of violence dating back to his childhood, so there is every reason to suppose Mavis was defending herself from his assaults, verbal and physical. And when Valerie saw her father and stepmother tussling on the balcony of Hiriartia—as she did— it was hard to say whether Mavis was threatening to jump or Horace to push her over.

In extremis, she too appealed to Jim Cole for help. 'He is much too lazy to do anything himself,' she wrote of her husband, 'and can only pass the time away by being as abusive as possible, and creating a most unpleasant atmosphere, that I find is quite impossible to go on living in.' Mavis's emotions were further confused by the insistent and passionate advances of a Spanish aristocrat called Count Nana de Tajo, whom she had met in a local bar. For a time they secretly corresponded, the count vowing to save Mavis from her 'blustering, mendacious husband'. 'There is something *unusual* about your beauty,' he rhapsodised,

> something rich and strange that irradiates from your heart. Yes, that's what you are, a girl with a great big soul, a marvellous heart, living in an epoch of intellectual professors and clever politicians with dried up, crusted hearts. You were made to step out of one of El Greco's paintings or to live in Shakespeare's sonnets, and who should you find to sing your praises but two cranks, your husband and myself.

But Mavis was tired of poetic outpourings and false promises. She wanted a secure future, a home and normal family life. She thought she had escaped the poverty of her childhood. Instead she found herself sinking back into it with a man who appeared morbidly to relish the tragedy of his situation.

Wisely Jim declined to get involved in his brother's marriage, leaving Horace at a loss as to what to do, not having the money to do anything. He spoke aimlessly of divorce, or of making Valerie a ward in Chancery as her mother Denise had been. He could neither live with Mavis nor survive without her. He had so idealised his relationship with Mavis, and beatified her image, that he was confused now that it was all falling apart before his eyes. Mavis was his 'inner light', his 'sun at noon that puts out the light of stars, planets, universes, constellations'. He pictured their souls and bodies entwined in a metaphysical way. She was 'dans ma peau'—in his flesh.

So when Mavis walked out for good at Easter 1934—'My word you were a brave and courageous girl to bear it so long,' wrote a friend—Horace was tortured by remorse and self-loathing. 'Wrecked! Wrecked! Wrecked! Wretched, Wretched, Wretched me!' he cried, '*I am in the dust.*' The timing of his wife's going away was steeped in religious symbolism; all the contradictions of his spiritual life were resolved in one simple desire.

> I wish I could become a Christian of deep and simple faith. I might acquire a vicarious happiness that way, for real happiness I'll never know again, not without Mavis and a returned and renewed love and forgiveness. Mavis could, I think, acquire a simple faith which would fortify her. Can a real desire for faith lead to faith itself? For with Faith might come Hope and

Jim Cole, who did his best to save his brother from himself (John Cole).

Charity and if I had even the rudiments of the latter (oh, how I hate myself in retrospect!) I could never offend my beloved, or anyone else, with my tongue again.

For the first time in years, he prayed, kneeling before the crucifix in his sparsely furnished room seeking revelation and divine peace. He fumbled for the right words, with two phrases in particular working endlessly through his chaotic imaginings: 'Faith, Hope and Charity' and 'Though your sins be as scarlet'. 'How terrible to kill such a rare offering, offered to an ageing man too and of no fame,' he wept. It was melodramatic and heart-rending. In his agony he ripped off those layers of disguise which had sheltered him since childhood. In a final plea to Mavis, he abased himself, laying himself utterly broken and torn at her feet.

All I know is that I love you worlds without end, that I have cried my eyes out for you (that is nothing), that I know all self-realisation and knowledge of you, that if any love is left for me in your heart we will be happy. I just love love love and worship you. To say I want you is feeble. I long for your presence every second. Waking to reality is a horror. I am more in love with you, in all ways, than I ever have been; and I did suffer when you left me, but this going is a nightmare. May I write to you? Will you send me even one short letter. Couldn't you telegraph me one or two words? You have imagination will you realize I am suffering the agonies of the damned because I know how culpable I am and how easily I could have made everything right. I have been the world's greatest fool, and you mock me by calling me a genius! Me a genius! I'm dirt and you cast the pearls of your love before this swine.

Horace shaped his agony into this poem for Mavis:

I am the well of ages;
No thirst can drain me dry;
My name is lust; and sages
Have drunk of me to die;

And youth has drunk its measure,
And left its heat to rust,
Mistaking me for pleasure,
When my sole name is lust:

All forms and shapes of women
Are mirrored in my spring;
And all are vain—for no man
Can grasp a mirroring;

He can grasp a fancy
Volatile as the wind;
And, through my necromancy,
Know not his eyes are blind.

Valerie reported to Mavis that after her father returned from seeing her off at the station 'his hands were all shaking and his eyes almost popping out of his head'. His behaviour was wildly erratic. One moment he was manically singing, the next slumped asleep in a chair. He blamed himself entirely for driving his wife away. 'He said he knew that you were not happy at home and that your people were not popular in the town. I suppose he's so vain that he's trying to get me to think that you did not want to go,' Valerie wrote, complaining that her father was being 'very oily and is obviously trying to get round me, but I'm not having any.' Aged fifteen, Valerie, suffering from neglect and with the clothes literally falling off her, was now alone in a hell of her father's own making. 'I wrap my flames round me, cuddle them up. Long live mental torture, remorse and life without hope!' he cried.

Salvation arrived not, as Horace pleaded, from above but from the British Consul in Bayonne, Paul Shoedelin. He placed Valerie in a convent school and spirited Horace away from Ascain and his most pressing debts. With Hiriartia under siege, Horace ordered the destruction of all his remaining papers, including his correspondence with his beloved mother. He had a horror of people picking over his effects and reading his most intimate thoughts after he was gone. He took only a drawing of Dick Innes which he had clung on to since his friend died. In a further symbolic sign of casting himself adrift, Horace lost his gold signet ring swimming off the Côte des Basques. Engraved with the Cole family crest, a hand grasping a scorpion, its loss symbolised an irretrievable break with his past and former self.

Shoedelin found Horace a bed-sitting-room a dozen miles away or so in Bayonne. With Mavis gone and Valerie at boarding school, his remittance was reduced to £2 or 154 francs a week by his family back in England. Eating regularly now became a struggle. With rent of over 100 francs a week there was precious little left for food, about a shilling a day in English terms. 'I won't say I miss steak and kidney puddings, sirloins and Irish stew; eggs and bacon, boiled eggs etc, my mouth waters at the thought of them!' He lived on oranges, tins of sardines, dates and raisins. His shoes went unmended and his clothes unwashed. The conditions were so bad he even started to feel nostalgic for Ascain. 'There was something friendly about "Hiriartia", in spite of bugs, rotten linen, floors and ceilings, kitchen and range accessories. Anyway one didn't feel lost in that little village: here I feel absolutely so. I've never felt so utterly lonely in my life.' From time to time he opened a long-empty box of cigars his brother had given him years before to 'waft a wistful smell to my innards!' Without the help of Shoedelin and his wife, Horace thought he might have starved. 'And to think I used to have houses and servants in London I didn't use when abroad!!!' he wrote in exasperation, '*What* a mess! My prime mistake was investing so heavily in Canadian real estate.' He drafted an appeal to King George V for the reinstatement of his army disability pension, surrendered to a fund for war widows and orphans. 'I know I once, with others, played a little joke on your late father's Fleets,' he began, 'BUT *I have good reason to believe that you, Sire, at any rate, saw the humour in it.'*

He felt like a prisoner, unable to go out, and thinking only of getting through the coming day, then hour, then minute (except prisoners were better fed). He was 'horribly lonely, wholey lost and livingly dead'. Deafness and his inability to speak French fluently made it difficult to meet people. He considered returning to England to live on the dole in a hostel or 'as an ex-officer of yeomanry' in the Royal Hospital at Chelsea. He was completely cut off from all society. He told Jim,

> There's Biarritz but you can't go into that set at my age, a come down on the world, with patched shoes, and clothes in the state mine inevitably are in. Also poverty cries louder than murder is supposed to do. Anyway it will out, especially in an elderly gentleman of fair education and intelligence who has had his clubs and houses and friends and wives etc and now is a living corpse. If I say I am living on £2 a week charity from relations they'll think I've committed some crime, and am exiled for that!

Horace had always loved the cut and thrust of argument, the thrill of conflict. Quoting Café Royal stalwart G.K. Chesterton's admiration for the 'ancient Christian custom of men arguing their heads off and shouting each other down for the glory of reason and the truth'; he bemoaned to Jim that 'I'll never argue with a friend again; or see London or England or you or anyone else.' He only had Shoedelin to talk to, and he soon grew tired of him: 'He has no imagination and is without any reading or interests. I believe he collects stamps.' The Consul did, however, reveal, with lascivious relish, that Mavis had been seen as little better than a prostitute locally, and that he 'couldn't understand why Mrs Cole was always trying to paint you as black as possible'. Horace refused to listen to Shoedelin's malicious gossip. He still loved Mavis and wanted her back 'with all my heart'. He wrote constantly to her, but had few replies. When Mavis did answer she told her husband she had been going to the Eiffel Tower with Nina Hamnett and Augustus, and been voted 'the most beautiful woman in the Café Royal'. She also told her husband, or so he queried Jim, that it was only the fear of stigma that prevented his family from having him 'shut up' in an institution.

Fear of madness had stalked Horace for years. He was haunted by the childhood memory of one of his English relatives casually saying aloud that his mother was 'mad and all Irish people were!!!' ('There *was* a period when the Irish were considered mad,' he commented savagely, 'especially by English shopkeepers and tradesmen and royalties and other bloody snobs.') He did not consider himself insane, though 'memories are scorching my brain to the torture of madness'. The only madness he had ever felt was his love for Mavis. There was insanity enough already in Europe with the rise of 'Macaroni' Mussolini and Hitler. Nevertheless the jibe stung. Before the war, Horace and his close friend Arthur Hay, son of the Marquess of Tweeddale, had dispatched an unpopular house-guest to a lunatic asylum using a signed but blank committal form stolen from a doctor (unfortunately, the denouement to this joke, which might have come straight from the pen of Saki, is not known). Now a similar fate was presented to him. Over the years plenty of people, from Ezra Pound to Neville Chamberlain, had adjudged him mad. Yet Horace always stoutly defended his reason. 'I am fully aware of my sanity; a sanity quite as sound as yours!' he fired back at Mavis.

Allow me to give a growl of dissent! I have done nothing for which you could divorce me, and no doctor would certify me. If one tried to I'd have *him* certified! And I don't know where you got this information about the intentions of my relations. You hardly know them. Surely your imagination is running away with your common-sense (of which you have a goodly amount). But supposing, my dear, that you *are* right—you'd better hurry up about your divorce: for if I'm shut up *first* you can never get one!!

What Mavis did not reveal in her letters was the affair developing between herself and Augustus, though Horace must have guessed at it. His wife spoke of the painter's 'wonderful eyes' and how he 'made suggestions' to her. Horace had left England owing his friend £20. As Augustus later admitted to Wyndham Lewis, he now resolved to recover this debt in kind. He seduced Mavis in erotically charged letters addressed to his 'Pirani' (Romany for 'Sweetheart'—how Horace would have hated that!) which he signed 'stiff and strong' and 'yours to the last half inch'. He even sent her, in July 1934, a poem in crude imitation of 'the eloquence of Horace':

> Sweet Perdita, the loveliest of Girls
> With lustrous eyes set in a frame of curls
> Of golden brown translucent like the prawn
> Grows hot with playing tennis on the lawn
>
> So to her room she hurries all a sweat,
> Tears off her pretty knickers now quite wet,
> And with immodest fingers 'gins to press
> The incandescent seat of her distress.
>
> Now her loud sighs announce the divine orgasm,
> And furiously she rubs her burning chasm,
> Till in a spate of mucous the young bitch
> Allays the sweet intolerable itch.

Mavis was ready to be seduced. Months of unhappiness, loneliness and anxiety over money made her vulnerable to the comfort of uncomplicated sex and attention. She could breathe again after being suffocated by Horace's misery. Once more, she luxuriated in the adoration of men, posing for Augustus and other artists who clustered in the pubs and clubs she frequented.

Hearing of this, Horace wryly commented that 'She always wanted to do that (and for photographers for private sale but I forbade it) long before she got married. She loves showing herself "in the nood"…And she *has* something to show, but so have thousands of other girls.' Yet always in the back of Mavis's mind was the figure of her husband alone in France, and how and when it would all end.

29

I have not flatter'd its rank breath, nor bow'd,
To its idolatries a patient knee
Nor coined my cheek to smiles, nor cried aloud
In worship of an echo; in the crowd
They could not deem me one of such; I stood
Among them, but not of them; in a shroud
Of thoughts which were not their thoughts, and still could,
Had I not filled my mind which thus itself subdued.

I have not loved the world, nor the world me,
But let us part fair foes I do believe,
Though I have found them not, that there may be
Words which are things, hopes which will not deceive,
And virtues which are merciful, nor weave
Snares for the failing; I would also deem
O'er others' griefs that some sincerely grieve;
That two, or one, are almost what they seem,
That goodness is no name, and happiness no dream.

Horace considered suicide. His life had been littered with the self-destruction of others, many of them relatives of his in Ireland. It was a subject which held a morbid fascination for him; the combining of violence with passion. He was haunted by the memory of John Davidson, a lyrical poet who, in similar desperate straits, had walked into the sea in 1909, leaving his young family with friends of Horace. 'He said he'd probably not come back but try and get to America! They understood.' He had compiled a list of the 15 people he had known to kill themselves: from his cousin Rose Lawless, who drowned herself in a lake, to Darrell Figgis, who shot himself when his mistress got pregnant. All appeared normal beforehand, and when questioned, a doctor confirmed to Horace that the act of suicide was a reasoned one. 'It required a sane brain to reason out and carry out the death sentence on itself,' he had informed Horace. 'Madmen generally lived on, and rarely slew themselves.' This gave him courage, as he knew he was sane. Moreover his mother had once told him she contemplated killing herself, giving the act legitimacy. Lacking a gun, he picked which train to lie down in front of (as Max Lobkowitz's brother had at Cannes). 'I may as well "shuffle off this mortal coil",' he resolved, 'tho' I am sure I'd make a bungle of the business with a "bare bodkin", like I—somewhat stupidly maybe—imagine I would on the line. It would be awful to be only mutilated and not immediately squiffed out.'

Only his 'ridiculous interest in life' held him back. Not fear of death. He had long ago lost that. Too many people he had loved were in their graves for him not to want to embrace his own. Early violent death had destroyed his generation, and it was a wonder he had survived as long as he had. 'This worm should never have recovered from that expanding bullet in July 1900!' Yet 'While there's life there's hope! I'm full of life, tho' underfed *and hoping for hope*, though I quite well know the whole business is futile, and I'd better end the farce as hundreds are doing daily on their own account, and thousands willy-nilly!' So he soldiered on, unable to end it himself but wishing that 'I'll get cancer from cold pork and eggs and thus free myself and my relations from the impossible position'.

Horace finally lost contact with Mavis during that summer. He still loved her, but his passion had been drained to the bitter dregs by her rejection. She had taken away his few remaining books, his poems and last hope of happiness. His

final letter to his wife was full of hurt, anger, disappointment
and injured pride.

> Your contempt does not hurt me for you, least of anyone, have
> a right to despise me for my present financial position and its
> consequences. Sympathy I never expected from you. *I do love you*
> and I have written to you so fully before that anything more I
> should write would only be repetition. Probably—judging from
> the whole tone of your last letter—I've said too much. Exposed
> my heart too clearly; for there is no response from you, and you
> led me to believe there might be.

He expected no reply and got none. He was now almost entirely dependent on Jim for money, news and comfort. In May
1935 Horace reached the age of fifty-four. He passed his
birthday—'my funniest ever, I think'— in complete silence:
speaking to no one, thinking only of his dead mother and
treating himself to the guilty extravagance of a small brandy
and soda.

Few of his old friends tried to reach him, or even knew how;
to many he was already dead. He sent Augustus a postcard,
which may have prompted a stab of guilt in the artist but
produced no reply. Someone who did have 'too much affection
and admiration for you not to be horrified at the thought of not
seeing you again' was the painter Geoffrey Nelson, a veteran
of several of Horace's jokes who had urged him not to marry
Mavis. He had struggled since his Slade School days to establish
himself as an artist, and now taught painting in France. In July,
Geoffrey discovered Horace living at Bayonne and offered
him a cottage at Honfleur in Normandy for 100 francs less a
month than he was currently paying in rent. Horace leapt at
the chance, seeing it as an opportunity to start afresh, perhaps
even to resurrect his abandoned book. Jim forwarded money
for the journey, and he went energised, carrying his portrait of
Dick Innes and the hope of renewal.

In reality, the cottage was more like a hovel, with bare earth floors and no running water, electricity or fireplace. The lavatory was housed in a drafty shed in the tiny, overgrown garden. Every morning, Horace had to walk a quarter of a mile into Honfleur to fetch water and milk. But he was happy. It was a rather small estate compared to West Woodhay, but at least he could afford it and call it his own. The sea air was bracing, the cider cheap and delicious, and the town, which had always attracted painters, had a quiet, unassuming air, in contrast to the seedy glamour of St Jean. Jim, kind as ever, sent over a steady stream of books. One package contained 'King Cole', a poem by John Masefield about an ancient king granted reprieve from heaven to walk the earth, 'the friend of man':

> So since that time, he wanders shore to shire,
> An old, poor, wandering man, with glittering eyes
> Helping distressful folk to their desire
> By power of spirit that within him lies.
> Gentle he is, and quiet, and most wise,
> He wears a ragged grey, he sings sweet words,
> And where he walks there flutter little birds.

'Am I "King Cole"?' Horace wondered, 'All I know is that a robin has attached himself to my tiny "garden"—I give crumbs—and also two blue tits. Still I don't play a flute or make anyone happy.'

The winter took its toll. Horace developed a persistent bronchial infection and suffered a bout of 'flu. He lay in bed for days on end, surviving on dry rusks and water. When his paraffin ran out, he lay in the dark and silence. His pulse raced and his heart pounded in his chest. He urged it to stop, for good. He watched the rats scurry across the floor, idly imagining how they would feed on his corpse. He knew no one, and no one came to see him. He was 'outside everything and everyone'. Geoffrey Nelson had gone to Paris with a speculative article Horace had written for the papers as an insurance policy against his funeral expenses. As he told Jim, 'I don't see why a hopelessly insolvent and bitterly cursed-and-be-bloody-damned-to-him-by-all-his-so-respectable-relations individual should not pay for his own funeral expenses in an original way.' Horace was preparing for death, willing it upon himself. Even before his illness, he had informed Jim, more in regret than sorrow but with utmost certainty, that he would never see his family or home or London ever again. 'Still,' he consoled himself, 'I've had enjoyable bits and enjoyed them.'

The infection eased, but it had aggravated his rheumatism, leaving him barely able to write, shave or light the fire. To cap it all, he had gout. However, a cheerful letter from Jim 'acted like a cocktail—a thing I ain't tasted for a while—for you send me news and you made me laugh'. Reports of the death of King George V made Horace reflective and strangely sad. He revealed to Jim,

> It's odd but I *really* feel I've *lost* someone, and I feel much older, never having had a sovereign younger than myself before! I think H.M. had quite a rare gift of, in theatrical parlance, getting his personality over the footlights. An ordinary face: but an unforgettable one. (There's a fine 'Poem in Prose' by Turgenov on this subject. But it deals with Christ Rex not George Rex. An American writer, Henry James, told me he considered it one of Turgenov's finest things. It's only two hundred words long, or so. Now if one could write like *that*?!)

On the day of the King's funeral Horace stood to attention for two minutes in his damp, little kitchen.

In January 1936, Horace heard from Jim that Mavis had had a child, a boy called Tristan. He was indifferent to the news. He knew the baby could not be his—his wife had been gone for two years, and the child was barely one. Giving a hint of his own suspicion, Horace directed Jim to Arnold Mason, the painter who had been with him when he first set eyes on Mavis at the Café Royal. Mason idolised Mavis, and later painted her. He 'would know who the father of Mavis' child is,' said Horace meaningfully, before adding, with some of the old sparkle, 'so would many other Chelseanites!' Mavis, if she knew the father, never told. If pressed, she always said it was Horace 'of course'. Augustus always believed Tristan was his, and treated him as such. Why should Mavis argue?

On 25 February 1936, Horace was sufficiently recovered from illness to venture out. That afternoon he was seen walking up the hill from town singing, recalled a neighbour, 'comme d'habitude'. In the morning, the boy who delivered his milk could get no answer. He fetched the wife of a local farmer, and together they found Horace dead in his chair. He had died, noted the coroner, 'décédé d'une crise cardiaque', though in truth his heart had broken long before. As he sat in his chair, the colour draining from his world, his 'merry sky voyage done', did Horace see again all the characters he had played? Did Herbert Cholmondeley enter the room and fussily place his umbrella by the bed? With a flurry of silks, did the Abyssinians cluster around him, laughing and singing? And was the Sultan of Zanzibar standing there, gazing at himself with an indulgent smile? Calling him, as Horace had once put it in a poem, to 'the hidden world beyond'.

30

When the end is indeed the end
In what fashion will you come to me?
Full tide passion? Or just spirit-free
As friend would come to friend?

Then, dear, will I not recognise
The dream-light, and the mysteries
That gleamed within those sun-flecked, western eyes?

For the dream must wake from its dream,
And visions live that were once half-true,
And you will give for the years we rue
Life like a golden beam;

And then, as through a mirage haze
We will look back on those slumber days
When we lived, but knew not the other's ways

News of Horace's death was greeted with a flurry of obituaries in the French, British and Irish press. Inevitably, the articles focused on his jokes, to the great regret of Aunt Eily, as these were '*such* a minor portion of his life, the portion which I somehow feel as having been prompted by an *enemy* spirit choking off the spirit of genius which was in him'. Neville Chamberlain had been the first member of the family to be told, as he was the easiest to find. He and Annie arranged for Valerie to be fetched from the convent at Bayonne and placed into their care at 11 Downing Street. He thought his niece an 'exceptionally pretty girl with a very attractive smile', and doted on her. When Neville became

Prime Minister in 1937, Valerie moved with the Chamberlains to number ten. She was there for the shortlived triumph of Munich and for the outbreak of war, an invisible presence among the crowds which packed Downing Street on both occasions. She even had dinner with the King and Queen when they were entertained by the Chamberlains in March 1939. Among the many other dignitaries at the table was Admiral of the Fleet Lord Chatfield, who was possibly unaware that he was sitting close to the daughter of the architect of the Royal Navy's most embarrassing hour.

Valerie says now that after the misery of her existence in France, moving to Downing Street was like 'falling into heaven'. Before her husband's premiership was destroyed by war, Annie Chamberlain was a popular if slightly chaotic political hostess. 'I have to create a home atmosphere of peace and cheerfulness,' she told the *Daily Express* in her 'pleasant, faintly drawling, musical voice.' As her brother would have wanted, Annie 'brought out' Valerie in the last glittering season before the war, taking her to the palace to be formally presented to the King and co-ordinating the endless round of dinners, receptions and dances she had to attend. The press called her 'Mrs Chamberlain's protégée'. She certainly caused quite a stir. Escorting his niece to a house party hosted by the Astors at Cliveden, Neville noticed how Valerie produced 'devastating effects on the younger and not only the young members of the party. The fact is that she is an exceptionally pretty girl with a very attractive smile and people want to talk to her.' Today, Valerie is remarkably matter-of-fact about this extraordinary change in her life, mainly recalling the warm affection of her aunt and uncle, despite the mounting political pressure they were under. She stayed in London throughout the Blitz—as her father would have expected—meeting then marrying a French pilot.

Like some terrible trophy to profligacy, Horace's body was carried back to England by the Coles and planted beside Uncle Alfred in the graveyard of West Woodhay. Augustus watched the interment. 'As the coffin was slowly lowered into the grave,' he wrote in his autobiography, 'in dreadful tension I waited for the moment for the lid to be lifted and a well-known figure to leap out with an ear-splitting yell. But my old friend disappointed me this time.' Mavis, clutching violets, was late. She left the church with Augustus, and remained his mistress for years. Augustus instructed Mavis 'to fill that pail' after Horace died but, as she knew, there was nothing left except a couple of boxes of papers recovered from France.

Mavis by society
photographer
Vivienne, circa 1940
(Tristan de Vere Cole).

Mavis collected this ephemera from the Chamberlains in Downing Street in the glare of the world's press. In 1939 she married the celebrated archaeologist Sir Mortimer Wheeler, though they divorced just three years later, after she was caught having an affair. In 1954, following a sensational trial, she was jailed for shooting and wounding another lover, Lord Vivian. Until her death in 1970, Tristan never once heard his mother criticise Horace. 'He was an aristocrat through and through,' Mavis told him. She remembered her husband as

A sincere man with his illusions about him. He had believed in the natural victory of talent; had been shown the superior advantage of well-placed friends. He had seen what he regarded as toadying accepted as friendship; what he considered corrupt justified as courtesy; cowardice called tact; deceit made to look like sincerity with a sophisticated veneer. He had looked for compassion; found only occasional people who felt sorry.

It is a good epitaph.

Note on sources

The Sultan of Zanzibar is based on the disparate groups of Horace de Vere Cole's papers remaining in the possession of his family. These include his fragmentary notes for the preparation of his uncompleted book, his diary for 1909 and letters of various dates to friends and members of his family, especially to his brother Jim. The principal source, however, is the remarkable run of lengthy letters written by Horace to his wife Mavis between 1927 and 1935 and carefully preserved by her. These candid papers contain a great deal of autobiographical detail and are highly revealing of his state of mind in the last years of his life. Mavis also retained various letters sent to her and her husband by Augustus John. I am very grateful to the owners of all these papers for permission to quote from them.

Other manuscript sources consulted include the Augustus John Papers at the National Library of Wales in Aberystwyth, official documents relating to the *Dreadnought* hoax in the National Archives at Kew and letters from Alfred Cole to Alfred Jenkinson in the collection of the University Library, Cambridge. Where appropriate these are cited in the text.

In addition, Horace's papers revealed a mass of newspaper clippings describing his activities, taken from the *Globe*, *Daily Mail*, *Daily Express*, *Sunday Express*, *Daily Telegraph*, *Daily Mirror*, *Irish Times* and other newspapers. The *Strand*, *Graphic* and *Tatler* magazines provided further useful background material.

Unattributed quotes at the openings of chapters are by Horace.

Notes on the text

p. 74, Andrei Bely's letter
1906, to Alexander Blok, from the Bely–Blok correspondence published in Russian (1969), quoted in Wikipedia entry 'Moulin Rouge'.

p. 93, Adrian Stephen's diary entry
1 July 1909, quoted in Jean MacGibbon, *There's the Lighthouse: A Biography of Adrian Stephen* (London, 1997), pp. 63–64.

p. 116, Adrian Stephen's recollections of the arrival at Weymouth
Adrian Stephen, *The 'Dreadnought' Hoax* (London, 1936), p. 20.

p. 128, Virginia Woolf's little-known 1921 short story
'A Society', published in *Monday or Tuesday* (London, 1921), a collection of Woolf's short stories. The story is mentioned in Kennard, 'Power and Sexual Ambiguity' (see Select Bibliography for full details).

p. 184, the theatre joke
There are differing accounts of how the effect was achieved. Richard Davenport-Hines, in the *Oxford Dictionary of National Biography*, has it that, rather than a letter written on each head, 'He gave tickets to a large number of bald men whose pates seen from the dress circle spelt out an expletive; characteristically he even remembered to dot the "i".'

p. 203, Oliver Gogarty's letter
2 October 1918, to Augustus John, National Library of Wales, MSS 22781D f11.

Acknowledgements

This is not the book I was asked to write or, indeed, intended to write. But it is the book I wanted to write. That it was written at all is due to my editor and publisher at Black Spring Press, Robert Hastings, who picked up my idea of a book about Horace and urged me to realise it. That we have succeeded where so many before us have failed is entirely owing to members of Horace's family, who have been an unending source of encouragement, support and hitherto hidden Horaciana: from letters and photos to daggers and diaries. They include Lady Selby, who sent a bundle of faded newspaper clippings and painstakingly photocopied a valuable series of letters from Horace to his mother, and Francis Chamberlain, who provided some wonderful images from the family albums. Francis also dug up a rare recording of BBC Radio's 1962 programme on the *Dreadnought* hoax originally broadcast when two of the original participants were still alive.

In particular, I should like to thank James and Yvonne Cole at West Woodhay for delving deep into their family papers (and memories) and emerging with so many undreamt-of treasures. James patiently answered all my usually trivial questions about the Coles, volunteering some essential family lore which has added brilliant colour to the written record. This was bolstered by the vivid personal recollection of Horace by James's father, Major John Cole. Eighty-five or so years on, John can still recall his uncle in full flight, hair flying as he leapt up from behind a sofa. No letter could offer a better impression of Horace.

As the text relates, this book had its genesis in a conversation I had with Tristan de Vere Cole in his beautiful garden near Newbury. Over several wildly entertaining lunches since, Tristan and his wife Prue fed body and mind with great food, wine and new, often scandalous, thoughts. Tristan's close interest in the project from beginning to end has seen it to fruition, while the generous loan of his mother's collection of letters from Horace and Augustus John has made it possible. Now that it is done, I hope that *The Sultan of Zanzibar* might be seen as a pendant (or prequel?) to his co-authored account of Mavis de Vere Cole's life, *Beautiful and Beloved*.

Further afield, I owe much to Pat Davies, the daughter-in-law of Denise Cole's indulgent landlady at Penywyllt, who still retains Denise's hastily abandoned suitcase (and unpaid bills). Also to John Buxton, son of Anthony Buxton, and Sylvia Lister, daughter of Leland Buxton, for their memories and portraits of their fathers. In addition, Mike McClintock kindly provided an image of West Woodhay, whilst in America Richard Kimball unearthed a wedding photograph of his grandmother Mildred Pasolini. Publication of the first edition prompted Lynn Lindsay to contact me with the surprising news that in the 1920s Horace briefly taught at the Central Foundation School for boys in the East End of London, her father being among his pupils. It also opened a fascinating and rewarding correspondence (continued over coffee in London) with Danell Jones, Associate Professor of English at Montana State University, who is engaged in a long-overdue full study of Virginia Woolf's role in the *Dreadnought* hoax. Much closer to home, I'd like to thank Helen Baron, an early reader of the manuscript, for telling me to write the whole thing again. You can't judge—but she was right.

Inevitably, and apprehensively, however, my greatest debt is to the one person alive who knew Horace de Vere Cole at his best (and worst)—his daughter Valerie. Meeting Valerie, staying with her in France and then escorting her around some old haunts of her father's in Cambridge are among the most fascinating, moving and inspiring days I have ever spent. Her own life story more than equals that of her father's for glamour, adventure and tragedy. Yet she has triumphed in glorious rebuke to his failings but tribute to his spirit. This book is dedicated to her with love and in the certain knowledge that her father would have done the same with his (had he finished it).

Finally, a word of apology to my own family, especially to my long-suffering wife and inspiration, Sam. Yet again they have had to cope with a perpetually distracted husband and father. It is offered with all my love and the promise it won't happen again (for now).

Select bibliography

BACKGROUND/BIOGRAPHY

Bell, Quentin, *Virginia Woolf: A Biography*, vol. I (London, 1972)

Bence-Jones, Mark, *Twilight of the Ascendancy* (London, 1987)

Brooker, Peter, *Bohemia in London: The Social Scene of Early Modernism* (London, 2004)

Browse, Lilian (ed.), *James Dickson Innes* (London, 1946)

Cross, Tom, *Artists and Bohemians: 100 Years of the Chelsea Arts Ball* (London, 1992)

David, Hugh, *The Fitzrovians: A Portrait of Bohemian Society 1900–55* (London, 1988)

De Vere White, Terence, *The Anglo-Irish* (London, 1972)

Deghy, Guy and Keith Waterhouse, *Café Royal: Ninety Years of Bohemia* (London, 1955)

Dilks, David, *Neville Chamberlain*, vol. I: *1869–1929* (Cambridge, 1984)

Fielding, Daphne, *The Rainbow Picnic: A Portrait of Iris Tree* (London, 1974)

Gardiner, Stephen, *Epstein: Artist Against the Establishment* (London, 1992)

Goldberg, Rose Lee, *Performance Art: From Futurism to the Present* (New York, 1988)

Greenwall, Harry J., *The Strange Life of Willy Clarkson: An Experiment in Biography* (London, 1936)

Haycock, David Boyd, *A Crisis of Brilliance* (London, 2009)

Holman-Hunt, Diana, *Latin among Lions: Alvaro Guevara* (London, 1974)

Holroyd, Michael, *Augustus John* (Harmondsworth, 1976)

James, Admiral Sir William, *Admiral Sir William Fisher* (London, 1943)

Klein, A. (ed.), *Grand Deception: The World's Most Spectacular and Successful Hoaxes, Impostures, Ruses, and Frauds* (London, 1956)

MacGibbon, Jean, *There's the Lighthouse: A Biography of Adrian Stephen* (London, 1997)

Marder, Arthur J., *Portrait of an Admiral: The Life and Papers of Sir Herbert Richmond* (1952)

Marr, Andrew, *The Making of Modern Britain* (London, 2009)

Moss, Norman, *The Pleasures of Deception* (London, 1977)

Nicholson, Virginia, *Among the Bohemians: Experiments in Living 1900–1939* (London, 2002)

Owen, Roderic and Tristan de Vere Cole, *Beautiful and Beloved: The Life of Mavis de Vere Cole* (London, 1974)

Reid, Benjamin, *The Man from New York: John Quinn and His Friends* (Oxford, 1968)

Reilly, Paraclita, *Aubrey de Vere: Victorian Observer* (Dublin, 1956)

Spalding, Frances, *Duncan Grant* (London, 1997)

Stansky, Peter, *On or About December 1910: Early Bloomsbury and its Intimate World* (Cambridge, 1996)

Taylor, D.J., *Bright Young People: The Rise and Fall of Generation 1918–1940* (London, 2007)

Wees, William C., *Vorticism and the English Avant Garde* (Manchester, 1972)

Wilson, Elizabeth, *Bohemians: The Glamorous Outcasts* (London, 2000)

LETTERS/MEMOIRS/DIARIES

Campbell, Roy, *Light on a Dark Horse* (London, 1951)

Carrington, Dora, *Carrington: Letters and Extracts from Her Diaries*, ed. David Garnett (London, 1970)

Colum, Mary, *Life and the Dream* (London, 1947)

Devas, Nicolette, *Two Flamboyant Fathers* (London, 1966)

Dunsany, Lord, *Patches of Sunlight* (London, 1938)

Epstein, Jacob, *An Autobiography* (London, 1955)

Fingal, Elizabeth Countess of, *Seventy Years Young* (London, 1937)

Garnett, David, *The Golden Echo* (London, 1953)

Glenavy, Beatrice, *Today We Will Only Gossip* (London, 1964)

Goldring, Douglas, *Odd Man Out* (London, 1935)

Gonne, Maud and William Butler Yeats, *The Gonne–Yeats Letters, 1893–1938: Always Your Friend*, ed. Anna MacBride White and A. Norman Jeffares (London, 1992)

Grantley, Lord, *Silver Spoon: Being Extracts from the Random Reminiscences of Lord Grantley* (London, 1954)

Gray, Cecil, *Peter Warlock: A Memoir of Philip Heseltine* (London, 1934)

Gregory, Lady Augusta, *Lady Gregory's Journals*, ed. Lennox Robinson (London, 1946)

— *Lady Gregory's Diaries, 1892–1902*, ed. J. Pethica (Gerrard's Cross, 1996)

Hamnett, Nina, *Laughing Torso* (London, 1932)

— *Is She a Lady?* (London, 1955)

John, Augustus, *Chiaroscuro: Fragments of Autobiography* (London, 1952)

King, Viva, *The Weeping and the Laughter* (London, 1976)

Leslie, Shane, *Long Shadows* (London, 1966)

— *The Film of Memory* (London, 1938)

May, Betty, *Tiger Woman: My Story* (London, 1929)

McClintock, Mary Howard, *Portrait of a House* (London, 1948)

Nevinson, C.R.W., *Paint and Prejudice* (London, 1937)

Pound, Ezra, *Selected Letters of Ezra Pound to John Quinn, 1915–1924*, ed. Timothy Materer (Durham, 1991)

Stephen, Adrian, *The 'Dreadnought' Hoax* (London, 1936)

Strachey, Lytton, *Letters of Lytton Strachey*, ed. Paul Levy (London, 2005)

Winterton, Lord, *Fifty Tumultuous Years* (London, 1955)

Woolf, Virginia, *The Flight of the Mind: The Letters of Virginia Woolf*, vol. I: *1888–1912*, ed. Nigel Nicolson (London, 1975)

— *A Passionate Apprentice: The Early Journals of Virginia Woolf*, ed. Mitchell Leaska (London, 1990)

— *The Platform of Time: Memoirs of Family and Friends*, ed. S.P. Rosenbaum (London, 2008)

Young, Geoffrey, *Mountains with a Difference* (London, 1951)

POETRY/FICTION

Arlen, Michael, *Piracy* (London, 1922)
—*The Green Hat* (London, 1924)
Campbell, Ivar, *Poems*, with an introduction by Guy Ridley (London, 1917)
Castle, Tudor, *The Gentle Shepherd and other Poems* (London, 1908)
Lewis, Wyndham, *The Apes of God* (London, 1931)
Pound, Ezra, *Cantos* (London, 1954)
Shelley, Lilian, *Mary Bryant* (London, 1923)
Studd, Mary, *Poems* (Dublin, 1932)
Thomas, Dylan and John Davenport, *The Death of the King's Canary*
    (London, 1976)

SOUND

Duncan Grant recounts the *Dreadnought* hoax in conversation with Roy
    Plomley on BBC radio's *Desert Island Discs*, broadcast on 15 March 1975
    (available on The Bloomsbury Group, British Library Sound Archive
    CD, 2009)
Account of the *Dreadnought* hoax in the BBC radio series *The Imposters*,
    broadcast on 20 April 1962

JOURNALS

Hone, Joseph, 'Horace Cole: King of Jokers', *The Listener*, 4 April 1940,
    pp. 674ff
Kennard, Jean E., 'Power and Sexual Ambiguity: The *Dreadnought* Hoax,
    The Voyage Out, *Mrs Dalloway* and *Orlando*', *Journal of Modern Literature*,
    vol. 20, no 2 (Winter, 1996) pp. 149–64
Reid, Panthea, 'Stephens, Fishers, and the Court of the "Sultan of
    Zanzibar": New Evidence from Virginia Stephen Woolf's Childhood',
    Journal of Biography, vol. 21 no 3 (Summer 1998), pp. 328–40
Shwabe, Randolph, 'Reminiscences of Fellow Students', *Burlington
    Magazine*, 1943, pp. 6–9

Index